SYSTEMATIC INSTRUCTION OF FUNCTIONAL SKILLS FOR STUDENTS AND ADULTS WITH DISABILITIES

Published and Distributed Throughout the World by

CHARLES C THOMAS • PUBLISHER, LTD.
2600 South First Street
Springfield, Illinois 62794-9265

© 2011 by CHARLES C THOMAS • PUBLISHER, LTD.

ISBN 978-0-398-08625-1 (hard)
ISBN 978-0-398-08626-8 (paper)
ISBN 978-0-398-08627-5 (ebook)

Library of Congress Catalog Card Number: 2010038579

With THOMAS BOOKS *careful attention is given to all details of manufacturing
and design. It is the Publisher's desire to present books that are satisfactory as to their
physical qualities and artistic possibilities and appropriate for their particular use.*
THOMAS BOOKS *will be true to those laws of quality that assure a good name
and good will.*

Printed in the United States of America
MM-R-3

Library of Congress Cataloging in Publication Data

Storey, Keith, 1956–
    Systematic instruction of functional skills for students and adults with dis-
abilities / by Keith Storey and Craig Miner.
        p. cm.
    Includes biographical references and index.
    ISBN 978-0-398-08625-1 (hard)–ISBN 978-0-398-08626-8 (pbk.)–
    ISBN 978-0-398-08627-5 (ebook)
    1. People with disabilities–Education–United States. 2. People with dis-
abilities–Vocational guidance–United States. 3. People with disabilities–
Employment–United States. I. Miner, Craig. II. Title.

LC3981.S76 2011
371.91–dc22   2010038579

FOREWORD

Even before passage of the 1975 Education of the Handicapped Act (renamed Individuals with Disabilities Education Act [IDEA]) which mandated educational services for all students with disabilities (Federal Register, 1977), some school districts were already educating these students. For example, the Madison (Wisconsin) Metropolitan Schools' stated goal for students with severe disabilities was to maximize their independent functioning in the community where people without disabilities lived, worked, and spent time (Van Deventer et al., 1981). When follow-up studies showed that, after exiting school, only 2 percent of these students spent their days in integrated settings, the district changed the curriculum of students with severe disabilities to focus on naturally-occurring (i.e., functional) activities in naturally-occurring contexts, including general education and the community (Alper, Ryndak, Hughes, & McDonnell, 2010). The change to a functional curriculum resulted in 91 percent of new graduates spending their work day hours in integrated settings with co-workers without disabilities. Similarly, Benz, Lindstrom, and Yanvanoff (2000) demonstrated that a functional skills curriculum (Youth Transition Program) was associated with improved post-school outcomes for participating students, including higher rates of graduation, employment, and participation in postsecondary education.

More than 30 years after the first of these early demonstrations of the effectiveness of a functional curriculum for students with disabilities, the field of special education appears to be in a quandary about what composes an appropriate curriculum for these students. On the one hand, federal legislation (e.g., No Child Left Behind Act [NCLB] of 2002) calls for an increased access to general education curricula and focus on academic outcomes and standardized testing. On the other hand, special education is not producing the positive postschool outcomes nationwide demonstrated in the early studies. Having a disability is persistently associated with poor postschool outcomes, such as low graduation and postsecondary enrollment rates and increased unengagement, unemployment, and underemployment (Newman,

Wagner, Cameto, & Knokey, 2009). For example, Newman and colleagues (2009) reported that, after leaving high school, only 33 percent of youth with intellectual disabilities are employed (primarily part-time), only 7 percent attend postsecondary school as a sole postschool activity, only 14 percent live independently or semi-independently, only 26 percent have a checking account, and only 11 percent participate in a community group, such as a sports team or church club. One factor related to such poor post-school outcomes may be the inappropriateness of the prevailing special education curriculum, instructional strategies, and service delivery model.

To illustrate, employment and follow-up studies have indicated that since the 1980s that the primary reason people with disabilities lose their jobs is not because they cannot perform required tasks, but because of difficulty fitting in socially in the workplace (e.g., Brickey, Campbell, & Browning, 1985; Chadsey, 2007; Greenspan & Shoultz, 1981). Social validation studies conducted in employment settings indicate that employers of people with disabilities have expectations for their employees on the job (e.g., interacting with coworkers at breaks, requesting and providing assistance, responding appropriately to constructive criticism) and that little tolerance exists for behaviors such as yelling, complaining, assaulting others, invading privacy, or interrupting meetings unannounced (e.g., Agran, Salzberg, & Martella, 1991; McConaughy, Stowitschek, Salzberg, & Peatross, 1989). At the same time, employers do not believe it is their job to teach expected social skills; rather, employers typically hold that employees with or without disabilities should enter employment with "job-ready" social skill repertoires in order that supervisors can focus on training requisite skills to maximize job performance (Butterworth & Strauch, 1994). If employers' perspectives were heeded, a critical component of special education programs for students with disabilities should be teaching socially validated social skills. That is, we should be teaching skills that are considered valuable to and functional for participating stakeholders. However, doing so does not appear to be the case. Those who have the most at stake with respect to the postschool outcomes of special education (e.g., parents, students, employers) often have little or no input into curriculum goals, instructional procedures, or educational outcomes (e.g., Kolb & Hanley-Maxwell, 2003). For example, Guy, Sitlington, Larsen, and Frank's (2009) statewide study revealed that employment training, in general, is limited in special education programs. Even when employment training is implemented, its main focus is teaching technical skills versus job-related social skills.

Keith Storey's and Craig Miner's text *Systematic Instruction of Functional Skills for Students and Adults with Disabilities* comes at a time when increasing numbers of special educators are beginning to question the relevance of a curriculum strictly focused on achieving grade-level general education standards versus functional skills (e.g., Bouck, 2009; Patton, Polloway, & Smith, 2000; Wehman, 2009). Storey and Miner remind us that "although specific curriculum content decisions must be based on standards and benchmarks as well as more individualized preferences and interests, the general goal of all instruction must be to enhance a person's capacity to function successfully in the community" (*see* Chapter 1). Therefore, the curriculum should comprise skills that teach a person to function in employment, residential, community living, and recreational/leisure domains and that are personally meaningful and valuable to the individual (Storey & Miner, 2010). Similarly, the authors argue that the curriculum should consist of skills that are useful in an immediate (e.g., learning to operate a microwave in order to cook and eat breakfast) or future environment (e.g., learning to ride the bus to get to work). Although the authors acknowledge the importance of grade-level academic standards and skills, their focus on *skills that are functional for the individual* is refreshing, timely, and critical. When we consider the poor adult outcomes generally experienced by individuals with disabilities (e.g., Newman et al., 2009), an renewed emphasis in the curriculum on the "criterion of ultimate functioning"–the skills a person must possess "to function as productively and independently as possible in socially, vocationally, and domestically integrated adult community environments" (Brown et al., 1976, p. 8)–is invaluable as we enter an era of "curriculum wars" in special education.

Storey and Miner also fill a critical gap in the literature on "how to teach." Those of us who teach pre-service teachers know how often we are asked, "But how do I *teach* everything we've been talking about in class?" The authors argue that this is "where the rubber meets the road. . . . How to teach individuals with disabilities is the foundation on which special education provides services" (*see* Preface). Their book provides both pre- and in-service practitioners with an evidence-based instructional methodology–*systematic instruction*–that has been proven to be effective in teaching a gamut of skills to students and adults with disabilities across multiple settings, ages, disability labels, and skill levels. As described by the authors, a systematic instruction approach to education begins with curriculum decisions on what to teach as well as provides the means to address the scope, sequence, and context of instruction–issues that practitioners often struggle with in providing educational services. Thankfully, Storey and Miner have addressed their book to the *practitioner*. The writing is accessible, user-friendly, and well-illustrated with case studies and realistic examples. Future research issues, discussion questions, activity suggestions, and consistency in format make the book a given for college instructors and others who are educating teachers and direct service providers.

I've been waiting for a book like this for a long time. It took Keith Storey and Craig Miner, two educators who have their feet in both the world of research and that of practice, to compile a solid text, accessible to the practitioner, on not just *how* to teach but *what* to teach. At a time when we desperately need to examine the special education curriculum in relation to adult outcomes of students with disabilities, you can bet that *Systematic Instruction of Functional Skills for Students and Adults with Disabilities* will be a book both on my shelf and in my college classes.

CAROLYN HUGHES

REFERENCES

Agran, M., Salzberg, C. L., & Martella, R. C. (1991). Expectancy effects in social validation methodology: Are there differential expectations for employees with mental retardation? *Research in Developmental Disabilities, 12,* 425–434.

Alper, S., Ryndak, D. L., Hughes, C., & McDonnell, J. (2010). *Documenting long-term outcomes of inclusive education for students with significant disabilities: Methodological issues.* Manuscript submitted for publication.

Benz, M. R., Lindstrom, L. E., & Yanvanoff, P. (2000). Improving graduation and employment outcomes of students with disabilities: Predictive factors and student perspectives. *Exceptional Children, 66,* 509–529.

Bouck, E. C. (2009). No child left behind, the Individuals with Disabilities Education Act, and functional curricula: A conflict of interest? *Education and Training in Developmental Disabilities, 44,* 3–13.

Brickey, M. P., Campbell, K. M., & Browning, L. J. (1985). A five-year follow-up of sheltered workshop employees placed in competitive jobs. *Mental Retardation, 20,* 67–83.

Brown, L., Nietupski, J., & Hamre-Nietupski, S. (1976). Criterion of ultimate functioning. In M. A. Thomas (Ed.), *Hey, Don't Forget About Me!* (pp. 2–15). Reston, VA: Council for Exceptional Children.

Butterworth, J., & Strauch, J. D. (1994). The relationship between social competence and success in the competitive work place for persons with mental retardation. *Education and Training in Mental Retardation and Developmental Disabilities, 29,* 118–133.

Chadsey, J. (2007). Adult social relationships. In S. L. Odom, R. H. Horner, M.E. Snell, & J. Blacher (Eds.), *Handbook of Developmental Disabilities* (pp. 449–466). New York: Guilford.

Federal Register. Washington, D.C.: U.S. Government Printing Office, August 23, 1977.

Greenspan, S., & Shoultz, B. (1981). Why mentally retarded adults lose their jobs: Social incompetence as a factor in work adjustment. *Applied Research in Mental Retardation, 2,* 23–38.

Guy, B. A., Sitlington, P. L., Larsen, M. D., & Frank, A. R. (2009). What are high schools offering as preparation for employment? *Career Development for Exceptional Individuals, 32,* 30–40.

Kolb, S. M., & Hanley-Maxwell, C. (2003). Critical social skills for adolescents with high incidence disabilities: Parental perspectives. *Exceptional Children, 69,* 163–179.

McConaughy, E. K., Stowitschek, J. J., Salzberg, C. L., & Peatross, D. K. (1989). Work supervisors' ratings of social behaviors related to employment success. *Rehabilitation Psychology, 34,* 3–15.

Newman, L., Wagner, M., Cameto, R., & Knokey, A. M. (2009). *The Post-High School Outcomes of Youth with Disabilities Up To 4 Years After High School. A Report of Findings from the National Longitudinal Transition Study-2 (NLTS2).* Menlo Park, CA: SRI International.

No Child Left Behind Act of 2001, Pub. L. No. 107-110, 115 Stat. 1425 (2002).

Patton, J. R., Polloway, E. A., & Smith, T. E. C. (2000). Educating students with mild mental retardation. *Focus on Autism and Other Developmental Disabilities, 15,* 80–89.

Van Deventer, P., Yelinek, N., Brown, L., Schroeder, J., Loomis, R., & Gruenewald, L. (1981). A follow-up examination of severely handicapped graduates of the Madison Metropolitan School District from 1971–1978. In L. Brown, K. Baumgart, I. Pumpian, J. Nisbet, A. Ford, A. Donnellan, M. Sweet, R. Loomis, & J. Schroeder (Eds.), *Educational programs for severely handicapped students, Vol, XI.* Madison, WI: Madison Metropolitan School District.

Wehman, P. (2009, October). *Transition From School to Adulthood For Youth With Disabilities: Where Are We in 2009?* Paper presented to the U.S. Department of Education, Office of Special Education and Rehabilitative Services. Washington, DC.

PREFACE

Scope

The scope of the book is to provide an overview of systematic instructional strategies that is written in a format so that teachers and other service providers can immediately put the information to use. We have tried to write specifically regarding general systematic instruction components such as task analysis, prompts, error correction, and so one, as well as specifically for different instructional domains such as employment, community, and residential. This book is specifically focused on systematic instruction for individuals with disabilities (school age and adults). It is generic across age groups as well as disability labels and should be of interest to those working in the schools as well as those in transition and adult service settings.

Plan

In this book each chapter follows the sequence of Key Point Questions, Window to the World Case Studies, Best Practice Recommendations, Future Research Issues, Discussion Questions, and School and Community-Based Activity Suggestions.

This book is focused on improving instructional practices for students and adults with disabilities. All too often the assumption is that students and adults have reached their "potential," and they become stuck in a place or setting because of a lack of skills on their part due to the poor instruction that they have received. Practitioners may understand the importance of placing individuals in different settings (e.g., inclusive classrooms, supported employment sites) but not how to improve their skills once they are in that setting. This book is intended to give teachers and other service providers the instructional skills for improving the skills of the individuals that they are serving.

Purpose

The rubber meets the road in how to teach. Although issues such as inclusion are certainly extremely important, how to teach individuals with disabilities is the foundation on which special education provides services. The most unique feature of the text is that it is written specifically for practitioners in the field (teachers and adult service providers) as well as those in training rather than being written for other academics. An advantage of this book is that those preparing teachers and others can easily use it in methods courses because it covers instructional methodology that is seldom covered in detail in most texts.

College instructors are likely to choose our book based on

1. the consistent format throughout the book
2. the "readability" of the book for students
3. the comprehensive coverage of systematic instruction
4. the direct applicability to applied settings

In addition to college instructors, we hope that others providing instruction, supervision, and training to direct service providers will find this book useful.

CONTENTS

SYSTEMATIC INSTRUCTION OF FUNCTIONAL SKILLS FOR STUDENTS AND ADULTS WITH DISABILITIES

Chapter 1

COMMUNITY-REFERENCED FUNCTIONAL CURRICULUM

Keypoint Questions

1. What to teach?
2. What are functional skills?
3. What are scope and sequence considerations?
4. What are lifestyle routines, functional skill sequences, and skill specific analyses?
5. What is the relationship between systematic instruction of functional skills and integration/inclusion?
6. What is the criterion of ultimate functioning?
7. What is age appropriateness?
8. What is the competence-deviance hypothesis?
9. What is partial participation?
10. What are simulation and in vivo instruction?
11. What is normalization?
12. What are quality of life outcomes?

Window to the World Case Study One

Anna is a seventeen-year-old student who has been identified as having a learning disability. Her passion in life is horses, and her goal is a career working with horses in some capacity. She currently takes riding lessons at a stable. In school, Anna has an individualized education program (IEP) and is in general education classes except for English, for which she goes to a resource center for small group and individualized instruction. Her special education coordinator, Ms. Rowland, coordinates instruction and support with her general education teachers and helps to focus assignments on horses as much as possible because Anna is very motivated when this is a topic and much less so when it is not.

Anna has a transition specialist, Ms. Forte, who is working with her on employment skills. Ms. Forte has developed a variety of instructional and support opportunities for Anna. First, she has had Anna enroll in the "Horse Club" at her school, which helps to integrate her with her peers and develop social supports and networks. Because Anna has difficulty in reading, Ms. Forte and Ms. Rowland have focused parts of her English resource time on vocabulary and reading related to horses so that Anna has a better understanding of more advanced and technical terminology. Finally, Ms. Forte has developed a position for Anna as an assistant with a local veterinarian who works with horses as well as other animals. Anna works one afternoon and every other Saturday with the veterinarian.

Window to the World Case Study Two

Salomea is a twelve-year-old who has been diagnosed as having autism. Her teachers and parents are looking to the future, when all presume that she will have a full time job and live in an apartment in a supported living situation where she will be independent in some activities such as cooking and need help in others (such as paying her bills). Currently, Salomea is in seventh grade and divides her time between general and special education classes. Her special education teacher, Mr. Ziegler, has her for classes each afternoon.

Three times a week Salomea goes into the community with Mr. Ziegler and two other students. They take the bus to a variety of places, such as the local grocery and retail stores, where Salomea and the other students purchase groceries and other home living items from lists provided by their parents. On the afternoons when they are not in the community, Mr. Ziegler works with Salomea on important social skills (e.g., greeting others and asking for help to find an item), using money to make purchases, recognizing words, and other skills that she will need for employment and to live in an apartment.

Key Point Question 1: What to Teach

Independence, productivity, and integration are valued outcomes for all individuals with disabilities. The opportunity to live, be educated, and participate in normalized settings contributes to the development of skills that enhance community functioning and attainment of these outcomes. However, beyond opportunity, it is important to recognize the critical importance of effective instruction and the difference that it can make in the lives of individuals with disabilities. Without effective instruction, it is doubtful that individuals will develop their ultimate functioning potential for successful community living. Modifications (changes in the delivery, content, or instructional level of subject matter or tests) and accommodations (provide different ways for students to take in information or communicate their knowledge back to the teacher) are important, especially in inclusive educational settings. However, even with appropriate modifications and accommodations, learners need to acquire skills that will be useful in their immediate and future environments. As noted by Downing and Demchak (2002), all students can benefit from direct and systematic instruction and, for some students, this type of instruction is essential. No matter how many accommodations or modifications are made, without systematic or direct instruction of skills, some learners may be unable to acquire new skills and information. By systematic instruction we mean instructional procedures that involve antecedent and consequence manipulations, frequent assistance to the learner (e.g., cues), immediate correction procedures, and direct and ongoing measurements that are designed to increase specific skills (e.g., behaviors) for the learner. There are certainly many other instructional and academic issues that are important for learners with disabilities, and there are a variety of instructional methodologies (Browder & Spooner, 2006; Wood, 2002), and we do not mean to marginalize or trivialize their importance. The focus of this book, however, is on directly teaching functional skills through systematic instruction procedures. We would also like to emphasize here that systematic instruction is "evidence based" and there is an extensive empirical base for the effectiveness of these procedures for teaching new skills (Iovannone, Dunlap, Huber, & Kincaid, 2003; Vaughn & Linan-Thompson, 2003).

Independence, productivity, and integration are all based upon individuals having skills necessary to be competent in specific situations (e.g., shopping for groceries, interacting with coworkers, cooking meals, etc.). For many learners, such competence is not acquired incidentally. In other words, the emphasis of instruction must be to develop competence (Gold, 1980) to function in employment settings, residential environments, community living situations, and recreational/leisure activities. Thus, curriculum content and skill selection need to be referenced to one (or more) of these domains.

Key Point Question 2: What are Functional Skills?

"What to teach?" is the initial question to be addressed when making instructional decisions involving students and adults with disabilities. Although specific curriculum content decisions must be based on standards and benchmarks as well as more individualized preferences and interests, the general goal of all instruction must be to enhance a person's capacity to function successfully in the community. To that end, the curriculum should consist of skills that enable a person to function in employment, residential, community living, and recreational/leisure domains. Thus, any skill taught needs to be referenced to one (or more) of these domains and meet the test of being personally meaningful and valuable to specific individuals. When skills are selected in this manner, their functionality or practical utility is virtually assured. This focus on teaching functional skills is sometimes lost in today's focus on inclusive education and access to the general curriculum. Although we certainly support the strong emphasis on including students with disabilities in general education classrooms and teaching them the general curriculum, educators must not forget the importance of also teaching the kinds of practical skills that individuals need to function successfully in adult society.

Functional teaching activities are instructional programs that involve skills of immediate usefulness to individuals and employ teaching materials that are real rather than simulated (Wehman, Renzaglia, & Bates, 1985). In other words, the skills must be immediately useful (e.g., learning to greet peers appropriately) and useful in future and adult settings (e.g., learning to greet a job interviewer appropriately). In considering if a skill is functional or not you need to ask if that skill is necessary to function effectively in community settings (one of the four domains). For example, learning how to ride a bus to a job site is functional because the individual can immediately use the skill to get to work. Learning how to put pegs in a peg board (once you are over the age of 3) is nonfunctional because the individual is unlikely to need to use that skill in a community environment. Another way to analyze functionality is to ask—if the person cannot perform the skill—whether someone else will have to do it for them. For instance, if someone cannot brush their teeth then someone else will have to do it for him or her. If someone cannot stack blocks, it is not necessary that someone else stack the blocks for him or her. Table 1.1 provides further analysis of the context relevance in which skills should be taught.

Lewis (1997) provides examples of individuals being taught skills that are non-functional and age-inappropriate. These include the following:

- He can put 100 pegs in a board in less than 20 minutes, but he cannot put quarters in a vending machine.
- He can sort blocks by color, but he cannot sort clothes—whites from colors—for washing.
- He can walk a balance beam frontward, sideways and backward, but he cannot walk up the steps or bleachers unassisted in the gym to watch a basketball game.

Table 1.1
CONTEXT RELEVANCE

---

1. A skill to be learned has immediate utility for the student; it either produces something useful for the student or is part of a broader skill that does so.
2. A skill has desirability for the student; it produces something for the student that would likely be chosen by the student if an appropriate choice were arranged.
3. A skill is acquired in a social context; its acquisition is the product of interactions with more than a single (care-giving) person.
4. A skill is acquired in the actual, physical contexts in which the skin will ultimately be requested of the student.
5. A skill has practicality for the student; the skill is likely to be needed and practiced with some reasonable frequency.
6. A skill is appropriate to the student's age; it will facilitate the student's increasing movement into less dependent and more integrated circumstances.
7. A skill is adaptable; its cluster of topographical boundaries are sufficiently diffuse to enable the student to respond to the needs of different stimulus configurations (situations) with appropriate adaptations, including different exemplars of materials where needed.

Source: Research on community intensive instruction as a model for building functional generalized skills, by W. Sailor, L. Goetz, J. Anderson, P. Hunt, and K. Gee (pp. 68–69), in *Generalization and Maintenance: Life-Style Changes in Applies Settings,* R. H. Horner, G. Dunlap, and R. L. Koegel (Eds.), 1988, Baltimore, MD: Paul H. Brookes Publishing Co.

Key Point Question 3: What Are Scope and Sequence Considerations?

Beyond the initial curriculum decisions regarding what to teach, the scope, sequence, and context of instruction are additional considerations of great importance to the success of systematic instruction. First, ecological inventories should be conducted within the functional domains and relevant environments of interest for the target population. Next, skill-specific task analyses, functional skills sequences, and lifestyle routines should be identified. Finally, the curriculum must be further individualized by conducting personal interest and preference assessment as part of a curriculum prioritization activity. Once personalized priorities are developed for individuals, behavioral objectives must be written and systematic instruction (cues, correction, and reinforcement procedures) conducted to assist individuals in achieving valued competencies. The unit of instruction should be on integrated and functional skills sequences rather than on isolated skill development. For example, individuals need to learn more functional competencies on a longitudinal curriculum sequence, such as getting dressed for school, changing into gym clothes, or putting on one's work clothes, rather than on isolated self-care skills such as buttoning. This focuses attention on the delineation of more complex skills sequences or routines. Table 1.2 provides further information on components of a functional curriculum.

Key Point Question 4: What Are Lifestyle Routines, Functional Skill Sequences, and Skill-Specific Analyses?

Routines are activities that a person engages in throughout a day. Brown, Evans, Weed, and Owen (1987) provide examples of the behaviors needed to get to class: entering the school building, hanging up one's jacket in a locker, obtaining necessary materials, traveling to the classroom, and entering the room. Routines should lead to a function or critical effect. In the previous example, the critical effect would be that the student is in the classroom with materials ready.

It is helpful to analyze routines in terms of differences between form and function (Brown et al., 1987). Form in a routine refers to a specific motor act. For example, putting one's arm into a sleeve of a coat in order to put it on. Function, on the other hand, focuses on the outcome or effect that the activity is to achieve. Defining accomplishments ac-

Table 1.2
INGREDIENTS OF AN INTEGRATED COMMUNITY
INTENSIVE INSTRUCTIONAL MODEL

1. A primary focus on decreasing the differences between students with severe disabilities and nondisabled peers by keeping activities, settings, and instructional materials age-appropriate, and by keeping a natural ratio of persons with and without disabilities in all instructional contexts.
2. Instruction that occurs across many schools and surrounding community environments and is imparted by a variety of adults and peers.
3. Structured, sustained interactions among same age peers with and without disabilities are fostered and encouraged by teaching staff.
4. Instructional technology and adaptations that are utilized such that each student participates, at least partially, in a variety of age-appropriate activities in integrated domestic, recreational, school, and vocational settings.
5. Maintenance of a functional life skills curriculum focus in which all educational intervention is measured against the "criterion of ultimate functioning" or the degree to which the curriculum enhances the ability of a student to perform as independently as possible in current and subsequent natural environments.
6. An instructional model wherein teaching occurs as much as possible in the context in which the taught skills will ultimately be performed, in order to capitalize on naturally occurring stimuli, routines, and motivational factors.
7. An integrated therapy model in which teachers, parents, and therapists work together to determine basic skill needs and to provide appropriate intervention in natural contexts.
8. A commitment to the likelihood of a nonsheltered future that stresses work and maximally independent living circumstances.

Source: Research on community intensive instruction as a model for building functional generalized skills, by W. Sailor, L. Goetz, J. Anderson, P. Hunt, and K. Gee (pp. 72–73), in *Generalization and Maintenance: Life-Style Changes in Applies Settings,* R. H. Horner, G. Dunlap, and R. L. Koegel (Eds.), 1988, Baltimore, MD: Paul H. Brookes Publishing Co.

cording to function has the advantage of defining success by the outcome of the behavior. For instance, there are multiple ways of putting on a coat (e.g., putting arms in sleeves one at a time or laying the coat on a table with the inside facing up and putting both arms in from behind at the same time). Both forms, however, achieve the same function or outcome (the person has his or her coat on).

In addition, routines may be fixed or substitutable (Brown et al., 1987). Fixed routines are those such as dressing for which one cannot substitute another routine (you have to get dressed to go to work or school). Substitutable forms are those that can be accomplished in a number of different ways. For example, spending time with a friend may be accomplished by playing a board game, going out for coffee, or playing together on a play station (Brown et al., 1987).

Key Point Question 5: What Is the Relationship Between Systematic Instruction of Functional Skills and Integration/Inclusion?

One of the most important reasons for teaching functional skills to students and adults with disabilities is to increase their integration with peers without disabilities in school and community settings. Although there may be some distinction between the terms inclusion and integration we will use them interchangeably in this text.

Mank and Buckley (1989) described integration as "in its simplest and most elegant form as a degree of community presence and participation for persons with disabilities that is no different from that enjoyed by persons without a disability label." Beyond the simplicity of broad terms such as inclusion, it is helpful to address more specific components and illustrations of inclusive or integrated opportunity. Several authors have contributed to a more-specific conceptualizations of inclusion (Mank & Buckley, 1989; Ryndak & Alper, 2003; Storey, 1993). These five components of inclusion represent more specific conceptualization.

1. Physical Inclusion: This requires proximity to peers, coworkers, and others without disabilities. A student with a disability in a general education classroom is physically included. A worker with a disability who works alongside nondisabled coworkers at a regular job site is physically included.
2. Social Inclusion: This involves elective personal interactions between individuals with and without disabilities. Social integration has been defined as "regular access to interactions with individuals without identified handicaps and regular use of normal community resources" (Will, 1984). These interactions include greeting others, small talk, and so on.
3. Relationships: Relationships depend on ongoing social interactions and usually involve reciprocal participation in activities.
4. Social Networks: Social networks involve repeated contact with a number of people who identify the relationships that exist within the group as "socially important." The interactions are characterized by importance and reciprocity among members and occur in a variety of settings. Social networks are seen as espe-

cially important because of their correlation with physical and mental health (O'Connor, 1983).

5. Academic Inclusion: Access to normalized educational, recreational, and social activities that occur in school. This includes access to the general education curriculum.

From an instructional standpoint there are several basic principles underlying inclusion that we would like to highlight.

First, inclusion is not conditional, and programs must fit the individual rather than the individual fitting the program.

Second, students and adults with disabilities must be full and active participants in school and community, occupying socially valued roles.

Third, in academic settings, the intended outcomes of most inclusion models are for students to become a true part of the regular education class and for them to learn the skills that have been identified as priority learning needs and included on the IEP as well as local educational standards and benchmarks. Thus, achievement is measured relative to the IEP goals as well as the regular education curriculum.

Systematic instruction then takes place in teaching skills needed in current inclusive settings (such as the general education classroom or a supported employment situation) as well as future inclusive settings (a general education classroom at a higher grade level or playing on a regular soccer team through a recreational program in the community).

Key Point Question 6: What Is the Criterion of Ultimate Functioning?

The criterion of ultimate functioning is "the ever changing, expanding, localized, and personalized cluster of factors that each person must possess in order to function as productively and independently as possible in socially, vocationally, and domestically integrated adult community environments" Brown et al. (1976, p. 8). Thus, any instructional activity must be judged in terms of how it relates to the criterion of ultimate functioning. Table 1.3 provides six questions that should be asked prior to the initiation of instruction. If the activity or skill to be learned does not fit into the criterion of ultimate functioning then it should probably not be taught.

Table 1.3
SIX QUESTIONS THAT SHOULD BE ASKED
PRIOR TO THE INITIATION OF INSTRUCTION

1. Why should we engage in this activity?
2. Is this activity necessary to prepare students to ultimately function in complex heterogeneous community settings?
3. Could students function successfully as adults if they did not acquire the skill?
4. Is there a different activity that will allow students to approximate realization of the criterion of ultimate functioning more quickly and more efficiently?
5. Will this activity impede, restrict, or reduce the probability that students will ultimately function successfully in integrated community settings?
6. Are the skills, materials, tasks, and criteria of concern similar to those encountered in adult life?

Source: Criterion of ultimate functioning, by L. Brown, J. Nietupski, and S. Hamre-Nietupski (p. 9), in *Hey, Don't Forget About Me?*, M. A. Thomas (Ed.), 1976, Reston, VA: Council for Exceptional Children.

Key Point Question 7: What Is Age Appropriateness?

Age appropriateness refers to what students are taught and the materials used to teach skills. Age appropriate means chronological age, not mental age (mental ages are not functional or appropriate; forget them). It is important that individuals with disabilities be treated in the same manner as other individuals of the same age. They should be given the opportunity to engage in activities that are age appropriate and to use materials and equipment that other students their age use. The use of chronologically age-inappropriate materials decreases the social image and increases the stigma of individuals with disabilities (Ferguson & Baumgart, 1991). For example, a twenty-one-year-old should not be given stuffed animals as a reinforcer. Stuffed animals are age appropriate for someone around six years of age. Age appropriate reinforcers for a twenty-one-year-old might include going to a concert, having a drink in a bar, having a snack, going on a date, playing softball, eating in a restaurant, or having friends over for dinner. Age appropriateness also works the other way, younger children should be engaged in activities and using materials that typically developing peers use. For example, first-grade students might be exploring jobs and careers available in the community but not learning specific job tasks such as cleaning a motel room or clerical tasks.

When teaching skills and using materials and reinforcers, you need to consider the impact that they will have on other people in addition to the person being taught. How would employees in a factory view a forty-year-old coworker with a disability being given a "smiley face" sticker for completing a task? That employee would be stigmatized, and coworkers would be likely to value him or her less as a fellow adult and think of him or her more as a child. If you are not sure if a task, material, or reinforcer is age appropriate, it is probably best not to use it. Better to be safe than to stigmatize the person you are working with.

What are the consequences of ignoring age appropriateness? When parents, employers, community members, teachers, and others view 20-year-old Evan playing with Tinkertoys™ during the middle of the day, what conclusions will they draw? Of what educational significance is it to say, "Anna is chronologically 21 years old and yet developmentally 3. Does it mean that she should be dressed as normal 3-year-old? Does it mean that all instructional efforts should be designed to teach her to function as a normal 4-year-old?" (Brown et al., 1988).

Related to age appropriateness is the issue of developmental stages. Attempting to arrange for students or adults with disabilities (especially those with more severe disabilities) to progress through the same developmental stages that students without disabilities go through is a manifestation of a "Normal Development Curricular Strategy." Users of such strategies usually assume that a student will make sufficient progress through consecutively arranged levels, stages, phases, and sequences that will result in general functioning that is in reasonable accordance with developmental capacity. Brown and associates (1988) have outlined several problems with this strategy:

1. Students with disabilities (especially those with severe intellectual disabilities), rarely, if ever, move through stages which students without disabilities progress, even after 21 years of instruction.
2. At the end of their educational careers, many important skills and attitudes that are certainly within their capabilities are never acquired because functional skills have not been taught.
3. The numbers and kinds of environments and activities they are exposed to approximate those one would allow children without disabilities, ages 2–4 to experience. Consequently, performance variances and other differences are systematically increased rather than decreased over time.

Key Point Question 8: What Is the Competence-Deviance Hypothesis?

An important consideration in teaching functional skills is whether the skill learned increases an individual's competence and decreases the deviance. Deviance equals aspects of an individual that cause negative attention. Competence equals attributes and skills that not everyone else has and that are appreciated and needed by someone else (Gold, 1980). It is important to note that the more competence an individual has, the more deviance will be tolerated by others. The value placed on people is greatly influenced by how their deviance balanced against their competence in the eyes of others. Competence, then, depends on whether the employer, coworkers, teacher, or whomever wants and needs that competence and how widely that competence is available from others. Simply doing something well does not necessarily make one competent in the eyes of others—not if most other people can also do the same thing. Whether one is welcomed to, tolerated in, or excluded from vital school and community settings will be greatly influenced by the degree of competence one has to offer the people in those settings.

Gold (1980) points out that many people with disabilities may always have certain things about them that are noticed by people in society and that draw negative attention. If individuals with disabilities have no skills or attributes that are perceived as competencies or their deviancies outweigh their competencies, they will be much more vulnerable to exclusion in community settings, because their deviancies will dominate the perception others have of them. Another way of looking at this issue is that there is a range of competencies in various domains that a person needs to acquire. For some people, bathing and hair care are competencies as much as fixing a copier is for another person. However, it is important to focus on the fact that individuals learn the skills/competencies they need for success in many life roles (friend, worker, citizen, etc.).

An important point to consider is that often instruction focuses on skills such as self-care skills (bathing, hair care) or domestic skills (cooking). These may be legitimate skills for a person to learn and are likely to result in an increase in that person's quality of life. However, they are not examples of competencies that are desired by others because they are not skills that other people need and not everyone has. Basically, they are skills that focus on decreasing deviance. (It is generally considered deviant in our society for an adult to be unable to bathe, cook, etc.) If people learn to complete these "typical" tasks they are perceived to be less deviant but not more competent.

For example, it is expected by employers and coworkers that an individual comes to work groomed and dressed. This may eliminate deviance but not lead to competence. If that individual has skills operating a copier and can fix jams that others cannot, however, then that person will be seen as having competencies and will be more likely to be valued by the employer and coworkers. Thus instructional programs need to have a balance between teaching skills that are aimed toward reducing deviance and teaching those related to establishing competencies.

Key Point Question 9: What Is Partial Participation?

Partial participation means that students who might not be able to acquire all of the skills needed to completely participate in activities are still capable of learning enough skills to partially participate (Baumgart et al., 1982; Ferguson & Baumgart, 1991). In other words, partial participation involves everyone, even if they cannot do all of the task. Partial participation helps individuals with disabilities to go beyond more presence in a situation and can increase "membership."

As noted by Baumgart and associates (1982), partial participation requires the consideration of adaptations that enhance the performance of existing skills, compensate for missing skills that will not likely be acquired, and allow for the acquisition and utilization of alternative skills. There are four types of individualized adaptations that we would like to highlight.

UTILIZING/CREATING MATERIALS AND DEVICES. These adaptations refer to portable objects, equipment, or materials created for instructional purposes that enhance or allow partial participation. For example, an individual who cannot independently make a smoothie, may be able to hit an electronic switch with his or her hand to activate the blender.

UTILIZING PERSONAL ASSISTANCE. This refers to cues or supervisory assistance provided by another person. For example, an employee at a county courthouse who is deaf or blind with severe mental retardation can shred documents correctly when at the shredder but needs assistance in locating materials that are to be shredded.

ADAPTING SKILLS SEQUENCES. This involves using a sequence that is different from that used by most individuals without disabilities. For instance, carrying a loaded tray of food in a cafeteria may be difficult for a student. Making multiple trips (one for silverware, one for food, one for a drink), however, may allow the student to be able to complete the task of getting their food to a table independently.

ADAPTING RULES. Rules are prescribed guidelines, procedures, or customs for engaging in activities. An example of adapting rules is provided by Bernabe and Block (1994), who helped to include a twelve-year-old girl with moderate to severe disabilities in a softball league. One adaptation that was made for her was that she was allowed to hit off a tee rather than from a pitched ball.

A possible misuse of partial participation is where it is too easy to decide that a student cannot add new skills and have them relegated to partial participation activities as an excuse. Ferguson and Baumgart (1991) also stress the importance of achieving active instead of passive partial participation. This involves increasing opportunities for students to practice their behaviors multiple times in a situation or to partially participate at different times during a day.

Key Point Question 10: What Are
Simulation and In Vivo Instruction?

Concern has been raised that artificial instructional materials and settings do not allow people with disabilities to solve real-life problems or provide them with the skills needed for practical functions as much as natural and realistic settings, tasks, and materials do (Brown, Nietupski, & Hamre-Nietupski, 1976).

Simulated instruction refers to teaching that is designed to approximate the natural environment (e.g., noncriterion settings, materials, and/or responses are employed) rather than teaching taking place in the criterion environment (Nietupski, Hamre-Nietupski, Clancy, & Veerhusen 1986). An example would be teaching street crossing using mock streets in a hallway.

Simulated instruction can have the advantage of (a) providing repeated practice over short periods of time, (b) being more cost effective, (c) being less time consuming, (d) reducing risk factors, (e) allowing for error correction more readily, and (f) reducing embarrassment by noncompetent performance in the community while a person is learning skills (Vogelsberg, Williams, & Bellamy, 1982).

In vivo instruction refers to teaching that takes place with actual materials in the criterion environment (e.g., a specific job site, a person's home, a grocery store where the person shops). For instance, teaching students to cross actual streets in the community would be in vivo instruction.

In vivo instruction can have the advantage of (a) providing a realistic setting for skills acquisition and performance, (b) enhancing the generalization of skills, (c) being more cost effective in the long run, and (d) allowing for the use of naturally occurring cues and corrections (Vogelsberg et al., 1982).

It is not clear if it is better to use in vivo or simulated instruction, and advantages and disadvantages for either depend on a variety of factors, including where the individual is placed for instruction, such as a general education classroom (Billingsley & Albertson, 1999; Brown et al., 1989; Brown et al., 1991). Nietupski and colleagues (1986) have advocated that simulation not be considered as an alternative to in vivo instruction but that, where in vivo instruction alone is ill-advised, simulation be conducted simultaneously.

Nietupski and associates (1986) also offer several guidelines for effective use of simulations. We would like to highlight three of these guidelines.

The first guideline is to use community performance data to modify simulations. By taking the learner to the criterion environment it is possible to assess performance in that environment and note the types of errors that occur and the stimuli that are controlling those errors. This highlights the importance of knowing about the incorrect as well as the correct performance of the learner. Error analysis is covered in more detail in Chapter 2. When error patterns are understood, the simulated instruction can be modified to focus on the mistakes that the learner is making.

The second guideline relates to the first. Simulated instruction can provide the student with concentrated and repeated practice of the errors. For example, if a student has difficulty correctly sorting books by call number at his or her part-time job at the public library, then it would be possible to practice this skill in the classroom or in the school library.

The third guideline relates to the scheduling of simulation and in vivo instruction. It may be best to have simulation instruction occur before the in vivo instruction occurs (e.g., simulation in the morning and in vivo in the afternoon). In addition, it is necessary to consider the schedule on a weekly basis. Should in vivo instruction occur on a weekly basis for community instruction such as bus riding and grocery shopping, whereas employment instruction might occur every afternoon at a job site for an older student?

Ultimately, to know if simulated instruction work is effective you must analyze the learner performance in the criterion environment (generalization, which is covered in more detail in Chapter 3). This is also known as the zero degree inference strategy, in which no inferences are made that training to a criterion on any task in one situation will result in criterion performance in similar but different situations requiring similar or slightly different actions (e.g., a student may have learned to shop at one grocery store but that does not necessarily mean that he or she can then shop at a different grocery store). Each time a situation changes for a student with disabilities, it will be necessary to empirically verify that he or she can perform the skills required by that new situation (Brown, Nietupski, & Hamre-Nietupski, 1976).

Key Point Question 11: What Is Normalization?

The principle of normalization (the term social role valorization has also been used) develops a point of reference for instruction by comparing methods and outcomes for individuals with disabilities to those for individuals without disabilities. Normalization was originally conceived as making available to all individuals with disabilities patterns of life and conditions of everyday living that are as close as possible to the regular circumstances and ways of life of their society (Nirje, 1969).

This also includes the utilization of instruction and supports that are as culturally normative as possible in order to establish and/or maintain personal behaviors and characteristics that are as culturally normative as possible (Wolfensberger, 1972).

From an instructional standpoint this means that it is important to consider what is "normal" in a particular environment. Each school or community and subenvironment is unique in many ways as a normative comparison. Consequently, there are bound to be differences from community to community regarding what is considered normal and acceptable (Thurman & Fiorelli, 1979). For instance, in many employment situations it is "normal" to wear more formal attire, such as a suit and tie, and an employee not wearing such attire would stand out and run the risk of stigma, isolation, or even termination. In contrast, in other employment situations, it is "normal" to wear jeans and a t-shirt and a person wearing a suit and tie would stand out.

Key Point Question 12: What Are Quality of Life Outcomes?

Quality of life refers to how well a person's life is going and if he or she is satisfied with life. The ultimate purpose of good instruction is to teach functional skills that improve the quality of life of the individual.

Although there is no agreed upon definition of quality of life, what measures should be used, or how to best measure it, Felce (1997) has proposed six quality of life domains that provide a useful framework for understanding and assessment purposes. These domains are physical well-being, material well-being, social well-being, productive well-being, emotional well-being, and civic well-being (Table 1.4). Thus, when considering any skill to teach, it is useful to consider these domains as a reference regarding the potential functionality of the skill. For example, teaching an individual how to balance a checkbook would obviously be a financial skill for independent living in the productive living domain. Teaching a person (older than a toddler) to stack blocks is unlikely to improve the quality of life of an individual according to these domains and thus is a nonfunctional skill.

BEST PRACTICE RECOMMENDATIONS

1. Any skill taught should be analyzed in terms of its relevance to functional domains (employment, residential, community living, and recreational/leisure) as well as the criterion of ultimate functioning.
2. Activities and instructional materials must be age appropriate.
3. Skills taught should increase the competence of the individual, not just decrease deviance.
4. Skills may be taught in simulation and/or in vivo depending on a variety of factors.

Table 1.4
QUALITY OF LIFE MEASURES

Physical Well-Being	Material Well-Being	Social Well-Being
Health Nutrition Fitness Individual physical mobility Personal safety	Wealth-ownership • income Housing quality • privacy • possessions • meals/food • neighborhood Transportation and mobility	Interpersonal relationships • family and household life • relatives • friends and social life • social support networks Community involvement • activities and events • acceptance and support Lifestyle patterns • activity patterns • daily lifestyle
Productive Well-Being	Emotional Well-Being	Civic Well-Being

(includes job, homelife,
    leisure/hobbies, and
    education)
Personal development
• competence
• independence
Choice/control
 	
Constructive activity
Employment
• job satisfaction
• social integration
Independent living
• domestic skills
• self-care skills
• finance skills
• community living skills
• survival skills
	Happiness
	Contentment/life
	Satisfaction
	Mental health
	Freedom from stress
	Sexuality
	Religious belief
	Self-esteem
	Self-determination
	• personal control and
	    autonomy
	• preference and choice
		Privacy
		Protection under the law
		Voting
		Civic roles and
		    responsibilities
		State of the nation

Source: Adapted from *Defining and applying the concept of quality of life,* by D. Felce, 1997, *Journal of Intellectual Disability Research, 41,* 126–135; and from Quality of life, by C. Hughes, S. Copeland, S. Fowler, and P. Church-Pupke (pp. 157–171), in *The Road Ahead: Transition to Adult Life for Persons With Disabilities,* K. Storey, P. Bates, and D. Hunter (Eds.), 2002, St. Augustine, FL: Training Resource Network, Inc.

5. An individual may partially participate in an activity even if they do not have all of the requisite skills.
6. The purpose of good instruction is to increase the individual's quality of life.

FUTURE RESEARCH ISSUES

1. What percentage of students with disabilities should receive functional skills training?
2. How should the decision-making process for a functional curriculum versus academic curriculum change over time?

DISCUSSION QUESTIONS

1. What if a skill is needed in a school environment (e.g., cutting paper with scissors) but not necessarily needed in a community environment? Is it still a functional skill worth teaching?
2. What is the best way to get good criterion of ultimate functioning outcomes, inclusion in general education environments, or community-based instruction?
3. Do quality-of-life considerations change over a person's life?
4. How do you know if someone has a "good" quality of life?
5. Do we want people with disabilities to be "normal" like people without disabilities or do we accept and promote their differences?

SCHOOL AND COMMUNITY-BASED ACTIVITY SUGGESTIONS

1. Visit a classroom or adult service agency. Observe and analyze skills that are being taught in terms of functionality and the criterion of ultimate functioning. List activities as functional or nonfunctional, and describe skills that might be more functional.
2. Visit a community environment such as a grocery store, mall, or job site. Analyze how different individuals perform a task. Are there different forms to achieve the function?

3. Visit a program for persons with disabilities and analyze in terms of its relevance for persons with disabilities. Analyze the program in terms of the criterion of ultimate functioning, integration, and quality-of-life outcomes. (Analyze in terms of the six quality of life domains from Felce [1997]: physical well-being, material well-being, social well-being, productive well-being, emotional well-being, and civic well-being.)

REFERENCES

Bates, P., Morrow, S., Pancsofar, E., & Sedlak, R. (1984). The effect of functional versus non-functional activities on the attitudes/expectations of non-handicapped persons: What they see is what we get. *Journal of the Association for Persons with Severe Handicaps, 9,* 73–78.

Baumgart, D., Brown, L., Pumpian, I., Nisbet, J., Ford, A., Sweet, M., Messina, R., & Schroeder, J. (1982). Principle of partial participation and individualized adaptations in educational programs for severely handicapped students. *Journal of the Association for the Severely Handicapped, 7,* 17–27.

Bernabe, E. A., & Block, M. E. (1994). Modifying rules of a regular girls softball league to facilitate the inclusion of a child with severe disabilities. *Journal of the Association for Persons with Severe Handicaps, 19,* 24–31.

Billingsley, F. F., & Albertson, L. R. (1999). Finding a future for functional skills. *Journal of the Association for Persons With Severe Handicaps, 24,* 298–302.

Browder, D. M., & Spooner, F. (2006). *Teaching language arts, math, & science to students with significant cognitive disabilities.* Baltimore, MD: Paul Brookes.

Brown, F., Evans, I. M., Weed, K. A., & Owen, V. (1987). Delineating functional competencies: A component model. *Journal of the Association for Persons with Severe Handicaps, 12,* 117–124.

Brown, L., Nietupski, J., & Hamre-Nietupski, S. (1976). Criterion of ultimate functioning. In M. A. Thomas (Ed.), *Hey, Don't Forget About Me!* (pp. 2-15). Reston, VA: Council for Exceptional Children.

Brown, L., Schwarz, P., Udvari-Solner, A., Kampschroer, E. F., Johnson, F., Jorgensen, J., & Gruenewald, L. (1991). How much time should students with severe intellectual disabilities spend in regular education classrooms and elsewhere? *Journal of the Association for Persons with Severe Handicaps, 16,* 39–47.

Brown, L., Udvari-Solner, A., Schwarz, P., VanDeventer, P., Ahlgren, C., Johnson, F., Gruenewald, L., & Jorgensen, J. (1989). Should students with severe intellectual disabilities be based in regular or in special education classrooms in home schools? *Journal of the Association for Persons with Severe Handicaps, 14,* 8–12.

Brown, L., Zanella-Albright, K., Rogan, P., York, J., Udvari-Solner, A., Johnson, F., VanDeventer, P., & Loomis, R. (1988). An integrated curriculum model for transition. In B. L. Ludlow, A. P. Turnbull, & R. Luckasson (Eds.), *Transitions to adult life for people with mental retardation: Principles and practices* (pp. 67–78). Baltimore,

MD: Paul Brookes.

Downing, J. E., & Demchak, M. A. (2002). Determining individual abilities and how best to support students. In J. E. Downing (Ed.), *Including students with severe and multiple disabilities in typical classrooms.* Baltimore, MD: Paul Brookes.

Felce, D. (1997). Defining and applying the concept of quality of life. *Journal of Intellectual Disability Research, 41,* 126–135.

Ferguson, D. L., & Baumgart, D. (1991). Partial participation revisited. *Journal of the Association for Persons with Severe Handicaps, 16,* 218–227.

Gold, M. W. (1980). *Did I Say That? Articles and Commentary on the Try Another Way System.* Champaign, IL: Research Press.

Hughes, C., Copeland, S., Fowler, S., & Church-Pupke, P. (2002). Quality of life. In K. Storey, P. Bates, & D. Hunter (Eds.), *The road ahead: Transition to adult life for persons with disabilities* (pp. 157–171). St. Augustine, FL: Training Resource Network, Inc.

Iovannone, R., Dunlap, G., Huber, H., & Kincaid, D. (2003). Effective educational practices for students with autism spectrum disorders. *Focus on Autism and Other Developmental Disabilities, 18,* 150–165,

Lewis, P. (1997). A case for teaching functional skills. *TASH Newsletter, 23,* 19.

Mank, D. M., & Buckley, J. (1989). Strategies for integrating employment environments. In W. Kiernan & R. Schalock (Eds.), *Economics, industry, and disability: A look ahead* (pp. 319–335). Baltimore, MD: Paul H. Brookes Publishing Company.

Nietupski, J., Hamre-Nietupski, S., Clancy, P., & Veerhusen, K. (1986). Guidelines for making simulation an effective adjunct to in vivo community instruction. *Journal of the Association for Persons with Severe Handicaps, 11,* 12–18.

Nirje, B. (1969). The normalization principle and its management implications. In R. Kugel & W. Wolfensberger (Eds.), *Changing patterns in residential services for the mentally retarded* (pp. 51–57). Washington, DC: U.S. Government Printing Office.

O'Connor, G. (1983). Social support of mentally retarded persons. *Mental Retardation, 21,* 187–196.

Ryndak, D. L., & Alper, S. (2003). *Curriculum and instruction for students with significant disabilities in inclusive settings.* Boston, MA: Allyn & Bacon.

Sailor, W., Goetz, L., Anderson, J., Hunt, P., & Gee, K. (1988). Research on community intensive instruction as a model for building functional generalized skills. In R. H. Horner, G. Dunlap, & R. L. Koegel (Eds.), *Generalization and maintenance: Lifestyle changes in applied settings* (pp. 67–98). Baltimore, MD: Paul H. Brookes Publishing Co.

Storey, K. (1993). A proposal for assessing integration. *Education and Training in Mental Retardation, 28,* 279–287.

Thurman, S., & Fiorelli, J. (1979). Perspectives on normalization. *The Journal of Special Education, 13,* 339–345.

Vaughn, S., & Linan-Thompson, S. (2003). What is special about special education for students with learning disabilities? *Journal of Special Education, 37,* 140–147.

Vogelsberg, R. T., Williams, W., & Bellamy, G. T. (1982). Preparation for independent living. In B. Wilcox & G. T. Bellamy (Eds.), *Design of high school programs for severely handicapped students* (pp. 153–173). Baltimore, MD: Paul Brookes.

Wehman, P., Renzaglia, A., & Bates, P. (1985). *Functional living skills for moderately and severely handicapped individuals.* Austin, TX: Pro-Ed.

Will, M. (1984). *OSERS programming for the transition of youth with disabilities: Bridges from school to working life.* Washington, DC: Department of Education. Office of Special Education and Rehabilitative Services.

Wolfensberger, W. (1970). The principle of normalization and its implications to psychiatric services. *American Journal of Psychiatry, 127,* 291–296.

Wood, J. W. (2002). *Adapting instruction to accommodate students in inclusive settings.* Upper Saddle River, NJ: Merrill Prentice Hall.

Chapter 2

HOW TO ASSESS AND ANALYZE SKILLS

Keypoint Questions

1. How are environments analyzed to identify settings and skills to be learned?
2. What is the best way to break down a task for instruction?
3. How are behaviors defined?
4. How are instructional objectives written?
5. How are instructional data collected?
6. What are other types of direct observation data?
7. Who should collect instructional data?
8. How often should data be collected?
9. How are instructional data analyzed?
10. How are learner errors analyzed?
11. How is generalization assessed?

Window to the World Case Study One

Carlos, a fifteen-year-old student in Ms. Kirk's class, has been working on purchasing skills. Ms. Kirk asked Carlos' mother, Ms. Hernandez, if she would send $5.00 to buy lunch.

Ms. Kirk sent a note home to parents letting them know that she was available to answer questions or address concerns any day after student dismissal. Ms. Hernandez, Carlos' mother, picked him up from school one day unexpectedly. She expressed her concern that she had been sending money for him to purchase his lunch at food booths in the school cafeteria and was wondering if he was independent yet so that he would not be stigmatized for having an adult with him at lunch

25

time. Ms. Hernandez asked about Carlos' progress. Because Ms. Kirk had been collecting and graphing Carlos' performance data daily, she was able to show Ms. Hernandez the progress Carlos was making. Although he was not yet independent, he was on his way. The trend line on the self-graphing sheet showed that Carlos had been working on selecting preferred food items from the menu, presenting the cashier with $1.00 more than the cost of his selected food, waiting for his change, and putting the change in his pocket. The data sheet indicated that the trainer was fading his prompting and that Carlos only needed a model for the dollar-more strategy and indirect verbal prompts for waiting for change and putting it in his pocket.

Window to the World Case Study Two

Robert is a twenty-seven-year-old with diagnoses of learning disability, attention-deficit/hyperactivity disorder (ADHD), and Tourette's syndrome. He has difficulty staying on task, and this was proving to be problematic in his job processing patient records at the hospital office where he worked. In other words, his supervisor was not pleased with his productivity.

Robert consulted his case manager, Mr. Bates from the Department of Rehabilitation, and they decided to be proactive and to collect data to show Robert's supervisor about his improved productivity. Because workers in his department often listened to music (with headphones) while working, Robert programmed his cell phone to beep every five minutes (while he was listening to music on his phone with headphones). He had a small index card that he kept in his shirt pocket, and every time the phone beeped he marked if he was on task or not at the beep (momentary time sampling). He collected data for three days and found that he was on task only 45 percent of the intervals. (No wonder his supervisor was concerned!)

Robert came up with a reinforcement plan. After work he would show his index card to his wife, and they would graph the percentage of intervals using a software program on their computer. For each interval that was on task he would put 5 cents into a fund for "special dates" that he and his wife could spend together. This combined direct observation, positive reinforcement for on-task behavior, use of peer (spouse) supports, graphic feedback, and back-up reinforcers. Needless to say, this intervention was quite effective, and within a few days his on-task behavior was over 95 percent and he was able to demonstrate this to his supervisor by showing her the graph of his on-task behavior.

The assessment and analysis process for instruction of functional skills involves understanding discriminative stimuli, skills, potential reinforcers, potential problems, current learner status, and understanding progress being made or not being made by the learner. It is important to analyze learning environments so that instruction can be effectively utilized for teaching these skills. This is a complex process involving curriculum development, or critical skills to be taught, and instructional decision making using direct observation. Identifying personally and socially significant target behaviors and assessing the progress of the learner and adapting instruction as needed maximizes the learning process.

Key Point Question 1: How Are Environments Analyzed to Identify Settings and Skills to Be Learned?

One method for thoroughly assessing the learning environment is the use of an ecological inventory. Brown and his colleagues (1979) described the use of an ecological inventory to analyze the environmental demands and pinpoint relevant skills. This ecological approach, or top-down approach, includes identifying current and future environments, the critical activities, and the skills required. A top-down approach begins with the demands of an integrated adult lifestyle and analyzes the activities/skills that are required, identifying relevant skills and avoiding the teaching of inappropriate, non-functional skills. Figure 2.1 provides an example of an ecological inventory of a university gymnasium for attending a sporting event. The steps of the ecological inventory are discussed in the following.

Life skills fall into one or more of the major life areas, or domains: domestic, vocational, community, and recreation. Person-centered planning identifies an individual's preferences, interests, and priority environments. Current and future learning environments must be identified based on a person-centered approach that considers an individual's preferences and interests. This is a necessary first step regardless of the age or severity of disability of the learner. This is a collaborative process involving professionals, family members, other interested parties, and the individual. Person-centered planning is discussed in detail in Chapter 9.

Ecological Inventory

Name: Juan Castro

Domain: Recreation/Leisure

Major Environment University Gymnasium							
Subenvironment Ticket Window		Subenvironment Snack Bar		Subenvironment Restroom		Subenvironment Main Arena	
Activity #1 Purchasing ticket	Activity #2	Activity #1 Selecting snacks	Activity #2 Paying for snacks	Activity #1 Using restroom	Activity #2 Washing hands	Activity #1 Locating seat	Activity #2 Watching game

Skills	Skills	Skills	Skills	Skills	Skills
					Turn water on
					Put hands
					  under water
					Put soap on
					  hands
					Rub hands
					  together
					Rinse hands
					Turn water off
					Get paper
					  Towel
					Dry hands
					Throw away
					  towel
						Skills	Skills

Figure 2.1. Ecological Inventory Form.

Once the priority environments are identified, the instructor/team conducts an analysis through the ecological inventory process. The steps of the ecological inventory are as follows:

Step 1: Identify curriculum domains
Step 2: Identify and survey current and future natural environments
Step 3: Breakdown major environments into sub-environments
Step 4: Identify relevant activities
Step 5: Identify skills required

Completing the ecological inventory involves observing/analyzing an environment in which the learner currently participates or will participate at a later time. Next, the various subenvironments are identified. For example, if a learner wishes to increase leisure skills by going to basketball games at the local university, the ecological inventory is conducted at a university gymnasium (*see* Figure 2.1). The domain is recreation/leisure, the environment is the gymnasium, and the subenvironments would include ticket window, snack bar, restroom, and main arena. Activities, such as purchasing tickets at the ticket window, selecting and purchasing snacks at the snack bar, using the restroom, and locating a seat and watching the game are identified within the subenvironments. These activities may be broken down into individual skills required or task analyzed for instruction (see later).

Key Point Question 2: What Is the Best Way to Break Down a Task for Instruction?

For instructional purposes, a task analysis is the key to building instruction. The more thorough you are in constructing the task analysis, the more successful the person is going to be in learning the task. A task analysis is a process of breaking a task into its required component responses and listing these responses in an appropriate sequence (Bellamy, Horner, & Inman, 1979). In other words, it is a complete description of each and every behavior needed to accomplish a specific activity.

The purpose of task analysis is to facilitate instruction by focusing the instructor's attention on the specific demands of a task and by providing a method for gathering data during instruction about the acquisition of the task by the learner. The teaching of complex tasks proceeds most efficiently if the tasks are shaped by successive approximations. People learn simpler component responses and chain them together ultimately to perform the complex target behavior (Cuvo, 1978).

A task analysis is a tool for the person who will be teaching the person with disabilities. Construction of a task analysis before instruction begins meets three instruction needs: (1) it increases the likelihood that the instructor has a thorough understanding of the task, (2) the task analysis provides the basis for a system for data collection, and (3) the identification of discriminative stimuli from which to direct instructional strategies. In developing a task analysis, consider the following points:

1. The specific objective for the task should be identified and recorded.
2. The person who will be doing the teaching should perform the task several times before constructing the task analysis. (This is important because there is often more than one method of completing a task, such as putting on a coat.)
3. The person who will be doing the instruction should analyze the task and construct the task analysis.
4. The task should be broken down into response units small enough to instruct the learner successfully. For some learners, bigger "chunks" are fine as response units (or steps) of the task analysis (in cleaning a room such as empty wastebasket, empty recycling container, vacuum floor, etc.), whereas other learners might need more detailed response units (such as go to wastebasket, pick up, walk to cart, empty waste into waste container on cart, etc.).
5. The steps in the task should be sequenced in exactly the order in which they will be performed.
6. Mandatory steps in the task analysis should be identified (certain steps in the task analysis that are considered essential). If these steps are not performed or are performed incorrectly, the terminal goal is not achieved successfully
7. The discriminative stimulus for each step should be identified (Cuvo, 1978; Gold, 1976; Mank & Horner, 1988; Powell et al., 1991).

Table 2.1
NINE-STEP TASK ANALYSIS FOR HANDWASHING

1. Turn water on
2. Put hands under water
3. Put soap on hands
4. Rub hands together
5. Rinse hands
6. Turn water off
7. Get paper towel
8. Dry hands
9. Throw away towel

The ecological inventory shown in Figure 2.1 identified the activity of handwashing in the restroom subenvironment. Handwashing is an important skill that is often taught using a task analysis approach. Many restaurants and other businesses have signs in their restrooms reminding employees to wash their hands before returning to work. For many learners, handwashing may need to be broken down into teachable steps. An example of a task analysis for handwashing can be seen in Table 2.1.

Chains of Behavior

The task analysis represents a chain of behavior, or the sequence of what the learner must do. Once a task analysis has been developed there are three strategies for using the task analysis for instructional purposes; forward chaining, whole task or concurrent chaining, and backward chaining.

FORWARD CHAINING. This is a teaching procedure in which a sequence of responses is developed by first teaching and reinforcing the initial step in the task analysis, then teaching and reinforcing the addition of the second step and so on until the entire activity has been learned. It is a cumulative process; only the first step is taught initially and then additional steps are added one at a time. For example, in teaching a person put on pants, the instructor would teach the first step "put foot into the pant leg," and then stop the instruction at that step until the learner can independently perform that step. Then, at the next instructional session, the instructor would teach putting both feet into pant legs. Then adding one more step at a time until the learner is successful in completing all of the steps for putting on pants.

WHOLE TASK CHAINING/CONCURRENT CHAINING. This process is where all steps of the task analysis are taught simultaneously in a forward sequence from the initial step in the task analysis to the last step, all in one session. For most community activities, whole task chaining is the preferred method of instruction because the learner is performing the whole activity in the context in which it must occur.

BACKWARD CHAINING. With backward chaining, the last response in the task analysis is taught first, then the response that precedes it, and so on until the first response in the sequence is taught. The advantage of backward chaining is that the response closest to the terminal reinforcer is taught first. An example of backward chaining when teaching a learner to put on pants is to set up the activity to the last step by putting the pants on the learner and getting them ready to button or physically assist the learner up until the last step (the last step in the task analysis, put button through the button hole, would be taught first) and then provide cueing procedures. Backward chaining is an efficient way to teach a task but is often difficult to use in community settings.

Key Point Question 3: How Are Behaviors Defined?

Direct observation of learner performance requires target behaviors to be accurately defined, also known as pinpointing. All behaviors must be observable and measurable. The general rule is that anyone observing the learner should be able to agree with other observers with reasonable certainty whether or not a behavior is performed. Poorly defined target behaviors may result in inconsistent measurement. For example, if the learner is receiving social skills instruction for appropriate greeting and establishing eye contact is not included in the definition, the learner may learn the skill without this critical aspect or receive conflicting feedback across trainers. When defining target behaviors, the instructor may explain the definition to other individuals, such as paraprofessionals and ask them to observe and record occurrence of the target behavior along with the instructor for a brief period of time. If both observers agree as to the occurrence of the behavior, then the data collected using this measurement system would be considered reliable. Key Point Question 6 describes the process of training staff to ensure reliable data collection.

Key Point Question 4: How Are Instructional Objectives Written?

When the skill that is targeted for instruction is clearly defined, an instructional objective should be written to establish when mastery has occurred and instruction will cease. A technically adequate instructional objective requires the conditions under which the behavior will be performed, an observable, measurable behavior, and the criteria for mastery (Mager, 1997). For example, washing hands after using the restroom is required for employees and recognized as good hygiene for everyone. If Jaden's teacher has targeted handwashing for instruction, he would first write an instructional objective such as, "After using the restroom, Jaden will wash his hands, completing all steps of the task analysis independently for five consecutive trials." The condition in this example would be "*After using the restroom,*" the behavior is clearly defined as *Jaden will wash his hands by completing all ten steps of the task analysis,* and the criteria for mastery are *independently for five consecutive trials.* When Jaden has washed his hands without prompts for five consecutive training session, the skill will be considered mastered and instruction terminated.

The instructional objective serves as the measure for student progress and, as mentioned earlier, ultimate mastery of the skill. For this reason, the instructional objective may be included at the top of the data collection sheet to provide a basis for measuring progress on the part of the learner (refer to Figure 2.2).

Key Point Question 5: How Are Instructional Data Collected?

When utilizing systematic instruction of target skills involving multiple steps in sequence, a task analysis assessment may be most appropriate. This form of assessment has been best suited for functional living skills (Storey, Bates, & Hanson, 1984). Task analysis data may include performed (+) or not performed (−) for each step or level of assistance required to successfully complete the task analysis or a target step.

Baseline data may be collected by presenting the learner with the discriminative stimulus or natural cue and allowing the learner to independently perform the step. During baseline, the instructor does not provide prompts or reinforcement for completing steps. Instruction of

Student:　Cliff Bergen　　　　　　　　　　　　　　　　　　　Month/Year:　August 2010

Instructional Objective: When given the direction, will fold them, completing all eight steps of the task analysis without prompts for three consecutive sessions.

Steps	1	2	3	4	5	6	7	8	9	10	11	12	13	14	15	16	17	18	19	20
1. Fold towel side to side	+	+	+	+	+	+	+	+	+	+	+	+								
2. Shake towel	–	–	–	–	–	FP	FP	PP	+	+	+	+								
3. Place towel on table	–	–	–	–	–	FP	PP	+	+	+	+	+								
4. Smooth towel flat	–	–	–	–	–	FP	PP	G	Pp	+	+	+								
5. Fold towel in half	–	–	–	–	–	FP	PP	G	PP	+	+	+								
6. Fold towel side to side	–	–	–	–	–	FP	PP	G	G	+	+	+								
7. Fold towel to top	–	–	–	–	–	FP	PP	G	G	+	+	+								
8. Stack towel	–	–	–	–	–	FP	G	+	G	+	+	+								

+ Independent performance
– Step not performed
IV = Indirect verbal
DV = Direct verbal
G = Gestural
M = Model
PP = Partial physical
FP = Full physical

The instructor records a (+) if the learner completes the step independently, an (IV) for indirect verbal prompt, a (DV) for a verbal prompt, a (G) for a gestural prompt, an (M) for a model, a (PP) for a partial physical prompt, and an (FP) for a full physical prompt.

Comments:

Figure 2.2. Task Analytic Data Collection Form for Folding Towels.

target steps or unlearned steps can begin after assessment of what the learner can already do. When teaching someone to make a bed (as a domestic or vocational skill), it must first be determined which steps of the task analysis the person can perform. The instructor would provide the cue "make the bed" and wait three seconds to see if the learner initiates the task. If he does not perform the first step or performs it incorrectly, the instructor would score it as a minus (–) and complete the step to provide the discriminative stimulus for the next step to be performed. The instructor sets up each step of the task to allow the learner the opportunity to perform each step and records a plus or minus (*see* Figure 2.2). The instructor does not tell the learner what to do or provide any additional cues. This allows the assessment of each step of the task analysis because a learner may not be able to perform the first couple of steps of a task but be able to perform the remaining steps.

Data collection during instruction, or formative data, can simply be conducted by recording the occurrence or nonoccurrence of independent performance of each step in the case of whole step or concurrent chaining or for targeted steps in forward or backwards chaining. Formative data are collected throughout the instructional process and are necessary to monitor learner progress toward skill acquisition.

Instruction using a concurrent chaining technique requires recording data for every step of the task analysis. If the learner is being taught handwashing with whole task instruction with a system of least to greatest prompts (*see* Chapter 3), the instructor would provide the verbal direction, "wash hands," then wait to see if the learner performed the first step correctly, if not then the instructor would deliver a gesture prompt and continue delivering prompts from least to greatest until the learner performs the behavior correctly.

The instructor may also choose to record the level of assistance or prompting level required to complete each step or target step because this allows analysis of whether the learner needs fewer prompts over time. The instructor records a (+) if the learner completes the step independently, an (IV) for an indirect verbal prompt, a (DV) for a verbal prompt, a (G) for a gestural prompt, an (M) for a model, a (PP) for a partial physical prompt, and an (FP) for a full physical prompt. Figure 2.2 shows a data sheet with baseline data and instructional data for teaching towel folding using concurrent chaining.

Key Point Question 6: What Are Other Types of Direct Observation Data?

Direct observation data are commonly used to determine the strength of a target behavior. The most common methods for collecting direct observation data are frequency, duration, latency, and interval recording.

Frequency Recording

Frequency recording is an often-used method of direct observation data collection. The number of times a behavior is performed during an observation session is its frequency. Frequency data may also be referred to as event data. Discrete behaviors, those with a distinct start and stop, are required for this type of recoding.

Frequency recording is most appropriate for behaviors of relatively consistent duration and moderate occurrence. For example, if you counted the number of times a supported employee was out of the designated work area, one occurrence on Monday could be for three hours and five occurrences of two minutes each on Tuesday would appear to be more problematic when graphed. Thus, frequency counts in this instance would not be a good measure of the individual's behavior.

Collecting frequency data requires a data sheet including dates, times, and tallies for each occurrence of the target behavior. Figure 2.3

Learner: Shawan		Instructor: Mr. Howard		
Setting(s): playground		Target Behavior(s): contacts with peers		
Date	Length of Observation	Frequency	Total	Rate
11/17/09	30 min.	//	2	n/a
11/18/09	30 min.	/////	5	n/a
11/19/09	30 min.	///	3	n/a
11/20/09	30 min.	//////	6	n/a

n/a = not applicable

Figure 2.3. Data Collection Form for Frequency.

provides an example of frequency recording for the learner perform-ance of asking for assistance when in the community. The instructor would make a tally for each occurrence observed.

Duration and Latency Recording

Duration and latency data are related to time. Duration is the length of time a behavior is performed. Duration data usually have a begin-ning time and an ending time to gather the total number of minutes or seconds a behavior occurs. An example of duration recording would involve the instructor noting the time that the learner began to walk to the bus stop and the time that he arrived at the stop. The duration would be the number of minutes it takes the learner to walk to the bus stop. Figure 2.4 provides an example of a duration/latency data sheet for the learner's performance on duration of completing assigned work tasks and latency between supervisor direction and initiation of task.

Latency is the amount of time between the presentation of the cue or discriminative stimulus and the initiation of the behavior. For exam-ple, the amount of time between when the supervisor gives a support-ed employee a directive to unload a delivery and when the employee begins unloading the product would be latency. Latency recording, like duration, is only useful for discrete behaviors, and continuous ob-servation may be necessary. An appropriate alternative to frequency, duration, or latency recording would be interval recording.

Learner: Shawan					Instructor: Mr. Howard			
Setting(s): Casten's Warehouse				Target Behavior(s):		Duration – Work Tasks Latency – Initiating Task		
Duration					Latency			
Date	Start Time	Stop Time	Duration		Date	Start Time	Stop Time	Latency
5/27	8:15	8:48	33 min.		5/27	8:00	8:15	15 min.
5/28	8:07	8:45	38 min.		5/28	8:00	8:07	7 min.
5/29	8:04	8:40	36 min.		5/29	8:00	8:04	4 min.
5/30	8:08	8:39	31 min.		5/30	8:00	8:08	8 min.

Figure 2.4. Data Collection Form for Duration/Latency.

Interval Recording

When it is difficult to clearly observe the beginning and ending of a behavior or continuous observation is difficult, interval data are often used. Interval recording is also useful for collecting data behaviors of inconsistent lengths or extremely high frequency. Three types of interval recording are typically utilized: whole interval, partial interval, and momentary time sampling. Interval recording can be used for a wide variety of behaviors. Interval recording has been used to measure the strength of behaviors such as time on task, peer interactions, and eye contact.

Collecting interval data requires the observer to divide the observation period into intervals of equal length and record a (+) for occurrence or (–) for nonoccurrence of the target behavior. The determination of occurrence or nonoccurrence varies depending on the type of interval recording. Accuracy of interval data is increased with shorter intervals. The length of an interval is usually between five and thirty seconds.

Whole interval recording requires that the behavior be performed throughout the entire interval to be considered an occurrence (+). This type of recording works best for behaviors that are expected to be continuous or ongoing without interruption. An example of a behavior appropriate for whole interval recording would be time in work area. This behavior would be expected to continue for a long period of time and time away from the work area would be noted.

The observer would record a (+) for occurrence in partial interval recording if the behavior is performed at any time during the interval. The behavior does not occur throughout the entire interval in partial interval recording. Partial interval recording may be most appropriate for target behaviors that are brief or fleeting. For example, interval recording may be useful in analyzing the strength of a previously mastered behavior such as asking a coworker for assistance.

Momentary time sampling may be the most useful type of interval recording. The observer records an occurrence (+) or nonoccurrence (–) at the precise moment of the end of an interval. This frees the observer to provide instruction or supervision throughout the interval except at the precise moment interval ends. Momentary time sampling can be used for many different behaviors, such as completing a task, socializing with others, and engaging in a leisure activity.

Key Point Question 7: Who Should Collect Instructional Data?

Ideally, the individual providing instruction will collect data on a target behavior. If it is not possible to collect data during instruction, alternative observers may be utilized. These could be paraprofessionals, volunteers, parents, or other instructors. It is very important to train others in any data collection method and allow for a period of time to practice and adapt to the process. Observers should record data frequently, systematically, and unobtrusively. Permanent products such as videorecording may be used to increase accuracy because they can be scored later and also discussed while scoring and rescored if necessary.

As discussed in Key Point Question 3, a clear definition of a behavior is necessary to ensure accuracy of data. It is also important that staff be trained in the specific procedures in order to increase reliability. It is not always possible, or desirable, that one person do all of the training or data collection. It cannot be taken for granted that different staff will collect reliable data. The individual who designs the instructional program should train others by clearly defining the behavior and data collection procedures. For example, if a teacher and paraprofessional are both going to collect data for a student putting on her coat, the teacher should go over the task analysis and how data are to be collected. After this training, the teacher and paraprofessional can collect the same data simultaneously and compare. If they have agreement of approximatley 90 percent or better by dividing the smaller by the larger number (frequency or duration/latency) or agreements divided by agreements plus disagreements (interval), the data collection system can be considered reliable.

It is often difficult to collect data during instruction, especially if multiple behaviors are addressed simultaneously. Several "tricks" have been found to be useful for unobtrusive data collection. For example, the instructor can merely move a button, coin, or paper clip from one pocket to another when collecting frequency data or tape a small piece of paper around his wrist to make tally marks or write start and stop times. Data sheets can be shrunk to fit inside the instructor's planner instead of carrying a cumbersome clipboard.

Technology is continuously changing the way instructors can collect data as well. Some have suggested that teachers use personal digital assistants (PDAs) when collecting observation data in the classroom (Cihak & Alaimo, 2003), but handheld devices have been found to be especially useful in community settings (Fletcher, Erickson, Toomey, & Wagenaar, 2003; Gravlee, Zenk, Woods, Rowe, & Schulz, 2006). Smartphones are quickly becoming the preferred device for completing tasks such as collecting data in multiple settings, eliminating the need for paper and pencil data collection forms.

Key Point Question 8: How Often Should Data Be Collected?

There is no clear empirical evidence for how often an instructor should take data (Holvoet, O'Neil, Chagdon, Carr, & Warner, 1983). Data should be collected regularly during instruction in order to make decisions about instructional effectiveness (or lack of) and for adapting instruction. The more frequent the data collection, the more sensitive to change the analysis becomes. Data collection promotes a more systematic approach to instruction. Data should be collected prior to instruction (baseline) and frequently throughout the learning process.

Data cannot be collected on every skill that is being taught, and they should not be collected just for the sake of collecting data. The instructor must prioritize skills requiring systematic instruction and plan for the data collection that must occur throughout the training session. Behaviors or skills that are addressed more informally or assessed for generalization can be measured using probes at naturally occurring times without instructor prompts or reinforcement. A probe is merely a brief assessment that occurs intermittenntly instead of during every training session. During a probe session, the teacher observes the learner in context and collects performance data (+ or –).

Key Point Question 9: How Are Instructional Data Analyzed?

It has been noted that merely collecting data does not improve instruction unless it is analyzed. The best method to analyze data is to visually inspect trends by graphing them. The simplest, most efficient way is to use a time series line graph. Graphing data allows the instructor and others to analyze learner performance through visual inspection. A graph is a visual representation of the learner's progress or lack of progress towards the instructional goal. Line graphs are easily inter-

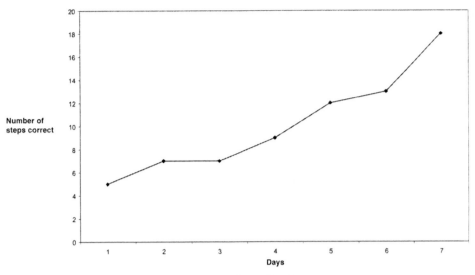

Figure 2.5. Line Graph.

preted and understood by instructors and other team members.

A line graph has a vertical and a horizontal line called the ordinate (y) and abscissa (x), respectively. The skill or target behavior is measured on the ordinate and the training sessions are identified on the abscissa. Figure 2.5 shows a line graph for John's number of steps completed on the purchasing a coffee task analysis.

When graphing data, a simple A-B design or case study can be used to analyze progress. A case study design involves comparing the individual's performance before instruction (i.e., baseline or A phase) to performance after instruction is implemented (B phase). When providing instruction and making data-based decisions about adapting instructional procedures, instructors may not be concerned with establishing a clear relationship between the intervention (i.e., independent variable) and the learner's performance of the skill (i.e., dependent variable) in the same way a researcher is. Alberto and Troutman (2009) provide a detailed description of designs that control for confounding variables that are primarily used for research purposes.

Baseline data should represent the learner's current level of performance. Baseline data are typically gathered for three to five days; however, the data must be consistent and stable to ensure an accurate measure of learner performance prior to instruction.

Data should be graphed in order to analyze the stability of baseline performance, learner progress during instruction, need for program modification, and ultimate mastery of the new skill. The data analysis process involves obtaining a stable baseline, implementing systematic instruction, continuing to collect performance data, analyzing trends, reviewing data collection sheets as necessary, modifying instruction, and reporting mastery to the team.

Key Point Question 10: How Are Learner Errors Analyzed?

As mentioned previously, data must be kept in order to conduct a deeper analysis of individual performance on a task. Steps on a task analysis that are repeatedly incorrect must be examined in order to make appropriate modifications to instruction. Primarily, the three types of errors are initiation errors, discrimination errors, and response errors. (*See* Chapter 3 for descriptions and strategies to address each type of error.) Data sheets should have a section for comments where the instructor can note the type of error the learner is making so a pattern can be identified. For example, during instruction in brushing teeth, if the learner performs the wrong action when brushing the inside of his teeth, the instructor would make a note in the comment section that the learner is making a response error. This step could be broken down in greater detail (i.e., turn wrist, place brush on inside of teeth, brush up and down) to teach the correct response.

Key Point Question 11: How Is Generalization Assessed?

To assess if a skill that has been mastered has generalized, it is necessary to assess performance in representative criterion environments after instruction has ceased. The instructor can reinstitute the direct observation data collection method that was used during instruction, ask others who are familiar with the individual's performance, or, in some cases, have the individual self-monitor. If the skill has not generalized, then instruction may be reinstituted as necessary. For example, Cliff learned to independently fold towels at his jobsite by performing all steps of the task analysis without prompts for three consecutive sessions. Cliff's instructor, Ms. Crocket, followed up three months later by collecting task analysis data in the same way she had during baseline for the instructional program. Cliff was incorrectly performing step 6 (a previously difficult step), resulting in towels that were folded with wrinkles. Ms. Crocket reinstituted training on smoothing out the towel, and Cliff performed it consistently (three consecutive sessions) after only five training sessions. Cliff continued to perform the entire task under Ms. Crocket's supervision for one week to ensure maintenance of the skill.

BEST PRACTICE RECOMMENDATIONS

1. Assessment should be an ongoing part of instruction.
2. Whoever is collecting data needs to be trained on how to collect the data.
3. Task analysis is the best way to break down a skill for instruction.
4. Data should be analyzed regularly regarding learner perform-ance and instruction should be modified based on this analysis.
5. Only collect data that you will use; do not collect data just to be collecting data.

FUTURE RESEARCH ISSUES

1. How can technology be used best for collecting data?
2. How can technology be used best for analyzing data and then for modifying and improving instruction?
3. What are the best ways for training staff in data collection?

DISCUSSION QUESTIONS

1. What data are most important to collect?
2. How often do data need to be collected?
3. What should you do if inaccurate data are being collected?

SCHOOL AND COMMUNITY-BASED ACTIVITY SUGGESTIONS

1. Write a task analysis for a common task, such as changing a tire, balancing a checkbook, or taking a shower. Ask someone you

know to write one and compare both task analyses. Note the differences in how steps are broken down, sequenced, and included or omitted.

2. Identify the measurement system that would be most appropriate for the following behaviors: (a) John will take turns while playing a video game, (b) Sabrina will share her toys during free play, (c) Joseph will practice the drums for one hour, (d) Wesley will use a fork to spear his food during lunch.

3. Provide three more examples of observable target behaviors and the type of measurement system that would be most appropriate for measuring the behaviors.

REFERENCES

Alberto, P. A., & Troutman, A. C. (2009). *Applied behavior analysis for teachers* (10th ed.). Upper Saddle River, NJ: Pearson.

Brown, L., Branston-McLean, M. B., Hamre-Nietupski, S., Pumpian, I., Certo, N., & Gruewald, L. (1979). A strategy for developing age appropriate and functional curricular content for severely handicapped adolescents. *Journal of Special Education, 13,* 81–90.

Bellamy, G. T., Horner, R. H., & Inman, D. P. (1979). *Vocational habilitation of severely retarded adults: A direct service technology.* Baltimore, MD: University Park Press.

Cihak, D. F., & Alaimo, D. (2003). Using personal digital assistants (PDA) for collecting observational data in the classroom. Atlanta, GA: Bureau for Students with Multiple and Severe Disabilities. The Department of Educational Psychology and Special Education, Georgia State University.

Cuvo, A. J. (1978). Validating task analyses of community living skills. *Vocational Evaluation and Work Adjustment Bulletin, 11,* 13–21.

Fletcher, L. A., Erickson, D. J., Toomey, T. L., & Wagenaar, A. C. (2003). Handheld computers: A feasible alternative to paper forms for field data collection. *Evaluation Review, 27,* 165–178.

Gold, M. W. (1976). Task analysis of a complex assembly task by the retarded blind. *Exceptional Children, 43,* 78–84.

Gravlee, C. C., Zenk, S. N., Woods, S., Rowe, Z., & Schulz, A. J. (2006). Handheld computers for direct observation of the social and physical environment. *Field Methods, 18,* 382–397.

Holvoet, J., O'Neil, C., Chazdon, L., Carr, D., & Warner, J. (1983). Hey, do we really need to collect data? *Journal of the Association for the Severely Handicapped, 8,* 56–70.

Mager, R. (1997). *Preparing instructional objectives: A critical tool in the development of effective instruction* (3rd ed.). Atlanta, GA: The Center for Effective Performance, Inc.

Mank, D. M., & Horner, R. H. (1988). Instructional programming in vocational education. In R. Gaylord-Ross (Ed.), *Vocational education for persons with handicaps* (pp. 142–173). Mountain View, CA: Mayfield Publishing Company.

Powell, T. H., Pancsofar, E. L., Steere, D. E., Butterworth, J., Itzkowitz, J. S., & Rainforth, B. (1991). *Supported employment: Providing integrated employment opportunities for persons with disabilities.* White Plains, NY: Longman.

Storey, K., Bates, P., & Hanson, H. (1984). Acquisition and generalization of coffee purchase skills by adults with severe disabilities. *Journal of the Association for Persons with Severe Handicaps, 9,* 178–185.

Chapter 3

TEACHING SKILLS

Keypoint Questions

1. What is behavior?
2. What is the difference between cues and corrections?
3. What do you do if the learner is having difficulty learning steps of the task?
4. How does reinforcement influence learning?
5. Can learners generalize what they have learned?

Window to the World Case Study One

Jeremy is a four year old with autism. His teacher, Ms. Fassel, has been teaching him to follow two-step directions. She offers him a variety of reinforcers when he correctly responds to her requests. Jeremy often repeats (echolalia) the name of the reinforcer when offered by his teacher.

On Thursday, the class had a birthday party for one of the students in the class, and some of the cake was leftover. Ms. Fassel offered Jeremy a small piece of cake as a reinforcer during his instructional time. Jeremy enjoyed the cake and worked very hard to earn a second piece.

Ms. Fassel began working with Jeremy on Friday morning and offered him leftover birthday cake as the reinforcer. Jeremy repeated "piece of cake" but threw the cake and screamed when she gave it to him. Jeremy was upset for the rest of the morning.

Ms. Fassel called Jeremy's mother and found out that he had gotten sick during the night but seemed fine in the morning. Jeremy's mother and Ms. Fassel concluded that he may have had too much cake on Thursday and seeing it on Friday brought back memories of getting sick. Ms. Fassel and Jeremy's mother agreed to increase their communication regarding his reinforcement preferences.

Window to the World Case Study Two

At twenty-eight years of age, Antonio had a history of achieving many goals over his school career and in the community-based adult service program he attended. Unfortunately, many of these goals were not maintained or transferred to nontraining settings.

At an earlier time, Antonio had mastered purchasing a drink at a coffee shop, grocery shopping at a Super Center, and cleaning tables in the school cafeteria. None of these skills were practiced after mastery. Mr. Washington, Antonio's job coach found that Antonio could not independently complete cleaning tables at a local restaurant. The assisted living trainer, Ms. Fink took Antonio to the coffee shop and grocery store and assessed that he was completing less than 10 percent of the steps of the task analyses for both settings. The trainers reviewed past IEPs and determined that it took Antonio a similar amount of time to master all three skills at this point in his life as it had when he was younger.

The local transition planning committee discussed the need for school and adult services to work together to identify skills and natural settings for youth at the high school. All functional skill objectives included a generalization statement for maintenance and follow-up.

Key Point Question 1: What Is Behavior?

The purpose of instruction is to develop competence for individuals (Gold, 1980). This competence may be thought of as individual skills or behaviors that the person can perform in specific circumstances. People may learn skills in a variety of ways but for many individuals with disabilities they will only learn skills with systematic instruction. Independence, productivity, and integration are all based upon having skills necessary to be competent in specific situations such as shopping for clothes, interviewing for a job, and riding the bus from one's apartment to work.

Behavior is observable actions that a person does, such as sorting clothes for the washer, engaging in conversation with a friend, or ordering a meal at restaurant. These behaviors are triggered by stimuli in the environment and maintained by consequences. These stimuli (technically known as discriminative stimuli or Sd's) may also be thought of as cues or clues for what to do. For example, when driving a car, having the light turn red is the discriminative stimulus to bring the car to a stop. A knock on the door is the discriminative stimulus to open the door to see who is there.

It is extremely important to understand that the point of instruction is to get the learner to respond appropriately to the naturally occurring stimuli in the environment. We often mistakenly think that the purpose of instruction is to get people to do what they are supposed to do and that if we prompt people and they then do the behavior that our instruction has been successful. However, the real purpose is to get the person to respond appropriately to the natural stimuli so that they can perform skills independently. For example, in teaching someone how to cross the street, it is possible to give a verbal cue "Cross the street" and the person would be likely to cross the street successfully. However, he or she may be responding only to the verbal cue and without the presence of the instructor and the verbal cue be unable to cross the street independently or, most importantly, correctly. But if the instructor were to give a cue that highlights the discriminative stimulus, "The walklight is green, what do you do now?" then the person is more likely to be able to respond independently to the discriminative stimulus of a green walk light in the future. Thus, instruction is giving the person information so that they can perform the behavior when it is appropriate to do so.

Key Point Question 2: What Is the Difference Between Cues and Corrections?

Cues and corrections are two different things. A cue refers to initial information provided to a learner **before** a behavior is performed. A correction procedure refers to supplementary or corrective information to communicate to a learner that a response **already performed** is inappropriate or that a different response is needed.

Cues

Cues (also known as prompts) are added antecedent stimuli that increase the probability of a correct response. Antecedent means that the cue is provided before the behavior is to occur. The reasoning for the use of cues is that they occur before the behavior should happen and thus increase the likelihood of a correct response. Then, the response can be reinforced and thus increase the likelihood that in the future the behavior will occur in response to the natural cue (the green/walk light) without the cue. The purpose of cues is to assist the learner in performing behaviors (skills) in response to naturally occurring discriminative stimuli. The learner is thus (1) alerted to important natural stimuli that provide information about behaviors to emit and (2) able to respond appropriately. As Steere and Pancsofar (1995) have written "The cue is the clue to do something new" (p. 37).

There are different types of cues that may be used to provide information to learners and they may be used in different ways.

VERBAL CUES. These are statements or questions provided by an instructor that draw attention to the discriminative stimuli. Verbal cues may state specifically what the individual should do such as "Spread the peanut butter on the bread" or "Here comes Tom Rover, be sure and say hello to him when he gets to you." Verbal cues may also be nonspecific questions (i.e., indirect verbal cues) that alert the learner that something should be noticed such as "What do you do after you have the peanut butter on the knife?" or "Here comes Tom Rover, what should you do when he gets to you?" Specific verbal cues provide more information than nonspecific verbal cues do.

MODELING. The instructor does the task to show the learner how to perform the task. For example, the instructor could spread some peanut butter on the bread and then hand the knife to the learner.

GESTURES. These are movements made by the instructor to draw attention to natural stimuli. Pointing, motioning, or shadowing movements are examples. For example, the instructor could point to the bread where the peanut butter is to be spread.

PHYSICAL GUIDANCE. This involves physical contact between the instructor and the learner. It may involve full physical prompting (hand over hand) to direct the learner's movements or just a light touch. For example, to spread the peanut butter the instructor could hold his or her hand over the hands of the learner and help her or him move the knife with the peanut butter across the bread.

Remember that (1) cues are sources of information, (2) you want to provide the minimal amount of information needed to get the correct responses, and (3) cues ideally focus attention on natural discriminative stimuli. You want to provide cues just before or at the time of the natural discriminative stimulus. For example, "See the bakery on the corner, here comes our stop; when the bus stops and the doors open we get off." Be sure to reinforce the learner for correct responding (e.g., "That was great the way that you stood up and got right off the bus when the doors opened.").

It helps if you label why people are getting reinforcement so that they clearly understand the connection between their behavior and the reinforcer. Use the minimally intrusive cue to obtain the correct performance. You do not want the cue to control the learner's behavior rather than the natural discriminative stimulus. This is known as "prompt dependency" or "learned helplessness," in which the learner passively waits to be told what to do.

TIME DELAY. Time delay is when a discriminative stimulus is presented to the learner to cue the learner's response and the prompt is given to elicit the correct response (Wolery, Ault, & Doyle, 1992). This procedure allows for the fading of the controlling cue by inserting a fixed amount of time between the task direction and the prompt, which then builds more independent performance from the learner. When initially teaching a skill, the instructor may have a zero-second delay between the instruction and the prompt for the correct response. For instance, if the learner is learning to recognize letters, then the instruction may be "Point to the letter A," and the instructor immediately provides a gesture prompt by pointing to the letter A. As instruction continues, the instructor can systematically build in a delay between the instruction and the prompt (e.g., one second for several trials, then two seconds, etc.). The logic behind providing this delay is so that learners are initially provided with information for the correct response before they are expected to respond. That way they are more likely to make the correct response. Building in the time delay between the cue and the response allows individuals to process the information and provide the correct response but not not allowing too much time to pass if the student does not make the correct response. This allows the individuals to learn quickly, with few errors. It also allows the instructor more opportunities to provide reinforcement for correct responding.

There are no set rules for the number of instructional trials for time delay sessions. The most important factor is how well the individual is learning. You want the individual to be consistently responding correctly before increasing the delay.

GROUP INSTRUCTION. Instruction may take place individually or in small groups. Wolery and associates (1992) have pointed out several advantages to small group instruction: (1) much instruction in general education settings takes place in small groups, and instruction for learners with disabilities in small groups will help them perform appropriately in those situations; (2) it is a more efficient use of instructor time; (3) it allows learners to learn social interaction skills; and (4) skills may be acquired through observational learning. In the small group setting, instruction may be directed toward one individual or all members of the group. Learner responses may then be individual or group (where the entire group responds in unison).

Correction Procedures

The basic assumption should be that errors are a function of the instructional approach, not inherent to the learner because of a disability label. Errors are not random. Few learners perform with unpredictable error patterns. The two most common errors are due to prior history (where the person has learned an inappropriate response to a discriminative stimulus) and incomplete instruction (Horner, Bellamy, & Colvin, 1984).

First, collect information on incorrect performance as well as correct performance. Errors are of equal, if not greater, importance for instructors to attend to (Horner, 1984). Second, design the instruction to minimize errors. This can be done by following the generalization guidelines in this chapter. Third, correct errors as soon as they are made. Finally, collect data that document error patterns.

When a learner makes an error, stop the learner immediately. It is important to interrupt the learner, in a nonpunitive manner, as soon as an error is initiated or observed. You do not want learners to continue on tasks after an error because they are learning incorrect performance. Second, recreate the situation in which the error occurred. Third, have the learner repeat the step using enough assistance to ensure success. Be sure to deliver praise for the correct response. Finally, repeat the step again using less assistance.

There are three types of errors that a learner may make: initiation errors, discrimination errors, and response errors.

INITIATION ERRORS. An initiation error is when the learner fails to initiate a behavior in response to the discriminative stimulus in the environment. For example, in making a peanut butter sandwich, an initiation error occurs when the learner stops after opening the jar of peanut butter and fails to initiate the next step of picking up the knife. Respond to initiation errors by

1. isolating preceding two steps and difficult step
2. identifying cues to ensure correct responding
3. pairing cue and task stimuli
4. fading cues
5. immediately reinforcing self-initiations
6. fading reinforcement

DISCRIMINATION ERRORS. These are errors in which the learner responds to the wrong discriminative stimulus in the environment. For example, in making a peanut butter sandwich, picking up a jar of pickles on the counter rather than the jar of peanut butter would be a discrimination error. Respond to discrimination errors by

1. increasing intensity and frequency of reinforcer
2. highlighting the relevant dimension of stimulus
3. presenting examples with very similar stimuli
4. fading reinforcement

RESPONSE ERRORS. These are errors in which the learner makes an incorrect response. For example, the learner could put the jar of peanut butter away in the freezer instead of in the refrigerator. Respond to response errors by

1. increasing intensity and frequency of reinforcer
2. identifying cues to ensure correct responding
3. presenting examples in cumulative sequence

In this example, you would increase both the intensity of the reinforcer (rather than just saying "good job" you would increase the enthusiasm and pat the person on the back) and the frequency (reinforce the learner every time that he or she put the peanut butter away correctly); identify cues that ensure the correct responding (you could label the freezer and refrigerator doors); and then present the examples in cumulative sequence (have the person make a peanut butter sandwich and then have her or him practice putting the peanut butter jar away).

Key Point Question 3: What Do You Do If the Learner is Having Difficulty Learning Steps of the Task?

No matter how well one teaches, there will be some tasks or parts of a task that are difficult for an individual to learn. A learner may perform most of a task accurately yet make consistent errors or require a consistent level of assistance on a few remaining steps. With these steps, modifying the kind, type, and amount of assistance and manipulating the kind and amount of reinforcement may not be effective in improving learner performance. A person's consistently poor performance on such steps functionally defines them as "difficult steps."

1. Provide Massed Trials

With massed trials, the learner does not practice the whole task but performs the difficult behavior or step of the task many times, which provides the learner with extra practice on the step that is difficult and maximizes the effect of training and feedback. This prevents other steps from occurring between feedback on one trial and the performance of the next trial. Naturally occurring tasks are preferable over unnatural tasks (i.e., emptying all wastebaskets in area versus putting on and taking off the same wastebasket bag).

For example, in learning how to empty wastebaskets, a person is having trouble learning the step of shaking the trash bag open. The instructor could then have the learner open up bags before doing the rounds. Because it is a short task, find a location where there are multiple wastebaskets (office) and provide many trials.

First, provide a discriminative stimulus for the step ("open the trash bag" or the natural discriminative stimulus of having the bag in hand while standing in front of trash can). Second, have the learner perform the step with or without assistance. Third, provide the learner with immediate feedback on performance. Finally, repeat the discriminative stimulus and the process.

2. Manipulate the Demands of a Step to Ensure Learner Success

One can reduce the difficulty for the learner by manipulating the task and need for assistance. It should be set up so the learner is performing correctly on 75 percent of the trials. This will help minimize uncooperative behavior and focus the training on what the learner can do instead of what he or she cannot do.

The learner should not experience repeated failure. You are trying to facilitate the performance of the response required or maximize the effect of the natural cue for breaking the sequence down in an easy to hard continuum. For example, open the bag part way if the learner is having trouble opening the bag.

3. Increase the Level of Reinforcement During Massed Trials Training

Although you might have increased the opportunity for reinforcement, because the step is difficult for the learner, it will require more effort to perform correctly. Increase the level of reinforcement to above that normally used when training the steps together. This is a step that has been frustrating for the learner. Massed trials should not be punishing or aversive. For example, when doing massed trials on bag opening, increase the amount of verbal praise, or if the learner particularly likes some part of the janitorial task, you may want to do that after massed trials.

4. Conduct Massed Trials in Short Time Blocks

Keep these massed trials shorter than normal training sessions (maybe ten to fifteen minutes long, two to three times per day). Give the learner access to the task but end before the learner begins to get bored by the task. For example, in using massed trials to teach a learner how to shake open the trash bag for emptying a wastebasket, go to an office with a lot of trash cans several times a day.

5. Systematically Include Mastered Steps in the Chain of the Task

It is of little use if the learner can do the difficult step in a mass trial session but cannot integrate it back into the natural chain. Adding the previous step in the chain during the practice sessions as the learner becomes more competent in the difficult step can accomplish this.

Then require the step immediately preceding the learned difficult step in the chain. Always perform the difficult step or isolated skill with the natural chain and context. This is the true test of learner performance because this is where the learner will need to use it. For example, if after many massed trials, the learner has finally mastered the step of shaking the trash bag open, add the steps before it back in.

6. Systematically Fade Your Assistance

Before providing any type of assistance, decide how you are going to fade it. It is easy to add something that will help the learner and then not be able to fade it and the learner becomes dependent upon the cue. Verbal directions are very difficult to systematically fade. You usually have to say it or not say it. For example, if you are assisting the learner by partially opening the bag, open it less and less during the massed trials as the learner acquires the skill.

Key Point Question 4: How Does Reinforcement Influence Learning?

Technically defined, positive reinforcement is an event presented after a response has been performed that increases the frequency of the behavior it follows (Kazdin, 2001). In other words, positive reinforcement is a process. You can see that reinforcement has happened only when you see change. An individual's behavior should increase following the delivery of the reinforcer. If the behavior does not increase, it is not a reinforcer.

Another way to analyze reinforcement is that you are arranging conditions under which someone gets things. Although reward and reinforcement are sometimes used interchangeably, an important distinction to recognize is that people are rewarded, but behavior is reinforced. Reinforcement can be used to teach new behaviors or to strengthen behaviors that the person already has. Not all items or events are reinforcers for everyone. One person may like Ian Hunter, another REM. One person may like iced tea, another soda.

General Guidelines for Using Reinforcement

1. Only reinforce correct responses. Reinforcement strengthens the behavior that it follows, so do not inadvertently reinforce incor-

rect performance.

2. If you provide assistance, also provide reinforcement. Reinforcement strengthens the response, so make sure that you deliver the reinforcement after the person performs the response correctly. It is okay to provide assistance but make sure that the reinforcement comes after the assistance and after the correct performance.

3. Use a positive tone.

4. Be brief. Do not interrupt people and take them off task.

5. Vary what you say. You do not always have to say "good job." It is easy to get in a rut of using the same word or phrase.

6. Make sure that you are reinforcing. You want to be pleasant and positive so that the person you are working with will want to interact with you and receive instruction from you. This will make praise from you reinforcing and other reinforcers less necessary. So be nice!

7. Do not reinforce simply attending to the task. It is correct performance (i.e., outcome) that you want to reinforce. Reinforcing attending to task (i.e., process) may not increase output.

Types of Reinforcers Useful in School and Community Environments

Participation and instruction in school and community settings is often activity based. Activity based means that a chain or sequence of behaviors is performed that produces an outcome that is functional for the individual (e.g., the sequence of behaviors for eating at a restaurant includes entering, waiting to be seated, ordering, eating, paying, and leaving). The focus should be on activities rather than on brief skill sequences because activities are outcome based and more likely to have a positive impact on the person's lifestyle (Wilcox & Bellamy, 1987). You need to be out in the real world (e.g., the criterion environment) teaching skills that are functional and usually a long chain of behavior sequences, so reinforcement must be used in the sequence and especially at the end of the sequence. For example, after completing the sequence of cleaning the offices in a complex, the worker might relax for a few minutes with something to eat or drink.

Selecting Reinforcers

1. One simple way to find out what a person likes is to ask! However, it may not always be that easy, and you may need a more structured interview to help the person think about the different reinforcers available.
2. If the person is not able to easily tell you what he or she likes, someone else who knows the person well might be able to. Family members, friends, roommates, significant others, or co-workers might be good resources. Each one might give you a different perspective on what the person likes in different situations such as at work versus at home.
3. Direct observations are very useful in assessing reinforcement preference. These include recording foods the person prefers, the type of activities engaged in, or with whom the person prefers to interact.
4. If people with disabilities have had limited exposure to activities and reinforcers in the community, they might not know what they like. Thus persons with disabilities take part in many community activities so that they are more likely to make an informed choice concerning reinforcers.

Considerations in Using Reinforcers

AGE APPROPRIATENESS. The reinforcer should be age appropriate for the person. Age appropriate means chronological age, not mental age. For example, a twenty-one year old should not be given stuffed animals as a reinforcer. Stuffed animals are age appropriate for someone around six years of age. Age appropriate reinforcers for a twenty-one year old might include going to a concert, having a drink in a bar, having a snack, going on a date, playing softball, eating in a restaurant, or having friends over for dinner.

When using reinforcers, consider the impact they will have on other people in addition to the person being reinforced. How would employees in a factory view a forty-year-old coworker with a disability being given a "smiley face" sticker for completing a task? That employee would be stigmatized and coworkers would be likely to value him or her less as a fellow adult and view him more as a child than as an adult. If you are not sure if a reinforcer is age appropriate it is probably best not to use it and to come up with a different reinforcer. Better to be safe than to stigmatize the person you are working with.

HEALTH APPROPRIATENESS. When using edible reinforcers, it is important to consider whether they are good for the person's health. If edible reinforcers are necessary and appropriate, raisins, pieces of fruit or vegetable, or juice are good alternatives to candy, cereal, or cookies. Also, be aware of the person's medical history concerning allergies or special diets.

EASE OF DELIVERY. Be sure that the reinforcer can be delivered easily. One nice thing about using praise as a reinforcer is that it can be delivered quite easily and efficiently and you do not have to interrupt what the person is doing to deliver it. If you are using reinforcers such as tokens or food, the delivery may not be so easy. For instance, if an individual is working as a busperson in a restaurant and you want to deliver a piece of fruit as a reinforcer, you must stop the person on the job. He or she might have to set down some dishes or a tub and wash hands before you can offer the piece of fruit and praise for clearing the table. The person will eat it and then go back to work. This is not very efficient and not typical for the workplace. It could stigmatize that person in front of coworkers, the employer, and customers.

TIME OF CONSUMPTION. Not only do you want to deliver the reinforcer quickly, you also want the person to consume it within a reasonable amount of time. Giving people taffy as a reinforcer would probably not be a good idea if they are working a job where they need to use their hands.

SATIATION. Even if you like salted pretzels a lot, would you want to eat them all day long? After fifty pretzels you would probably not want any more. This is known as satiation. At this point something to drink would probably be more reinforcing than another pretzel. It is important that you use different reinforcers and mix them so that the person does not satiate on one reinforcer.

The following are some ways to prevent satiation:

1. Have different reinforcers available for different tasks.
2. Alternate reinforcers during instructional sessions.
3. Gradually decrease the size or amount of the reinforcer.
4. Be sure that the reinforcer you are using is not something the person has easy access to throughout the day.

5. Change the pool of reinforcers from which the person has to choose from so he or she cannott always pick the same reinforcer and possibly become satiated.

CONTINGENCY. Contingency means that when people do a certain behavior (such as correctly busing a table), they get a specific reinforcer (i.e., praise from the job coach). If they do not bus the table they don't get the praise. This is probably the most important consideration for delivering reinforcement: is the reinforcement contingent upon what the person does? If it is not, you have problems. One way to help make the connection between the reinforcement and the behavior is to label the reinforcement contingencies. In other words, tell the person why he or she is being reinforced. For example, if a person pays correctly when getting on a bus you could say "That was a great job of putting your dollar in the slot. Way to go!"

A person needs to be reinforced for what he or she does. A common mistake is when the instructor makes it too difficult for the person to get the reinforcer. What usually happens is that the person becomes frustrated or angry because of not being reinforced, so he or she does not do what the instructor expects. Be sure that you are delivering reinforcement often enough.

When to Reinforce in Behavior Chains

If you deliver reinforcement only at the end of a behavior chain, not all responses in the chain are equally affected. The reinforcer has a greater effect on responses later in the chain. The longer the chain is, the less likely it is that a reinforcer at the end of the chain will maintain performance of early responses (Bellamy, Horner, & Inman, 1979). You must take into account the number of responses within a chain when deciding on a reinforcement schedule. You may want to deliver reinforcement at several points in the chain.

Suppose that Johann is learning how to clean an office. He might be responsible for emptying recycling and wastebaskets, vacuuming, sweeping, wet and dry dusting, and removing trash. If you wait until Johann completes all the tasks before reinforcing him, the reinforcement schedule might be too thin and he might slow down or stop working. You may want to make sure that Johann gets reinforcement at different times or points in the sequence of tasks (such as at the end of emptying the recycling and wastebaskets, vacuuming, etc.).

A reinforcer delivered at the end of a chain does reinforce all responses in the chain, however, although not equally, as pointed out. If Johann makes a mistake in the chain and still gets reinforced at the end, he might be more likely to make the same mistake again. If Johann does make a mistake, stop him, provide feedback (i.e., "the recycling goes in the blue bag"), have him do it the right way, and then reinforce him. Because reinforcement increases the probability that the person will behave in the same manner in the future, you want to be sure that you are reinforcing only correct responses. The opportunity to perform each subsequent step in the task analysis will effectively reinforce the learner's behavior only if the series of behaviors ultimately produces reinforcing events. For example, you might want to reinforce Johann with a snack break following completion of tasks.

Key Point Question 5: Can Learners Generalize What They Have Learned?

If a person learns how to purchase an item in a specific grocery store, it does not necessarily mean that he or she will be able to purchase the same item in a different grocery store.

People with disabilities often have difficulty generalizing what they learn. Generalization is demonstration of skills in situations other than those in which the original instruction occurred. Generalization may be across time, persons, settings, and behaviors (Stokes & Baer, 1977). From an instructional standpoint, generalization just does not happen; it must be planned for. Instructors need to make generalization part of most, but not all, instruction (a person probably needs to know how to operate only one set of washer and dryers, not all washers and dryers). There are a number of strategies for facilitating generalization, but we would like to focus on seven of these strategies. More detailed information on generalization and general case analysis may be found in Horner, Dunlap, and Koegel (1988).

Train in the Natural Setting

Teaching is conducted directly in at least one type of setting in which the skills will be used (the criterion environment). For example, in teaching how to set a table at a restaurant, you could do the actual instruction at the restaurant.

Sequential Modification

Teaching is provided in one setting and generalization is probed in other settings. If necessary, teaching is conducted sequentially in more and more settings until generalization to all desired settings is observed. For example, one could teach appropriate greeting skills toward different people (teachers, school staff, peers, community members), environments (the lunch room, the playground, the hallway), and times of the day and different types of greeting behaviors (appropriate verbal greetings, handshakes, etc.).

Program Common Stimuli

This requires selecting a salient, but not necessarily task-related, stimulus from the situation to which generalization is desired and including that stimulus in the training program. For example, when teaching an individual exercise skills to participate in aerobics class, use the music from the class when teaching the skills outside of the aerobics class.

Multiple Exemplars

Several examples of the stimulus class to which generalization is desired are trained at the same time. For example, when teaching exercise skills, teach three types of skills and generalization may occur to untaught skills.

Incidental Teaching

This also is called naturalistic teaching, nonintensive teaching, or minimal intervention. Settings, cues, prompts, materials, response definition, and other features of the training situation are purposely varied to avoid a ritual, highly structured, invariate program that might inhibit generalization.

Mediate Generalization

Teach a secondary behavior or strategy that will help an individual remember or figure out how and when to generalize or that will dispel the differences between the teaching and the generalization situations. An example is using picture prompts for cooking skills (picture prompts are a series of pictures or drawings showing the person what to do). Once Eliza understands how to use picture prompts to cook a hot dog, she may be likely to use picture prompts to pop popcorn or make a smoothie.

Use Self-Mediated Stimuli (e.g., self-management strategies)

Self-medicated stimuli (e.g., self-management strategies) can be very effective for facilitating generalization. These strategies are covered in Chapter 10.

GENERALIZATION ERROR PATTERNS

Learners can make mistakes in generalization and it is very important to analyze why they are making these mistakes in order to increase their ability to generalize information that they have learned.

Irrelevant Stimuli Control the Target Response

To avoid this problem, use both positive and negative teaching examples. A positive teaching example is modeling or showing the person what he or she is supposed to do. A negative teaching example is modeling or showing the person what he or she is not supposed to do). For example, if a person learns that the discriminative stimulus for crossing a street is initiation of crossing by another person, present the learner with situations in which another person crosses the street first and situations in which nobody crosses in front of the learner.

Irrelevant Stimuli Control Irrelevant Responses

Following successful teaching, the learner does not perform the target behavior under novel conditions because irrelevant stimuli in the novel conditions exerts more powerful control over irrelevant responses than the relevant stimuli exert over the target response. An example would be a learner who yells and grabs to obtain things although he or she was taught to use sign language (but not in that setting). To avoid this problem, teaching should occur with a set of positive and negative examples that include those irrelevant stimuli that control irrelevant responses.

Because it may not be possible to conduct a general case analysis of all learning situations from an instruction standpoint, try using at least three examples for as many skills as possible. This involves conducting teaching in three different settings, with three different sets of materials, and three different teachers. This will increase the chances of successful generalization without having to take the time to conduct a general case analysis. For example, you may teach a student how to appropriately greet others in a classroom setting, but you cannot safely assume that the student will be able to successfully generalize the greeting skills to other people, settings, times, and behaviors. Therefore, you might teach the skills with three other people (a nondisabled peer, another teacher, and a parent volunteer), across three settings (the cafeteria, the playground, and in the library), at three different times of the day (first thing in the morning, at lunch, and in the afternoon), and across three different types of greeting behaviors ("Hi, how are you?" "What is new?" "Nice to see you.").

Use of Technology in Systematic Instruction

Video modeling has been increasingly used to teach skills to individuals with disabilities. Video modeling uses observational learning to provide multiple examples of stimulus and response variation across a variety of settings (Mechling, 2005).

Video feedback involves the viewing of one's own performance on a task and then evaluating and/or receiving feedback on that performance. For example, Embregts (2003) combined self-management strategies with video feeback (videotape segments from the previous week of the individual interacting with others) to increase appropriate behaviors and decrease inappropriate behaviors for four individuals with mild mental retardation.

Video modeling involves the performance of a skill by a model, and the learner watches the video demonstration and is then asked to perform the skill at a later time and setting.

Advantages for the use of video modeling include repeated observations of the same model and repeated review for maintenance (Mechling, 2005).

BEST PRACTICE RECOMMENDATIONS

1. Skills are best taught by teaching the learner to respond to discriminative stimuli in the environment. The purpose of instruction is to give the learner information to perform skills.
2. Use cues to provide initial information to a learner before a behavior is performed. Use correction procedures to provide additional or corrective information to a learner that a response already performed is not correct or that a different response is needed.
3. If the learner is having difficulty learning steps of the task analysis, the general guidelines are to (a) provide massed trials, (b) manipulate the demands of a step to ensure learner success, (c) increase the level of reinforcement a learner receives during massed trials, (d) conduct massed trials in short time blocks, (e) systematically build a step back into the chain after it has been mastered, and (f) systematically fade assistance.
4. Persons with disabilities often have difficulty generalizing what they have learned across behaviors, settings, people, and time. Although there are various methods of increasing generalization, general case programming is the most effective strategy.

FUTURE RESEARCH ISSUES

1. There needs to be a better understanding of how to best use cues for instruction. For instance, what type of cueing hierarchy is best?
2. How do we teach cueing to instructors?
3. The use of self-management and self-reinforcement strategies offers promising methodologies to help learners become more independent in community settings, but further research is needed in this area.

DISCUSSION QUESTIONS

1. If a person is not learning a task, is it more likely that it is not being taught correctly or that the person cannot learn?

2. Can all people, no matter how severe their disability, be successful in community settings with appropriate supports?
3. How do support needs vary from person to person?

SCHOOL AND COMMUNITY-BASED ACTIVITY SUGGESTIONS

1. Bring in materials for teaching a self-care/domestic task using a task analysis. Teach the task three times to someone once using a concurrent (whole task) chain, once with a forward chain, and once using a backward chain. For the task analysis:
   a. list the natural cue and response for each step.
   b. indicate which steps are mandatory.
   c. list the materials necessary to complete the activity and
   d. list three possible modifications/adaptations for relevant steps of the task analysis.
2. At an employment site, interview someone who is involved in training new workers on how to complete job tasks. Ask that person how they break down tasks and do the instruction.
3. Go to a community setting (such as a laundromat) and observe the different ways in which people there complete a task. Determine which way might be most efficient for teaching a person with a disability and how modifications and adaptations might be useful.

REFERENCES

Bellamy, G. T., Horner, R. H., & Inman, D. P. (1979). *Vocational habilitation of severely retarded adults: A direct service technology.* Baltimore, MD: University Park Press.

Embregts, P. J. C. M. (2003). Using self-management, video feedback, and graphic feedback to improve social behavior of youth with mild mental retardation. *Education and Training in Developmental Disabilities, 38,* 283–295.

Gold, M. W. (1980). *Did I say that? Articles and commentary on the try another way system.* Champaign, IL: Research Press.

Horner, R. H. (1984). The value of student errors. *Direct Instruction News, 3,* 13.

Horner, R. H., Bellamy, G. T., & Colvin, G. T. (1984). Responding in the presence of nontrained stimuli: Implications of generalization error patterns. *Journal of the Association for Persons with Severe Handicaps, 9,* 287–295.

Horner, R. H., Dunlap, G., & Koegel, R. L. (1988). *Generalization and maintenance:*

Life-style changes in applied settings. Baltimore, MD: Paul H. Brookes.

Kazdin, A. E. (2001). *Behavior modification in applied settings* (6th ed.). Belmont, CA : Wadsworth/Thomson Learning.

Mechling, L. (2005). The effect of instructor-created video programs to teach students with disabilities: A literature review. *Journal of Special Education Technology, 20,* 25–36.

Steere, D. E., & Pancsofar, E. L. (1995). Cues, prompts, and correction strategies. In W. W. Woolcock & J. W. Domaracki (Eds.), *Instructional strategies in the community: A resource guide for community instruction for persons with disabilities* (pp. 35–53). Austin, TX: Pro-Ed.

Stokes, T. F., & Baer, D. M. (1977). An implicit technology of generalization. *Journal of Applied Behavior Analysis, 10,* 349–367.

Wilcox, B., & Bellamy, G. T. (1987). *A comprehensive guide to the activities catalog: An alternative curriculum for youth and adults with severe disabilities.* Baltimore, MD: Paul Brookes.

Wolery, M., Ault, M. J., & Doyle, P. M. (1992). *Teaching students with moderate to severe disabilities: Use of response prompting strategies.* White Plains, NY: Longman.

Chapter 4

FUNCTIONAL ACADEMICS

Keypoint Questions

1. What are functional academics?
2. Why are functional academic skills important?
3. Where are functional academics best taught?
4. How do you determine which functional academic skills to teach?
5. What are functional reading skills?
6. What are functional writing skills?
7. What are functional math skills?
8. How are functional academic skills taught?

Window to the World Case Study One

Ramana is a nine-year-old student who has been diagnosed with multiple disabilities. He has been in a self-contained classroom at school since age five. This year he is receiving an inclusive educational experience in the fourth-grade general education classroom. His past preacademic goals in the self-contained program involved pointing to letters, shapes, and colors. These are goals Ramana has worked on for four years. He is able to point to the lower case letters (a through k), colors (red, blue, green, yellow), and shapes (square, circle, and triangle).

His fourth-grade teacher, Mr. Morreau, and his inclusion teacher, Ms. Emig, realize that the academic skills that he has previously learned are by themselves (in an isolated context) nonfunctional. Ms. Emig shared the book *Including Students With Severe and Multiple Disabilities in Typical Classrooms: Practical Strategies For Teachers* (Downing,

2008) with Mr. Morreau. They realize that they need to consider being literate as more than just recognizing, decoding, and comprehending the written word and that Ramana needs to be able to obtain information from a variety of alternative formats. He then needs to be able to produce literary output in a variety of formats as well.

Therefore, they decide that Ramana will obtain information from recorded information (e.g., LeapPad books), having peers read to him (which also benefits the peers), and through the use of magazines when he is shown pictures in group activities related to career exploration and the pictures/careers are discussed. For assessing Ramana's understanding of the information (so that he is not just a passive recipient), he is engaged in cooperative learning strategies in which the group members are asked comprehension questions about the career exploration lessons. Ramana responds to the questions by using his Picture Exchange Communication System (PECS). In addition, he asks peers questions as well using the PECS.

Window to the World Case Study Two

Martha is a thirty-eight-year-old woman with dyslexia. In school she was taught to read using whole language instruction, which was ineffective in teaching her to read. In part because of her functional illiteracy, Martha has difficulty reading and thus has had difficulty holding jobs. Her dream career has always been to be a pastry chef in a fancy restaurant.

After meeting with a counselor at her local One-Stop center, Martha decides on a multifaceted approach to her career goal. First, she enrolls in a chef training program at her local community college. Second, she accesses supports at the college's Disability Support Services office. There she is assessed by the Learning Disability specialist, Ms. Sanchez, who realizes that academics will be a challenge for Martha both at the college and in her restaurant work. For the college courses, Martha and Ms. Sanchez agree on a variety of supports, such as the use of peer notetakers in classes, the use of auditory text books for classes, a peer support group, and a peer tutor from the learning support center. A reading specialist from the Disability Support Programs and Services (DSPS) assesses Martha's reading ability and decides to include Martha in a reading group teaching her to read using the Keyword Method (Mastropieri, 1988), which she believes will be most effective in teaching Martha to read.

As part of the training program at the college, students do internships at the local culinary academy and several restaurants. Ms. Sanchez realizes that there will be words in those environments that Martha will need to be able to understand in order to be successful on the job. So she and Martha do a pretour of the culinary academy and restaurants where Martha is likely to intern. At those sites both Martha and Ms. Sanchez take pictures of any words or signs that Martha may have to read. Back at the learning center a peer tutor works with Martha on recognizing words in the pictures. Because they are using actual pictures of the words in context it makes generalization easier for Martha than, say, reading words from index cards. Martha also learned to use a speech synthesis system to read back reports and memos and other written materials from classes and work.

Key Point Question 1: What Are Functional Academics?

The purpose of learning functional academics is to respond appropriately to stimuli in order to perform employment, community, and independent living skills related to the criterion of ultimate functioning (*see* Chapter 1). It is reasonable to believe that education should focus on content that is relevant and useful in "real life." Many high school students have asked the teacher in their algebra class, "Why do we need to know this stuff?" Students and adults with disabilities need to ask the same questions for any academic skill they are being taught. The best teachers can explain that the academic content they are learning can be used immediately or in the future. However, it is possible that some of the standards that have been identified in public education are of limited use to individuals with disabilities in community settings. This challenge of relevancy must be addressed when deciding what academic skills are to be taught to individuals with disabilities. Additionally, decisions must be made about when, where, and how the academic skills are to be taught.

Academic standards refer to what students should know or be able to do when they have completed each grade level. These standards have been set up by each state and vary from state to state. Generally, these standards focus on academic domains such as literacy, mathematics, science, and social studies. Although academic standards for students with or without disabilities have been hotly debated (Ravitch,

2009; Salend, 2009), this chapter focuses on academic skills that individuals with disabilities need in employment, community, and living situations, and thus they may or may not be directly related to school academic skills and academic standards.

Functional academics primarily fall into the three Rs: reading, writing, and arithmetic. These are skills that are typically learned in early grades by students without disabilities. For example, telling time is a skill that is taught in first grade at a time when many children with disabilities have yet to master number identification, which was taught in kindergarten. The traditional approach to teaching this skill is to have students identify hour, then half hour, quarter hour, and so on. If a student with a disability is still working on those preskills, he or she may not benefit from instruction on more advanced skills, such as telling time to the minute or telling time before the hour. The lack of adequate progress in academic skills leads to a greater and greater discrepancy between grade level standards and performance skills of many students with disabilities.

The instruction of functional academic skills in general education classrooms is not the focus of this chapter although many of the strategies for embedding instruction into functional activities can be implemented in any setting including inclusive classrooms. Functional academic instruction in general education settings is covered in-depth in Downing (2008).

Key Point Question 2: Why Are Functional Academics Important?

The Individuals with Disabilities Education Act (IDEA) (9sec, 300.600[b][1]) requires that there be "improved educational results and functional outcomes for all students with disabilities." Thus, academic skills are important because they allow individuals to function as independently as possible in school environments as well as in adult environments (employment, community, independent living). It is necessary to identify what academic skills are critical for future environments (e.g., the criterion of ultimate functioning). It is also important to consider if these skills are useful across life skill domains. For example, telling time (whether digitally or through a traditional mode) can be a very important skill to have across all domains, including school. For example, Isaac is a twenty-seven year old with Down syndrome. When he was in middle school and continuing into high school, he worked on telling time on a digital clock at the end of each class session. In high school, he used his analog watch to plan for completing tasks within a specific time frame. He would use a self-management data collection sheet to keep track of the amount of work in completed in the last fifteen minutes of class. Now that he is working at an automobile repair shop, he uses that functional academic skill to monitor his task completion before going to lunch and for clocking out at the end of his shift.

Key Point Question 3: Where Are Functional Academics Best Taught?

The best answer to this question is "where they need to be used." Functional academic skills are used across all domains. These skills are useful at home, in the community, during recreation, and at school or work. Instruction often must occur across all domains as well (if generalization may be difficult for the learner). For example, a student may be learning to identify the men's room signs (important to remember that different criterion environments will use different signs, wording, etc., and the student must be able to generalize skills across environments) at school, local restaurants, the gym, and other community environments. This specific reading skill would not be required at home.

Training in functional academics is embedded in natural routines in order to provide natural contextual cues. For example, if Jackson is learning how to use both the school and the community library for checking out books, DVDs and CDs, then he will need to learn relevant academic skills such as looking up catalog information on the library website, finding items by call number, and using the checkout system. Thus, instruction should take place in the criterion environment (e.g., the library) and involve the whole sequence of behaviors and academic skills (such as searching by books by topic in the catalog on the web site, finding the book, and checking it out). Some of these skills may be initially taught in a classroom environment (such as using the catalog on the web site) following the instructional guidelines by Nietupski, Hamre-Nietupski, Clancy, and Veerhusen (1986).

The focus ideally should be on teaching "real world" skills in the context in which they are required or demanded. If simulation is utilized, it must replicate actual conditions as closely as possible. For example, in teaching banking skills such as depositing a check, it is possible to practice the subskills of signing a check, completing a deposit form, waiting in line, and giving the check and deposit form to a cashier. These skills could be practiced in a classroom setting using photocopied forms and with role playing. Generalization assessment could then take place in the criterion environment (e.g., the bank) with further instruction in that environment if necessary.

Systematic instruction of math skills in the same setting that they are required has been found to be extremely effective (Browder, Spooner, Ahlgrim-Delzell, Harris, & Wakeman, 2008). Many individuals without disabilities find the acquisition of math skills difficult and depend on assistive technology such as a calculator to perform basic math skills. One of the difficult aspects of basic math acquisition is the application of specific tasks to each situation. When Clarence goes to the deli to buy his lunch and unexpectedly finds that there is a daily special that costs about the same amount as his usually preferred sandwich, he must be able to determine if it is more or less than his usual order and decide if he can afford it. This is also an example of the need for generalization of a functional math skill and the advantage of instruction in the natural environment.

Key Point Question 4: How Do You Determine Which Functional Academic Skills to Teach?

Table 4.1 provides an analysis of factors to consider in deciding academic goals for individuals with disabilities. Some functional academic skills will be useful in both school and community settings, such as telling time, signing one's name, and so on. Other academic skills will be specific to settings, such as reading words that are specific to a work site. For example, an individual working in a hospital would need to know how to read and understand words such as oxygen, nurse call button, or defibrillator that would probably not need to be known in other work environments, such as the local bank.

Preacademic skills include identifying shapes, counting, reciting the alphabet, and so on. Although these teaching these skills to younger students with disabilities might be appropriate (if nondisabled students are also being taught these skills), it becomes less appropriate as students get older and is inappropriate for adults with disabilities due to

Table 4.1
FACTORS TO CONSIDER IN DECIDING ACADEMIC GOALS
FOR INDIVIDUALS WITH DISABILITIES

1. Current and future academic needs. Prioritize what skills are most important, both currently and in the future.
2. Skills needed in domain areas other than school (employment, community, domestic) that involve academic subskills
3. The chronological age of the learner
4. The prior rate of learning of academic skills
5. The preferences of the student and parents
6. Consider the scope and purpose of educational standards. Maximize the flexibility of the curriculum and opportunities for instruction by connecting the standard to functional skills.

Source: Adapted from Functional academics, by D. M. Browder and M. E. Snell (pp. 442–279), in *Instruction of Students With Severe Disabilities,* M. E. Snell (Ed.), 1993, Upper Saddle River, NJ: Merrill/Prentice Hall; and

a variety of factors. Table 4.2 provides analysis of this issue. These preacademic skills may not be essential skills in criterion environments, especially when accommodations or modifications are appropriate and can be easily used.

It is difficult to predict how much a younger student may learn in academic areas. Programmatic goals should not be made based on disability or labels. For example, not too many years ago it was assumed that individuals with Down syndrome could not learn to read. However, this is not true, and individuals with Down syndrome have learned to read to differing levels of proficiency (Lemons & Fuchs,

Table 4.2
CONCERNS WITH TEACHING PREACADEMIC SKILLS
TO OLDER STUDENTS OR ADULTS WITH DISABILITIES

1. Age Appropriateness: It will be stigmatizing for older students or adults to be working on these preacademic skills.
2. Teaching Time: After a certain amount of teaching time and different strategies it is likely that the individual is not going to learn the academic skills and modifications, and accommodations may be more appropriate.
3. Role of Accommodations and Modifications: If a learner does not learn academic skills, then it is important to consider alternatives to those skills that lead to the desirable outcome (such as not being able to tell time but having the outcome of knowing what time it is).
4. Criterion of Ultimate Functioning: Many preacademic skills are of doubtful value in order to function as an adult in society.

2010). Thus, instructors should assume that individuals with disabilities can learn academic skills, especially for younger students.

All learners progress to different levels of proficiency. If a learner is not making adequate progress, then it is important to try a variety of remedial instructional strategies. An important, although difficult issue, is at what point do you decide that a learner is not progressing even with appropriate remediation? There is no clear answer to this question, and what you do not want to do is to continue with instructional strategies that are not working. (For instance, after two years of teaching an individual to recognize letters do you continue even though the learner still does not recognize letters?) In other words, academic goals such as literacy are not abandoned, but greater amounts of time may be committed to teaching functional academic skills.

Key Point Question 5: What Are Functional Reading Skills?

Functional reading is broadly defined as "reading" visual stimuli that cue action in the learner (Valletutti, Bender, & Baglin, 2008). For example, reading the words "preset oven to 350 degrees" prompts the person cooking food to turn the oven on to 350 degrees. If an individual can respond appropriately to a visual stimulus that helps with completion of a task (such as cooking a meal, completing forms, using a computer program), it can then be considered a functional reading skill. Ultimately it is reading or recognizing words and then using or demonstrating understanding in completing a task that determines functionality.

The goals of functional reading are in some ways more limited that teaching complete reading and literacy skills. The focus is more on teaching individuals to be able to read and respond appropriately to a limited number of words in performing specific skills such as completing a job application. Often instructors will teach students "survival words" or "sight words" in a classroom setting using cards or other printed material. However, it may be difficult for the learner to then read and recognize the word in a different context. For example, the learner may read the word "boys" on a card but be unable to read the same word in a different color and font on a bathroom door (e.g., the criterion environment). Also, common lists of "survival words" often include words that the learner is unlikely to actually ever need to read, such as "lifeguard" or "no right turn." Thus, a better strategy

Table 4.3
STRATEGIES FOR INCREASING WORD RECOGNITION

1. The more frequently that a learner encounters, is taught, and uses a word, the more likely that they will understand and use the word in the criterion environment.
2. The use of words on flash cards, electronically, with pictures, or in games can provide the repetition necessary for automaticity (recognizing the word immediately and automatically); immediate recognition of words contributes significantly to fluency and understanding of words and text.
3. Retention over time can be difficult, and teaching and checking need to occur repeatedly.
4. Auditory skills (phonological awareness) may need to be directly taught.
5. Combine multisensory methods (visual, auditory, kinesthetic, and tactile).
6. Take literacy walks in local neighborhoods (e.g., the criterion environments) to read printed words and use as a teaching and discussion situation.

Source: Adapted from *Remediating Reading Difficulties* (5th ed.), by S. J. Crawley and K. Merritt, 2009, Boston, MA: McGraw-Hill; Reading instruction, by D. Gartland (pp. 233–256), in *Instructional Methods for Secondary Students With Learning and Behavior Problems,* P. J. Schloss, M. A. Schloss, and C. N. Schloss (Eds.), 2007, Boston, MA: Pearson; and *Commonsense Methods for Children With Special Needs: Strategies for the Regular Classroom* (4th ed.), by P. Westwood, 2003, New York: Routledge Falmer.

is to identify sight words through ecological inventory (*see* Chapter 6). This makes it more likely that relevant sight words from the criterion environment are being taught. It is important to remember that in order for the learner to understand and respond to sight words they must be in the learner's comprehension vocabulary. Thus, direct teaching of sight words may be necessary, and it may also be necessary to teach the understanding of what the words mean and how to respond (e.g., a learner may be able to read the word "exit" but not know what it means). Table 4.3 provides strategies for increasing word recognition skills.

Reading for leisure is also an important skill for individuals with a disability. In school or work environments, one generally reads for knowledge, either to learn material or to use skills learned from the reading material. At home or in community settings, one generally reads for pleasure, and the type of material to be read is often broader. For example, at home one may read magazines, cookbooks, novels, catalogs, and so on. Thus, the focus of the reading instruction may vary depending on the context in which the reading skills are to be used. For instance, reading a clothes catalog may involve less reading the words and more analyzing the pictures and then discussing them with others.

Key Point Question 6: What Are Functional Writing Skills?

Functional writing skills have traditionally included tasks such as an individual's signature, filling out job applications and other forms, writing a note, making a shopping list, and so on. In other words, putting pen to paper. Signing one's name in cursive is the most traditional example of "writing." However, advancements in technology have led to changes in analyzing what writing tasks are functional and in deciding what writing skills to teach. For example, keyboarding skills may now be more important than being able to write by hand. Text messaging is widely used among cell phone users and may be more useful to an individual with a disability than learning to write a note by hand. It is important to emphasize that writing ability is closely tied to reading ability for any individual, no matter what his or her reading and writing skill levels are.

When deciding which skills to teach, it is crucial that the instructor look at current demands rather than what has been taught traditionally. For example, how can an individual "write?" Are electronic signatures acceptable in the criterion environment, such as at a bank? Completing a resume online may be tied into keyboarding skills, cutting and pasting from an electronic document, and the ability to navigate commands on the online page. Writing for content is still important for many individuals, but electronic supports such as spelling and grammar checkers, the use of macros, and other word processing supports have helped to assist all writers.

Technology advances have greatly increased the ability to get around poor or even non-existent writing skills. For example, putting a voice reminder into a cell phone application instead of writing a reminder note to oneself means that the individual does not have to write at all to achieve the functional outcome (being able to read and respond to the note in the future). In this example, using the features on the cell phone is more important than traditional writing skills are. Even keyboarding skills may not be a critical skill because the use of voice recognition software allows individuals to use word processing applications without using a keyboard (although again, the ability to use and understand other functions of the computer would be critical skills rather than traditional writing skills).

Key Point Question 7: What Are Functional Math Skills?

Math covers a wide area, such as recognizing numbers, being able to count, performing addition or subtraction, understanding place values, and performing mathematical calculations. The goal of functional math then becomes giving an individual skills to perform math-related skills in the criterion environment related to money, measurement, and time management. If mathematical content is to be relevant to the learner, it must be presented (and perhaps taught) in real world contexts. For example, although algebra is commonly taught in schools, it has no real relevance in real world settings because it is not used in employment, community, or living situations and mainly involves memorizing meaningless mathematical procedures. In contrast, understanding the basic mathematical concept of "more than" can be very useful in real world settings such as the "dollar plus" strategy for making purchases (Denny & Test, 1995). Table 4.4 provides some important instructional issues related to teaching functional math skills.

Table 4.4
IMPORTANT INSTRUCTIONAL ISSUES RELATED TO
TEACHING FUNCTIONAL MATH SKILLS

1. Mathematical concepts and operations are hierarchically ordered. An individual must have mastered necessary preskills to build upon, such as understanding addition facts before learning subtraction facts.
2. Instructor modeling of math skills is a powerful instructional strategy.
3. Teach math skills to mastery (where the learner uses the math skills in the criterion environment without hesitating to compute the answer such as "this drink if $1.50 so I need to give the cashier two $1 bills"). Brief instructional exposures are generally ineffective.
4. Teach math skills that are directly tied into career and life activities.
5. Encourage learners to use adaptive devices such as calculators in both teaching situations and the criterion environment.
6. Use pictorial or written prompts to increase likelihood of learner success.
7. Use concrete materials as much as possible, especially when introducing abstract concepts.
8. Use mnemonic instructional aids to help learners remember concepts, vocabulary, steps, and formulas.
9. For classroom token economies, use currency-based units (e.g., cents, dollars, etc.) rather than points. Use classroom paychecks, checking accounts, savings accounts, and other types of options for learning real-world math skills.

Source: Adapted from Mathematic instruction, by D. Majsterek, R. Wilson, and E. D. Jones (pp. 257–276), in *Instructional Methods for Secondary Students With Learning and Behavior Problems,* P. J. Schloss, M. A. Schloss, and C. N. Schloss (Eds.), 2007, Boston, MA: Pearson; and *Teaching Students With Learning Problems* (7th ed.), by C. D. Mercer and A. R. Mercer, 2005, Upper Saddle River, NJ: Pearson.

Part of functional mathematics is the use of money in community settings. For example, calculating a tip, paying for an item at a store, and buying a sandwich all involve math skills. These functional math skills are necessary to participate successfully and independently in cash transactions. Although many transactions involve the use of credit or debit cards, individuals still need to be able to use money in community settings. Thus, being able to calculate monetary transactions is a functional skill that can be taught in classrooms as well as in the criterion environment in the community.

Measurement skills are also part of math skills. For instance, following recipes involves math skills related to adding, dividing, and so on. Thus, in order for people to cook using recipes, they will need to understand and be able to follow the written instructions.

Time management involves time measurement skills to facilitate the ability of an individual to manage his or her time effectively, such as turning on the television at the time that a favorite show begins.

Key Point Question 8: How Do You Teach Functional Academic Skills

The systematic instructional approaches described throughout this text apply to functional academic skills as well as other skill areas. Although academic skills are often taught in classroom settings, it is important to remember that instruction in simulation environment (the classroom) must be as closely approximated as possible to actual demands in the criterion environment. For example, using labels of actual items to teach product safety leads to greater generalization than flash cards of labels do (Collins & Stinson, 1995; Collins & Griffen, 1996). If academic skills are taught in simulation environments, it becomes critical to assess for successful generalization to criterion situations and then to teach in those situations if necessary.

Teaching functional academic skills in a systematic way utilizes the strategies described throughout this text. Although there is not a single way to teach the variety of functional academic skills, the basic steps include the following:

1. Determine strengths and preferences through person-centered planning
2. Identify current and future environments

3. Conduct ecological inventory of environments
4. List functional academic demands
5. If socially valid, begin instruction by labeling items in environment to connect words to objects
6. Systematically teach words that require action along with specific behaviors
7. Identify and provide assistive technology or other modifications as appropriate to improve skill acquisition or accommodation.
8. Promote and assess generalization

As discussed previously, one of the often-overlooked areas of functional academics for individuals with disabilities is reading for leisure. A large discrepancy between reading grade level and age of the person has resulted in lack of access to high-interest, age-appropriate reading materials. The definition of literacy may need to be broadened to allow individuals with disabilities to read for leisure. Instructors can begin instruction by utilizing text to speech, closed captioning, and other forms of available technology. Individuals with limited reading proficiency can utilize free programs, such as ReadPlease® (http://www.readplease.com), which can be downloaded, allowing the user to cut and paste any text into a window that can be read aloud or have any web page read. Secondly, whenever watching a movie on DVD or other media, most televisions have a closed captioning option. The individual without specific reading skills can follow along with the captions as he or she enjoys the video.

One of the most promising options for enjoying books and other print materials without the requisite literacy skills is the e-book reader. E-books and other digitized materials can be rendered and displayed with technologies such as the Amazon Kindle and iPad. These devices give the individual with a disability the opportunity to download desirable reading materials that can be read aloud as he or she follows along with the text. The use of online resources such as www.reading a-z.com may also be beneficial for leisure reading.

BEST PRACTICE RECOMMENDATIONS

1. Any academic skill taught needs to be considered in the context of the criterion of ultimate functioning for the learner.

2. When teaching functional academic skills, it is important to assess for generalization to the criterion environment and to teach in the criterion environment if necessary.
3. Use technology to support learners who might otherwise struggle with academic skills.
4. Use academic accommodations and modifications to help individuals be successful.

FUTURE RESEARCH ISSUES

1. How can technological advances best be used to teach academic skills and also to be used as accommodations and/or modifications.
2. How can functional academic skills best be taught to students with disabilities in the age of high-stakes testing?
3. How should teachers of students with disabilities be evaluated concerning the academic success of their students?

DISCUSSION QUESTIONS

1. Do students with disabilities best learn academic skills in general education settings, special education settings, or community settings?
2. Because learners need to be able to generalize academic skills, how can skills best be taught to increase this generalization?
3. Are some academic skills taught in school settings environments "nonfunctional?"
4. What is the best method for teaching reading and other academic skills to students with disabilities?
5. Does what is considered functional academics change depending on whether the learner is a student or an adult with a disability?
6. Are academic skills best taught by credentialed teachers or paraprofessionals?
7. Does technology enhance or replace good teaching?

SCHOOL AND COMMUNITY-BASED ACTIVITY SUGGESTIONS

1. List the steps of your morning routine and identify the activities in which reading, writing, or mathematics were required? How important are these functional academic skills in your life?
2. What activities required reading, writing, or mathematics during a typical day in your life?
3. Go to a job site or community setting. Analyze what functional academic skills are required in that setting. Also analyze accommodations and/or modifications that might be made.

REFERENCES

Browder, D. M., Spooner, F., Ahlgrim-Delzell, L., Harris, A. A., & Wakeman, S. (2008). A meta-analysis on teaching mathematics to students with significant disabilities. *Exceptional Children, 74,* 407–432.

Collins, B. C., & Griffen, A. K. (1996). Teaching students with moderate disabilities to make safer responses to product warning labels. *Education and Treatment of Children, 19,* 30–45.

Collins, B. C., & Stinson, D. M. (1995). Teaching generalized reading of product warning labels to adolescents with disabilities through the use of key words. *Exceptionality, 5,* 163–181.

Denny, P. J., & Test, D. W. (1995). Using the one-more-than technique to teach money counting to individuals with moderate mental retardation: A systematic replication. *Education and Treatment of Children, 18,* 422–432.

Downing, J. (2008). *Including students with severe and multiple disabilities in typical classrooms: Practical strategies for teachers* (3rd ed.). Baltimore, MD: Paul Brookes.

Lemons, C. J., & Fuchs, D. (2010). Modeling response to reading intervention in children with Down syndrome: An examination of predictors to different growth. *Reading Research Quarterly, 45,* 134–168.

Mastropieri, M. A. (1988). Using the keyword method. *Teaching Exceptional Children, 20,* 4–8.

Nietupski, J., Hamre-Nietupski, S., Clancy, P., & Veerhusen, K. (1986). Guidelines for making simulation an effective adjunct to in vivo community instruction. *Journal of the Association for Persons with Severe Handicaps, 11,* 12–18.

Ravitch, D. (2009). *The death and life of the great American school system: How testing and choice are undermining education.* New York: Basic Books.

Salend, S. J. (2009). *Classroom testing and assessment for ALL students: Beyond standardization.* Thousand Oaks, CA: Corwin Press.

Valletutti, P. J., Bender, M., & Baglin, C. A. (2008). *A functional assessment and curriculum for teaching students with disabilities* (3rd ed.). Austin, TX: Pro-Ed.

Chapter 5

TEACHING EMPLOYMENT SKILLS

Keypoint Questions

1. Why is employment in real work settings important for people with disabilities?
2. What is the difference between supported and sheltered work?
3. How do you best assess employment skills?
4. What employment skills should be taught in school settings?
5. What employment skills should be taught in work settings?
6. What is a job analysis and why is it important for determining needed skills?
7. Why are interview skills important?
8. What are job site accommodations and modifications?
9. What is the role of technology in employment success?
10. What are point of transition strategies?

Window to the World Case Study One

Johann had just completed high school and was unsure as to what type of career he wanted. He had been diagnosed as having Asperger's syndrome in middle school. In high school he had always gotten good grades and was fully included in general education classes. He and his parents felt that he was not ready to go to a four-year college because of some social issues he was having and his anxiety in handling new situations, especially ones in which he was required to interact with people he had not met before.

Johann went to his local community college, where Jean, the career counselor at the DSPS, met with him about his academic and career interests. She had him do informational interviews with employers in different career areas in which he was interested. From these interviews he decided that he was most interested in a career in library services. Jean arranged an internship for him at the local library, where he worked in different departments so that he could get a "hands on" understanding of the job duties. Johann found that he really liked working in the cataloging department because the job tasks did not vary greatly from day to day and he was not required to interact with others much as part of his job duties, which helped him in regard to his anxiety in social situations. He also joined a support group for individuals with Asperger's syndrome at the community college where he was able to received supports and instruction around his anxiety as well as other issues in his life related to his Asperger's syndrome and some that were not. Through his internship, Johann was offered a part time job at the library in the catalog department, and he started taking classes in library science at the community college with the plan of transferring to a four-year college and majoring in library studies.

Window to the World Case Study Two

Kristin was diagnosed as having a profound intellectual disability, being deaf and blind, and engaged in self-injurious behavior. She was twenty-seven and had spent the last five years in an adult day program doing prevocational work such as stuffing envelopes. She did not earn any money at the day program and lived at home with her parents.

Kristin's brother-in-law Bob was obtaining his special education teaching credential and one of his classes was "School to Adult Life," which made Bob realize that Kristin was more capable of working than she had been given credit for. Bob contacted the local supported employment agency, Bay Area Innovations, where the director Tom agreed with Bob's viewpoint that Kristin could work if given appropriate instruction and supports. Tom and his team met with Kristin and her family to assess her skills and interests. Tom had several supported employment placements at the county judicial office, and from this he knew that the offices had secretaries and other support staff bringing documents to an office to shred but were having to do the shredding themselves which as inefficient.

Lori, Bay Area Innovation's supported employment director conducted a job analysis and met with office managers of the different departments and proposed that Kristin be hired to man the shredding room. The managers agreed that this would increase the efficiency of their staff, and Kristin was hired as a county employee (her civil service exam was waived as part of an agreement between the county and the union to increase diversity by hiring people with developmental disabilities). A job coach was provided by Bay Area Innovation to instruct Kristin on the job duties and to support her in other areas, such as using the cafeteria. Kristin enjoyed the job very much, her self-injurious behavior stopped, and she was earning minimum wage (with pay increases), was paying into the county retirement program, and had good benefits.

Key Point Question 1: Why Is Employment in Real Work Settings Important for People With Disabilities?

If, and where, people with disabilities should work has been an issue that people with disabilities and their families, school systems, adult service systems, and governments have struggled with (Wehman, 2006). Questions concerning whether or not people with disabilities are capable of working, whether the focus needs to be first on prevocational skills, whether they need to get "ready" to work, whether they should work in sheltered or integrated environments, and the type of supports that are appropriate are issues confronting the field and have not been clearly resolved (Mank, 1994).

We believe that work in integrated (e.g., supported employment) settings is important for the reasons that follow. (These have been discussed in more detail in Storey, 2000.) It is a philosophical/ethical judgment that people with disabilities should work.

A. Civil rights. Work and integration for persons with disabilities has been an extension of the civil rights movement, and the importance of integration applies for adults as well as for students with disabilities.

B. Normalization. Normalization broadly refers to what is "typical" behavior of peers. It is expected or normal that as an adult one becomes employed in some capacity.

C. Community participation. It is important that people with disabilities be part of their communities, whether it be where they live, shop, recreate, or work. Through work, people with disabilities are more likely to be involved in their community.

D. Influencing society. Work and integration can be very powerful factors in changing attitudes and expectations toward people with disabilities. If employers, coworkers, customers, and others see people with disabilities performing competently in real jobs then people with disabilities are more likely to be seen as competent in their abilities and more likely to be accepted as equals.

E. Work is valued. Work is commonly valued, and an individual's status or worth often is based on their employment and economic status.

F. Helps individuals through stress and difficulties. When people are having a difficult time, they often turn to coworkers for support, and we all need an adequate social support network.

G. Economic independence. With good wages and good benefits, people with disabilities can avoid the poverty and dependency in which the vast majority of people with disabilities live.

H. Professionals cannot meet all needs of persons with disabilities. Although professionals may be important, professionals come and go. Friends, coworkers, and family members are more likely to be stable in the lives of people with disabilities and more likely to provide reciprocity and social networks.

I. Life-long learning. Life-long learning is important in terms of factors such as intellectual stimulation and learning new skills that may be important in future work environments.

J. Contribution to society. Through work, people with disabilities are productive members of society.

K. Economic reasons in terms of wages and health and other benefits.

Key Point Question 2: What Is the Difference Between Supported and Sheltered Work?

Two (sheltered or supported work) basic, but very different, types of employment services have been developed for adults with disabilities. The differences between these two are discussed in the following.

Sheltered Work

Sheltered work encompasses a variety of options and titles, such as work activity, day activity, day treatment, community rehabilitation programs, and day habilitation (Schalock, Kiernan, McGaughey, Lynch, & McNally, 1993). Sheltered workshops typically involve only individuals with disabilities (often hundreds working in one building) who work on contracts (such as making license plates or stuffing envelops) or other types of piecework. Individuals are usually paid below the minimum wage and receive no health or retirement benefits. The vast majority of adults with intellectual disabilities are served in segregated settings such as sheltered workshops.

Sheltered work has been criticized because of a lack of integration, wages, benefits, and other meaningful outcomes for the people with disabilities (Dileo, 2007; Murphy & Rogan, 1995). For many people with disabilities, especially those with intellectual disabilities, a flow-through model of employment services was set up in the 1950s and 1960s. This model was based on the "readiness" paradigm in which it was believed that a person had to get "ready" to work and that there were prerequisite skills that were necessary for successful employment. Thus the focus was on prevocational skills. For example, one individual may get a tray of nuts and bolts and assemble them, pass the tray of assembled pieces to another individual who takes them apart. That person then passes them to another person who assembles them, and so on. The "logic" of prevocational skills is that the individual will gain generic skills that will lead to eventual employment.

Supported Employment

Supported employment (also referred to as competitive employment) has been developed as an alternative method of providing employment services. With this model the emphasis is on outcomes mentioned earlier (wages, integration, etc.) of employment with appropriate supports in real jobs in the community (Wehman & Kregel, 1995). Rather than being stuck on getting people ready to work, the emphasis is on placing people and then training them ("place and train") and providing supports (also known as the "choose, get, and keep" model of employment). This is in contrast to the "train and place" model of the sheltered workshops.

Supported employment has been promoted as more desirable than sheltered service delivery systems are because it is more capable of delivering the desirable outcomes mentioned earlier (Wehman & Kregel, 1995). In this chapter we are discussing skills that are important for supported employment because we see this model as much more beneficial than sheltered workshops are for individuals with disabilities (Storey, 2000).

Key Point Question 3: How Do You Best Assess Employment Skills?

Assessment should be used to learn about the skill needs and support needs of the individual and assessment needs to focus on how to make the individual successful. Every person needs skills to perform required job tasks correctly (learned before and/or on the job) and every individual at work has support needs (such as learning to use new computer software, learning about policies and procedures, etc.). It is very important that assessment be used to understand what individuals need to be successful at work, not to keep people from working. Assessment must be nonexclusionary. It is of course all too easy to find a reason to exclude an individual with a disability from employment. For instance, Dileo (2007) provides an example of an adult with autism spectrum disorders who started a job as a data entry person. He often started singing television commercials at the job site. Rather than seeing this as a deficit to be eliminated, his nondisabled peers at the site found it to be fun (as the job was rather boring) and would join in. Productivity and morale went up at the job site thanks to this worker and his singing. Vocational assessment may be thought of in terms of either standardized or contemporary assessment. Standardized assessment refers to measures of prior learning "assuming that already learned aptitudes, interests, and traits can forecast subsequent learning, performance, and adjustment" (Browning & Irvin, 1981, p. 375). In contrast, contemporary assessment measures "applied performance within the context in which the performance is expected" (Browning & Irvin, 1981, p. 379). It is important to note that standardized assessment tools are generally not effective for predicting future employment success for people with disabilities. This is due in part to their reliance on the responder's academic ability, awareness of potential jobs, reliance on receptive language skills, intact neurological functioning, absence of sensory deficits, and inability to match skills and support needs to individual work sites.

Assessment should be ongoing and dynamic. People change and work situations change. An assessment of an individual at age sixteen is not still relevant when he or she is thirty and has fourteen years of

Table 5.1
ASSESSMENT OF INDIVIDUALS WITH LEARNING DISABILITIES

1. Do not assume that an individual has a thorough, accurate understanding of his or her disability or its ramifications. Of the students with previously identified learning disabilities, 65 to 80 percent cannot articulate what having a learning disability means or describe its implications.
2. Review all assessments with the individuals.
3. Many people with learning disabilities perform well in the quiet, orderly, systematic environments of classrooms but fail in the noisy, hectic environments of jobs. Understanding the conditions under which jobs must be performed is a critical component for success of many individuals with disabilities in the work world.
4. Be sure to address social and interpersonal skills in assessments for transition planning purposes.
5. Review the eligibility criteria for adult services agencies and comply whenever possible in order to minimize repetitive and unnecessary testing.

Source: Adapted from Applications for youth with learning disabilities, by E. E. Getzel and J. J. Gugerty (pp. 301–355), in *Life Beyond the Classroom: Transition Strategies for Young People With Disabilities,* P. Wehman (Ed.), 1992, Baltimore, MD: Paul Brookes.

work experience. Jobs do not necessarily remain the same. Job duties may be added, new software used, personnel changes may happen, and so on, which may have an impact on the ability of people to do their jobs. It is also important to review vocational assessments with the individuals being assessed. This will help individuals understand their strengths and support needs related to work and also to understand their disability in terms of modifications and accommodations that may be necessary. Table 5.1 provides guidelines for helping individuals to understand their assessment information.

The purposes of vocational assessment are many, but need to consider these points:

1. To provide relevant information on individual competencies such as work habits and attitudes.
2. The support needs of individuals in specific vocational areas— that is, skills for specific job duties instead of training on generic "tool use" or "equipment operation."
3. Characteristics of instructional and support strategies that are effective for an individual.
4. Placement options during and at the end of training. (Irvin, 1988)

Effective Assessment Strategies

There are many effective assessment strategies that have been used for individuals with disabilities in employment settings. These may be used individually or in conjunction with each other, depending on the individual and the situation.

1. Detailed job analyses

The logic for a job analysis is similar to that for task analysis, in other words, tasks associated with successful job completion must be identified and sequenced (Mank & Horner, 1988). A job analysis is conducted to ensure that the requirements of the employment position are met. In other words, the tasks must be performed at the proper time and in an acceptable way in order to result in completion of the entire job. The job analysis looks at

    A. the motor tasks that define the job
    B. the social skills that enable the person to fit into the workplace
    C. the self-management skills that help the person to be autonomous and adaptable
    D. academic skills that the person needs to be successful

2. Direct observation (on-the-job evaluation)

Direct observation procedures have been described in more detail in Chapter 2. These procedures can provide realistic, work-oriented methods for assessing individuals.

3. Work experience evaluations

Work experience involves the individual's working a job for a limited time period (one day to a week) in order to assess his or her ability to perform the job duties. For example, a person who is interested in working in an office may work for a day with a file clerk at an office, which would allow the evaluator to get a better idea of that individual's ability to perform the job duties in an actual situation rather than in a simulated environment such as a classroom.

4. Previous research

There is an extensive body of research over many decades demonstrating that individuals with disabilities can be successfully employed with appropriate supports. Relevant journals in this area are in the appendix to this book, and there are many books that provide an overview of the research (Baker, 2005; Bakken & Obiakor, 2008; Blalock, Patton, Kohler, & Bassett, 2008; Clark & Unruh, 2009; Luecking, Fabian, & Tilson, 2004; Rusch, 2008; Szymanski & Parker, 2010; Test, Aspel, & Everson, 2006; Wehman, Inge, Revell, & Brookes, 2007).

5. Work samples

Work samples are a simulated task or work activity designed to test the individual's use of materials and tools to do tasks that are similar to those in an actual job or cluster of jobs. Work samples (such as circuit board assembly, bench assembly, horticulture) have been used to assess vocational aptitude, worker characteristics, and vocational interests. An advantage to work samples is that they can easily be used in classrooms and other situations.

Drawbacks are that work samples fail to take into account variables such as social skills, generalization ability, personal hygiene, or self-help skills. Also, work samples almost exclusively measure motor responses rather than assessing the ability of the individual to work successfully in an employment position.

6. Situational assessments (also known as ecological assessments or on the job evaluations)

With situational assessments, the student spends a short time (half a day to a day) at a job site. This can also be at different job locations within a site (for example at a veterinarian's office it could include the front desk, assisting the vet, cleaning cages, etc.). The purpose of the situational assessment is to obtain an evaluation of the individual's skills in the context of the environment and routine where skills are typically performed. From the situational assessment, you want to create a positive student profile that includes

    a. Who is the student?
    b. What are the student's strengths?
    c. What are the student's greatest challenges and needs?
    d. What supports are needed?

ADVANTAGES TO SITUATIONAL ASSESSMENTS
    a. Provides an opportunity to evaluate skills and preferences. Indication of how individual responds to environmental factors.
    b. Can reveal variation in individual's performance within and across days.

CHALLENGES TO SITUATIONAL ASSESSMENTS
    a. Finding and negotiating real sites can be time consuming.
    b. Time involved to conduct assessment.
    c. Individual may not have prior experience with target setting. Skills may be unknown.
    d. Having adequate support for individual during assessment.
    e. Knowing how much is "enough."
    f. Summarizing the information.

Assessment Issues to Consider

    a. Work proficiency of the individual: Competency in performing tasks correctly
    b. Instructional assessment (how well the individual is learning with instruction): Work rate
    c. What the acceptable work rate is and how it varies (during "rush" times versus "slow" times for example)
      1. Work quality
      2. How well the task is completed
      3. Quality may be subjective. It is important to understand how it is being judged.
    d. Work repertoire
      1. Number of tasks worker can perform
      2. Degree of proficiency for each task
      3. At what rate each task is completed
      4. What quality level is present
    e. Work endurance: Selection of jobs should reflect analysis of physical requirements

How important these characteristics are varies from job to job. For instance, a job at a fast food restaurant is likely to care more about quantity than quality whereas a job at an electronics manufacturing plant is more likely to care about quality than quantity.

Importance of Assessing Individual Worker Skills and Generic Employment Skills

Not only must workers be able to perform job tasks, but they must also be able to perform a variety of more generic skills.

1. Transportation and mobility: A person needs to be able to get to and from work; otherwise, he or she obviously will not be successful at that job.
2. Communication: An individual needs to be able to communicate successfully with others on the job site. For some individuals this may involve augmentative communication systems, picture books, sign language, or other methods (McNaughton & Beukelman, 2010).
3. Self-care and appearance
4. Socialization
5. Functional reading and computation
6. Each skills cluster is only necessary as it relates to successful completion of the job in a given work environment. For instance, a person may have poor reading skills but if the job does not require reading then this deficit is unlikely to have a negative impact the person's performance.

Key Point Question 4: What Employment Skills Should Be Taught in School Settings?

Many generic employment skills (such as following directions, getting along with others, completing job tasks, appearance and hygiene skills, asking for help appropriately, etc.) can initially be taught to students in school settings. These can involve classroom jobs (such as answering phones, greeting visitors, getting materials ready) or school jobs (e.g., taking attendance forms to the office, filing in the office, working in the cafeteria).

We would like to emphasize three points regarding instruction in school settings.

1. It is never too early in the school years to start vocational instruction. As noted before, students at a young age can be involved in classroom and school jobs as well as studying and exploring career opportunities.

2. Vocational instruction needs to be integrated into all aspects of the curriculum.

3. Vocational instruction needs to occur throughout the school years with an increasing emphasis as the student gets older.

Identification and Exploration of Jobs

While in school, students can learn about job opportunities in a variety of ways, such as career days, having parents and other family members come in and talk about jobs that they do, having employers talk about work at their sites, having adults with disabilities discuss their careers, and field trips to work sites. These explorations can broaden a student's viewpoint of jobs and careers that are available and also help to break stereotypes about jobs that individuals with disabilities can do.

It is important to involve students in the transition process because, after all, it is their lives being planned. Table 5.2 provides information from Brown-Glover (1992) that offers a variety of strategies to use and not use in involving students in the transition process. Students can also be involved by being in charge of their own IEPs (Martin, Van Dycke, D'Ottavio, & Nickerson, 2007). Table 5.3 provides information on skills to be taught at different grade levels.

Table 5.2
STUDENT INVOLVEMENT IN THE LEARNING PROCESS

DOs

1. Ask each student the types of activities and skills that he or she would like to work to develop during part of every day.
2. Actively involve students in career education and job-seeking activities.
3. Invite outside speakers from different careers to come into the classroom and share information about their jobs. Encourage students to visit different jobs to gain an understanding of what is involved in holding a job.
4. Teach students how to complete job applications.
5. Teach students how to develop job resumes.
6. Make sure every student has a social security card.
7. Teach students how to look for jobs in the classified ads and online.
8. Teach students how to find different recreational activities and events in the newspapers and online. Take them to some of these activities and teach them how to involve themselves in community activities.
9. Teach students how to get around town using public transportation.

continued

Table 5.2–*Continued*

DON'Ts

1. Do not rely heavily on workbooks.
2. Do not rely on large volumes of ditto sheets and desk work.
3. Do not let students repeatedly fail tasks or activities.
4. Do not plan vocational curricula on the basis of a curriculum guide or book that comes from a state agency or book publisher. Plan curricula around the student's needs and interests.
5. Do not arrange teaching environments so that the teacher does all of the teaching and the students do all of the listening. Design environments where students are heavily involved in the learning process.

Source: Adapted from Applications for youth with mild retardation, by P. Brown-Glover (pp. 237–260), in *Life Beyond the Classroom: Transition Strategies for Young People* With Disabilities, P. Wehman (Ed.), 1992, Baltimore, MD: Paul Brookes.

Table 5.3
VOCATIONAL SKILLS TO BE TAUGHT AT DIFFERENT GRADE LEVELS

VALUES
K–3:   awareness of self and responsibility for own actions
4–6:   understanding concepts of quality, opportunity, planning one's time
7–12:   individual inquiry, importance and outcomes of work, and problem solving

HUMAN RELATIONSHIPS
K–3:   awareness of behavior standards, cooperative social behavior
4–6:   self-control and development of personal relationships
7–12:   socially responsible behavior

OCCUPATIONAL
K–3:   awareness of different types of occupational roles, respect for others and work that they do
4–6:   knowledge of occupational clusters, development of work attitudes/ethics
7–12:   knowledge of economic concepts, development of work environment behavior, identifying a range of jobs for work experiences

JOB AND DAILY LIVING SKILLS
K–3:   skill in using money and caring for equipment
4–6:   skill in home and safety, skill in classroom and school jobs, development of cooking and cleaning skills, personal care skills
7–12:   skill in banking and purchasing, skill in specific job requirements, service learning experiences.

Source: Modified from Vocational assessment in school and rehabilitation programs, by L. K. Irvin (pp. 111–141), in *Vocational Education for Persons With Handicaps,* R. Gaylord-Ross (Ed.), 1998, Mountain View, CA: Mayfield Publishing Company; and Career development: Developing basic work skills and employment preferences, by A. Renzaglia, M. P. Hutchins, S. K. Dymond, and D. L. Shelden (pp. 72–106), in *The Road Ahead: Transition to Adult Life for Persons with Disabilities* (2nd ed.), K. Storey, P. Bates, and D. Hunter (Eds.), 2008. St. Augustine, FL: Training Resource Network, Inc.

Key Point Question 5: What Employment Skills Should Be Taught in Employment Settings?

Whatever skills the individual needs to be successful! The major goal is to increase independent performance. An individual may not be able to complete all job tasks, complete them accurately, or complete them quickly when starting a job.

A critical skill that must be taught is the ability to handle change. Some individuals with disabilities have trouble handing change, especially when it is unexpected. At many jobs there may be changes in routines that are expected (such as moving from one task to another) and some that are not routine (such as the supervisor saying to stop a job task to take up another one in a different area such as moving from food preparation to helping in the dish-washing area).

Strategies such as social skills instruction, social stories, practices, advanced notice of change, and positive reinforcement may be effective in helping the individual deal with these important situations.

Key Point Question 6: What Is a Job Analysis and Why Is It Important for Determining Needed Skills?

In order to understand the work environment in terms of whether it is a good fit for the individual, what types of supports are most appropriate, what skills the individual needs, and the performance on the job, a job analysis is a very effective strategy for understanding the job and for developing appropriate instruction and supports for the individual.

The job analysis enables the trainer to learn the job. The bottom line is that the trainer is responsible for seeing that the tasks are performed correctly from day one. The trainer must know the job in order to teach the employee how to perform successfully.

The job analysis also uncovers less obvious components or aspects of the job. Jobs often vary from day to day. For instance, there may be times when there is a great deal of work or little work, and the employee must be able to perform and "fit in" with the variation.

With the job analysis, it is easier to understand

1. Task completion criteria (quality and accuracy)
2. Task variation (sequence/frequency)
3. Low frequency job events

4. Opportunity to figure out "company culture"
5. Opportunities for instruction and feedback (correction and reinforcement)

Key Point Question 7: Why Are Interview Skills Important?

All too often a person has good job skills, is a good candidate for the job, makes it to the job interview, and loses the job in the interview. There are many generic books available regarding job interviewing skills (Bolles, 2010; Bolles & Christen, 2006; Goden, 1998) as well as some specifically for individuals with disabilities (Bolles & Brown, 2001).

Interviewing skills can be broken down into a series of subskills. Preparing for an interview involves individuals in researching both themselves (what skills they have, what they contribute to the work site) and the job for which they are interviewing (not only the job but also the company, its mission, its culture, etc.). It is often beneficial to conduct mock interviews beforehand and to videotape them so that they can be analyzed for both good and bad aspects of the interviewee. Many business people are willing to conduct mock interviews (and provide feedback) with students and adults with disabilities which can be very beneficial for them to get "real world" interview experiences in a safe environment.

Informational interviews can be used to collect detailed, up-to-date, and personalized perspectives on a specific occupation. With informational interviews, the individual is not applying for a job but is seeking information about occupations. For example, someone interested in working in a hospital might interview the human resources director regarding the types of jobs available, the qualifications needed, the hiring process, and so on. A list of questions should be developed to guide the interview (e.g., employment outlook, educational or training requirements, description of a typical day, etc.). The informational interview itself should be short (fifteen to twenty minutes) and, if possible, include a brief tour of the business. A thank you note to the interviewee should be sent after the interview. Following the informational interview, the more the interviewee knows about the employer in future interviews, the more the interviewer will be convinced of his or her interest in the job.

THE ACTUAL INTERVIEW. Table 5.4 provides a list of questions the individual should evaluate before the interview. The goal for interviewer is to answer two questions: Why should I hire you and why would you be good for my organization? The individual must be prepared to answer these questions (although, of course, they may be asked in a variety of formats).

FOLLOW-UP. A short thank you note should be sent.

EVALUATE THE INTERVIEW. What questions were most difficult to answer? How could the individual have improved the interview?

Table 5.4
THINGS TO EVALUATE BEFORE THE INTERVIEW

What are the crucial facts about yourself that you want to be sure the interviewer knows?

What characteristics do you think the employer is most interested in?

What are your greatest strengths for the job?

What are your greatest weaknesses for the job?

What do you need to know about the job and organization to enable you to decide whether to accept an offer?

Key Point Question 8: What Are Job Site Accommodations and Modifications?

Employees with disabilities have the legal right to have accommodations and/or modifications made for them under the Americans with Disabilities Act as well as Section 504 of the Rehabilitation Act of 1973 (for any entity that receives federal funds).

Accommodations

Accommodations provide different ways for employees to take in information or to perform job tasks. Accommodation changes do not alter or lower the standards or expectations for job performance. Examples would be the use of large print in written documents or a note taker for meetings.

Modifications

Modifications are changes in what a person does at a job site. They result in changing or lowering expectations and create a different standard for employees with disabilities than exists for those without disabilities. Examples include a modified number of work tasks that the employee must perform or the amount of lifting that he or she does.

It is possible to use job restructuring strategies such as job carving or job sharing for individuals who might not be able to complete some of the essential tasks for a job. Job carving involves having the individual perform certain tasks of a job but not all of the tasks of a job. For example, in an office, many administrative assistants may be responsible for photocopying. Having one person responsible for the photocopying would be taking that one task from many and having one individual responsible for that task. With job sharing, two individuals are hired as a team. There is variability to job sharing, such as working together to complete a task, splitting responsibilities, or splitting the time worked (e.g., one in the morning and one in the afternoon). The overall purpose of these accommodations, modifications, and restructuring is to improve the efficiency of all of the workers at the site (not just for the person with a disability).

Key Point Question 9: What Is the Role of Technology in Employment Success?

A vast array of technology is used in workplaces that an individual may need to know how to use (the job analysis can be very helpful in determining this), but technology can also be used to help an individual with a disability perform job tasks. The term assistive technology is often used to describe the variety of devices that are available.

It can be helpful to divide assistive technology into low or high technology. Low technology refers to adaptations to materials or activities that are easy to make and/or low cost such as color-coded keys, pencil grips, or large key calculators (Thoma, Bartholomew, & Scott, 2009). High technology refers to devices or pieces of equipment that are more complex and often involve computers and software such as voice input software, braille printers, or switches for a computer (Thoma et al., 2009).

The key is to match the technology with the support needs of the individual. Often devices are provided directly by the employer (under the American with Disability Act requirements) or through the state department of rehabilitation. Because employers may not be aware of technology available to assist employees, the school system, the adult service provider, or the individual with a disability may need to provide information. Web sites such as www.rehabtool.com and the job accommodation network (www.jan.wvu.edu) can be useful starting places.

Key Point Question 10: What Are Point of Transition Strategies?

Point of transition strategies involve the bringing together of relevant service agencies (the school district, adult service agencies, department of rehabilitation, the individual and his or her family) *before* the student exits the school system in order to coordinate services and supports (Certo, Luecking, et al., 2008; Certo, Mautz, et al., 2003). The basic idea is that the last day of school for the individual should look no different that the first day of adult life. In other words, if the student has a job he or she will stay in that position and services supports will shift from the school district to the adult service provider. This avoids potential pitfalls in the transition process such as determining eligibility, having to complete new assessments, and so on.

BEST PRACTICE RECOMMENDATIONS

1. Assessment should be focused on interests, strengths, and support needs rather than deficits.
2. Individuals need to be taught how to do complete jobs, not isolated job skills.
3. Students need to exit the school system with marketable job skills.
4. Students need to be exposed through a variety of methods (job exploration, job shadowing, internships, part-time jobs) to a wide variety of job possibilities in order to expand their horizons and to help them make informed choices.

FUTURE RESEARCH ISSUES

1. How do you best match supports to the individual and the work environment?
2. How are federal, state, and local dollars best distributed for the employment of people with disabilities?

3. What are the best ways to support people who lose their jobs and are looking for work?

DISCUSSION QUESTIONS

1. Are some people too severely disabled to work?
2. Is there any role for sheltered workshops or other segregated vocational programs?
3. As students in the school system get older, should the focus be on academics or work and community living skills?
4. Can employment skills be successfully taught in the context of the general education classroom?
5. How do school systems and adult service agencies best coordinate their services?
6. Should individuals have jobs or careers?

SCHOOL AND COMMUNITY-BASED ACTIVITY

1. Develop a plan for implementing community connections for an individual with a disability who would like to form new relationships and community connections.
2. Interview the person about his or her likes and dislikes, hobbies, and values. Identify five to ten specific community connections the individual could make related to likes, hobbies, and values. (Connections are joining groups or organizations or being a part of the community in some way, in other words, being part of the community, not just being in the community.) Develop a support plan for each connection to assist the person in making each of the recommended community connections.
3. Visit a one-stop center and go on an official tour and orientation with a student or an adult with a disability. Spend time at the center using the materials and resources in conjunction with the person with a disability and also on your own.
4. Visit and evaluate the DSPS at a local community college. Analyze how a student with a disability qualifies for services, what the process is for applying, what services and supports are available, and what a student should do before entering the program (i.e., while he or she is still in high school).

5. Visit and assess sheltered workshop and supported employment settings. For each placement, write an analysis of what you saw in terms of wages, benefits, career advancement, meaningful work, hours worked, social integration, variety of tasks, choice, and community access.

REFERENCES

Baker, J. (2005). *Preparing for life: The complete guide for transitioning to adulthood for those with Autism and Asperger's Syndrome.* Arlington, TX: Future Horizons.

Bakken, J. P., & Obiakor, F. E. (2008). *Transition planning for students with disabilities.* Springfield, IL: Charles C Thomas.

Blalock, G., Patton, J. R., Kohler, P., & Bassett, D. (2008). *Transition and students with learning disabilities: Facilitating the movement from school to adult life* (2nd ed.), Austin, TX: Hammill Institute on Disabilities.

Bolles, R. N. (2010). *What color is your parachute? 2010: A practical manual for job-hunters and career-changers.* Berkeley, CA: Ten Speed Press.

Bolles, R. N., & Brown, D. S. (2001). *Job hunting for the so called handicapped or people who have disabilities.* Berkeley, CA: Ten Speed Press.

Bolles, R. N., & Christen, C. (2006). *What color is your parachute? for teens: Discovering yourself, defining your future.* Berkeley, CA: Ten Speed Press.

Brown-Glover, P. (1992). Applications for youth with mild mental retardation. In P. Wehman (Ed.), *Life beyond the classroom: Transition strategies for young people with disabilities* (pp. 237–260). Baltimore, MD: Paul Brookes.

Browning, P., & Irvin, L. K. (1981). The vocational evaluation, training and placement of mentally retarded persons: A research review. *Rehabilitation Counseling Bulletin, 24,* 374–408.

Certo, N. J., Luecking, R. G., Murphy, S., Brown, L., Courey, S., & Belanger, D. (2008). Seamless transition and long-term support for individuals with severe intellectual disabilities. *Research and Practice for Persons with Severe Disabilities, 33,* 85–95.

Certo, N. J., Mautz, D., Pumpian, I., Sax, C., Smalley, K., Wade, H. A., Noves, D., Luecking, R., Weschler, J., & Batterman, N. (2003). A review and discussion of a model for seamless transition to adulthood. *Education and Training in Mental Retardation and Developmental Disabilities, 38,* 3–17.

Clark, H. B., & Unruh, D. K. (2009). *Transition of youth and young adults with emotional or behavioral difficulties.* Baltimore, MD: Paul H. Brookes.

Dileo, D. (2007). *Raymond's room: Ending the segregation of people with disabilities.* St. Augustine, FL: Training Resources Network.

Getzel, E. E., & Gugerty, J. J. (1992). Applications for youth with learning disabilities. In P. Wehman (Ed.), *Life beyond the classroom: Transition strategies for young people with disabilities* (pp. 301–355). Baltimore, MD: Paul Brookes.

Goden, R. L. (1998). *Basic interviewing skills.* Long Grove, IL: Waveland Press.

Luecking, R. G., Fabian, E. S., & Tilson, G. P. (2004). *Working relationships: Creating career opportunities for job seekers with disabilities through employer partnerships.* Baltimore, MD: Paul Brookes.

Mank, D. M. (1994). The underachievement of supported employment: A call for reinvestment. *Journal of Disability Policy Studies, 5,* 1–24.

Mank, D. M., & Horner, R. H. (1988). Instructional programming in vocational education. In R. Gaylord-Ross (Ed.), *Vocational education for persons with handicaps* (pp. 142–173). Mountain View, CA: Mayfield Publishing Company.

Martin, J. E., Van Dycke, J., D'Ottavio, M., & Nickerson, K. (2007). The student-directed summary of performance: Increasing student and family involvement in the transition planning process. *Career Development for Exceptional Individuals, 30,* 13–26.

McNaughton, D. B., & Beukelman, D. R. (2010). *Transition strategies for adolescents and young adults who use augmentative and alternative communication.* Baltimore, MD: Paul Brookes.

Murphy, S. T., & Rogan, P. M. (1995). *Closing the shop: Conversion from sheltered to integrated work.* Baltimore: Paul Brookes.

Rusch, F. R. (2008). *Beyond high school: Preparing adolescents for tomorrow's challenges* (2nd ed.). Upper Saddle River, NJ: Pearson.

Schalock, R. L., Kiernan, W. E., McGaughey, M. J., Lynch, S. A., & McNally, L. C. (1993). State MR/DD agency information systems and available data related to day and employment programs. *Mental Retardation, 31,* 29–34.

Storey, K. (2000). Why employment in integrated settings for people with disabilities. *International Journal of Rehabilitation Research, 23,* 103–110.

Szymanski, E. M., & Parker, R. M. (2010). *Work and disability: Contexts, issues, and strategies for enhancing employment outcomes for people with disabilities* (3rd ed.). Austin, TX: Pro-Ed.

Test, D. W., Aspel, N. P., & Everson, J. M. (2006). *Transition methods for youth with disabilities.* Upper Saddle River, NJ: Pearson Merrill/Prentice Hall.

Thoma, C. A., Bartholomew, C. C., & Scott, L. A. (2009). *Universal design for transition: A roadmap for planning and instruction.* Baltimore, MD: Paul Brookes.

Wehman, P., & Kregel, J. (1995). At the crossroads: Supported employment a decade later. *Journal of the Association for Persons with Severe Handicaps, 20,* 286–299.

Wehman, P. (2006). *Life beyond the classroom: Transition strategies for young people with disabilities* (4th ed.). Baltimore, MD: Paul Brookes Publishing Company.

Wehman, P., Inge, K. J., Revell, W. G., & Brookes, V. A. (2007). *Real work for real pay: Inclusive employment for people with disabilities.* Baltimore, MD: Paul Brookes Publishing Company.

Chapter 6

FUNCTIONAL SKILLS IN COMMUNITY SETTINGS

Keypoint Questions

1. What is community-based instruction?
2. What are the benefits of instruction in community settings?
3. How can barriers to community instruction be overcome?
4. What skills are taught for community participation?
5. How do you determine which community skills to teach?
6. How is systematic instruction used to teach travel/mobility skills?
7. How is systematic instruction used to teach a functional skill in community settings?
8. How is systematic instruction used to teach recreation/leisure skills?
9. How is systematic instruction used to teach financial skills?

Window to the World Case Study One

Stephanie is a seventeen-year-old student with a diagnosis of autism. Her parents have expressed the desire for her to learn grocery shopping skills. Stephanie's transition plan includes a post school goal of going shopping with assistance from a caretaker. Her teacher, Mr. Gregory, has developed an individualized task analysis for shopping for Stephanie and has seen a great deal of success in her performance. The major barrier to mastery of grocery shopping for Stephanie is waiting in the checkout line to pay for the groceries. Stephanie places the items on the conveyer and pays the cashier but exhibits undesirable behaviors, such as making loud noises and bumping others with

the cart while waiting to get to the checkout. Mr. Gregory has targeted the steps causing Stephanie difficulty.

The manager of the store has begun sending a cashier to open up a
separate line to check Stephanie out when she becomes agitated. The
grocery store manager is well-intentioned but has taken away the
opportunity for Stephanie to learn this important aspect of shopping.
Mr. Gregory goes into the store on a day when he is not training one
of his students and expresses his appreciation for the store manager's
consideration but explains the need for Stephanie to perform the
shopping task under normal conditions. The store manager agrees to
refrain from opening a separate checkout lane just for Stephanie in the
future. After Mr. Gregory's conversation with the store manager,
Stephanie had multiple trials of identifying an open checkout with the
shortest line, getting in line, and waiting until she reached the counter
to begin placing items from the cart to the counter. Mr. Gregory used
a most-to-least physical prompting procedure for this portion of
Stephanie's training. While Stephanie pushed the cart, he would hold
the front of the cart and physically prompt her to the shortest line.
Then he positioned himself between the cart and shopper at the end
of the line so as to prevent Stephanie from hitting the person in front
of her. He also taught her relaxation techniques to use while waiting in
line (Lipsitt, Groden, Baron, & Groden, 2006). After six weeks of
"checking out" at the grocery store, Stephanie was independent in all
steps of the grocery shopping process. She could not have mastered
waiting in line to check out without experiencing the natural conditions encountered by typical shoppers.

Window to the World Case Study Two

Clarence is a thirty-year-old with a diagnosis of "intellectual disability." He lives in an apartment with one other man with an intellectual
disability. An adult service agency provides supported employment
services for Clarence's job at a "trendy" upscale clothing store and also
trains him in functional skills in the community. The community trainer, Zac, has been working with Clarence over the past six months.
Until this year, Clarence was placed in a sheltered workshop. When
he received his check from the workshop for $1.49, he would go to the
simulated store at the sheltered workshop and purchase candy or
some other snack. When Clarence was hired by the clothing store and

began receiving minimum wage, he cashed his paycheck and went to the store. Clarence wanted to spend the entire week's pay on snacks and candy. Zac quickly scheduled a team meeting to consider budgeting and banking skills for Clarence. It was obvious to everyone that Clarence preferred to spend his money immediately. An instructional plan that included depositing his paycheck into a checking account and keeping a small portion to purchase snacks at the local grocery store honored Clarence's spending preference and began the process of teaching him necessary budgeting skills. Each week, Clarence would monitor the balance in his checking account after depositing his paycheck by using a software program on the bank's web site. This became just as reinforcing as the trip to the grocery store to purchase a snack. After a couple of months, Clarence chose to skip the snack purchase. He decided that he wanted to save his money to purchase a new electronic gaming system that he and his roommate liked to play.

Key Point Question 1: What Is Community-Based Instruction?

Efforts to increase the amount of time students with disabilities spend in general education classrooms, although positive, have often limited the opportunities for students to receive instruction in community settings. As students get older, the need for learning functional skills in the community increases. This does not mean that high school students with disabilities cannot receive educational services alongside their peers without disabilities, but it does mean that consideration needs to be increasingly focused on adult outcomes in community settings. It could be argued that all students, including those without disabilities, need to be taught community living skills. Nevertheless, individuals with disabilities, both students and adults, require systematic instruction of those critical skills that are required in community settings. Past research documents the benefits to individuals receiving community-based instruction (Snell & Browder, 1986). The amount of time someone should receive training in the community versus school settings is much debated. The premise of this chapter is that regardless of the amount of time the team determines an individual should receive instruction in the community it should be as efficient as possible.

A variety of skills are needed to live successfully in the community. One needs to be able to get to and from work, to shop, to recreate, and so on. Each of these areas has a subset of skills that are required. Having individuals perform functional skills in natural environments is the goal of community-based instruction. The natural environment is the actual setting (e.g., the grocery store, the aerobics club, etc.) in which the person must function.

Simulated instruction is conducted in settings involving artificial stimuli. These settings may occasion responses that are different than what is expected in natural environments. Simulated instruction may be used to supplement instruction in the community, but it should replicate the stimuli and response demands of the natural environment as closely as possible (Nietupski, Hamre-Nietupski, Clancy, & Veerhusen, 1986). If learners can successfully generalize skills learned from the classroom (e.g., simulated environment) to the community, then they are set; otherwise, systematic instruction must take place in the settings in which the skills are expected to be performed, for example, the criterion environment. It is important to note that assessment of mastery of skills ultimately needs to be conducted in the criterion environment.

Key Point Question 2: What Are the Benefits of Instruction in Community Settings?

There are several important benefits to community-based instruction, both for individuals with disabilities and for the community at large. The major benefits for individuals with disabilities include (1) increased likelihood of generalization, (2) natural cues and corrections, (3) more community presence for people with disabilities, (4) more efficient acquisition of skills leading to greater independence, (5) opportunities for increased social competence and the development of social networks, and (6) inhibition of undesirable behaviors.

Instruction in community settings can promote generalization instruction across untrained settings, behaviors, people, and times. In addition to increased opportunities for generalization, community instruction also increases the probability that the learned skills will be maintained. For example, if the job coach teaches Isaac to locate the entrance of a store in order to buy his work uniform, it enhances the possibility that he may also be able to find the entrance to many other business (generalization across settings) and perform the untrained skill of purchasing a ticket at the local theater (generalization across behaviors), and he is more likely to continue these skills at other times with coworkers or friends (generalization across times and people).

Learning a new skill requires that it be performed in the presence of the discriminative stimulus (*see* Chapter 3). If simulated instruction is used, then the simulations must be developed as close as possible to the natural context with the discriminative stimuli as similar as possible in order to help facilitate generalization. Training in the community provides the natural discriminative stimulus that must occasion the response. For example, the announcement on the transit train for an individual's upcoming stop is the discriminative stimulus for getting up and exiting the train. The natural consequence (e.g., missing the appropriate stop) is an added benefit to the learning process; the learner is less likely to make the same mistake in the future. These natural conditions and consequences make learning more efficient.

As children age and mature, they usually go more places in the community. People with disabilities often spend time in a limited number of settings. Some individuals may not prefer novel environments, or they may exhibit behaviors that cause caregivers to avoid trips in the community. Many students with disabilities are bused to and from school without the opportunity to participate in other environments. More importantly, however, individuals with disabilities need exposure with appropriate supports and instruction in order to make informed choices and to be successful. Community-based instruction allows for increased exposure to multiple settings with careful planning by the instructor to avoid conflict and prevent problem behavior.

The efficiency of learning in the natural environments and generalization of untrained skills may lead to greater independence. Training in the community provides opportunities to increase the overall number of learned skills that caregivers would have to perform for the individual. For example, if Jonathan is taught to purchase a drink from the deli and generalizes that skill to buying his lunch to take to work each day, he gains autonomy over many choices that may have previously been made by residential staff (e.g., trying a new food item for lunch).

Social competence is a concern for many individuals with disabilities. A major argument for including students with disabilities in general education classrooms is that it promotes social competence due to exposure to same-age peers without disabilities (Carter & Hughes, 2007). Individuals in the community also provide good models for socialization as well as the natural cues and corrections for inappropriate social skills. Additionally, friendships are often established through common interests. When John, a young adult with Down syndrome, learned to go to the local recreation center to work out, he was greeted each day by someone at the desk. This greeting led to conversations with center staff. Over the course of many weeks of workouts, John began talking to another regular member, Andrew (a person without a disability), about different exercises that could be performed on various pieces of equipment. Now, John and Andrew work out together and then go out for a healthy snack after their workout.

As stated earlier, some interfering behaviors have inhibited community presence for many individuals with disabilities. Many of the factors discussed previously promote acceptable behavior in the community. The natural cues/corrections and social models are strong influences over an individual's behavior. When Lauren's parents pointed out that none of the other children at the park were "twirling," she began to use the swings as an appropriate alternative activity.

There are also benefits to the community when individuals with disabilities receive training in these criterion settings. Businesses, such as banks and restaurants welcome additional customers. Coincidentally, these training sites may also provide opportunities for future employment of individuals with disabilities. Potential employers can observe and interact with individuals with disabilities and recognize their competence. Additionally, training in the community demonstrates the ongoing support that job coaches can provide employees with disabilities. To illustrate, Jaclyn was a twenty-year-old student receiving community-based instruction for recreation at the local community college. The transition program supported her participation in a physical fitness course at the college. Over the course of the semester, staff at the recreation center observed Jaclyn's eagerness to learn new skills and the effectiveness of systematic instruction provided by the transition program staff. The athletic director for the college approached Jaclyn and asked if she would like to interview for a position as a staff member in the athletic department.

Important concerns have been regarding safety, supervision, and cost and transportation for community instruction, and these concerns need to be seriously considered for each individual. For example, team decisions must be made as to whether or not an individual will be safe if traveling alone in the community. Stakeholders, such as parents or other caregivers, should be involved in the decision-making process. If one-on-one supervision is deemed necessary anytime the individual is in the community, partial participation in community mobility might still be a priority. Learning to walk alongside another person when crossing streets or moving about in the community can be a crucial skill for increasing community presence.

Teachers and other providers must advocate for community instruction by highlighting the benefits, ensuring the safety of individuals, and planning for the effective use of instructional support. These issues must be addressed in allocating resources for training in the community.

Key Point Question 3: How Can Barriers to Community Instruction Be Overcome?

As discussed earlier, the barriers to community instruction must be overcome. Collaboration with families, administration, community members, and other professionals can be effective in overcoming these barriers. Many teams have found ways to address the barriers associated with supervision, cost, transportation, and safety/liability concerns.

SUPERVISION. One-on-one or small group instruction works best in community settings. Large group instruction is unnatural in such settings. It can be stigmatizing and result in missed or incorrect cues, responses, and reinforcers. Adequate supervision of learners may be difficult when typical ratios of instructor to learner are much higher. Many schools have solved this problem through the effective use of paraprofessionals. Paraprofessionals may be able to supervise larger groups at school while the teacher takes a small group into the community. In other circumstances, volunteers, peers without disabilities, or other staff may be used to provide necessary supervision.

COST. Additional expenses may be associated with community-based instruction. The first avenue to pursue for added costs would be to have instruction in the community included in the program budget. Making instruction in natural settings a priority is best demonstrated by the allocation of funds. In some cases, a school district or program may lack the resources to take on this expense. Under these circumstances, staff may need to solicit donations, hold fundraisers, or find other creative funding sources. For example, individuals learning to make purchases in the community may buy groceries for cooking classes or for teachers at the school.

TRANSPORTATION. Traveling to community settings is one of the barriers that must be overcome if individuals are going to receive community instruction. This barrier is closely associated with increased costs. Public transportation can be an ideal solution. Transit passes are often provided free of charge to individuals with disabilities receiving mobility training. Utilizing other transportation options that are available, such as a school/agency van that is not used during program hours, may address this dilemma. Selecting instructional settings within walking distance is also an option but may restrict opportunities for natural contexts.

SAFETY/LIABILITY. Necessary supervision is required to ensure the safety of individuals with disabilities in the community. Liability of the school district or agency must be addressed in the planning process. Districts and agencies must have policies regarding supervision of individuals receiving instruction in community settings. Staff must be trained to ensure the safety of learners and adhere to district/agency policies. The cellular phone is a useful tool in the community. Staff and learners can carry cell phones programmed with emergency numbers and information. Cell phones can also include global positioning systems (GPS) that can be used

Key Point Question 4: What Skills Are Taught for Community Participation?

The environments in which community-based instruction occurs are as varied as the skills themselves. Functional skills are carried out in stores, recreation centers, and banks, among a multitude of other settings. Four major types of skills that are taught in the community include (1) travel and mobility (e.g., street crossing), (2) community skills (e.g., shopping), (3) recreation/leisure (e.g., karate class), and (4) financial skills (e.g., cashing a check). Community participation includes specific skills such as grocery shopping, ordering and eating at a restaurant, making a deposit and/or withdrawal at a bank, going to the movies, playing bingo, and riding mass transit. The list is endless.

Skills need to be taught that are specific to the situation and needs of the individual. For example, if the learner has a grocery store near their home then it might be more appropriate to teach the individual to shop there rather than at a variety of grocery stores in the town.

Key Point Question 5: How to Determine Which Community Skills to Teach?

In Chapter 1, the criterion of ultimate functioning was introduced (Brown, Nietupski, & Hamre-Nietupski, 1976). Of course, a multitude of community skills meet this criterion for adults with disabilities. Obviously, all of the skills associated with community presence cannot be taught simultaneously. Due to the vast array of possible skills to be taught and the criterion environments for these skills, community skills must be prioritized. Some of the considerations for prioritizing community skills include the following.

1. Individual and Family Preference

Individual preferences can be generated through self-determination curriculum (*see* Chapter 9) and other strategies such as interviewing key stakeholders and direct observation. Individuals with disabilities often have difficulty communicating preferences and interests, although their behaviors communicate a great deal about what they would like to do or avoid. Caregivers often serve as joint consumers in expressing a desire to participate in a community living skill. If the individual and family want her or him to be able to make a purchase at the local coffee shop, this may be chosen over other possible community skills. If the individual does not perform the skill after training because either family or caregivers do not provide the opportunity or the person simply does not want to purchase coffee, it does not meet the definition of a functional or priority skill.

2. Age Appropriateness

Community living skills are learned at various stages of life. Choosing skills to be learned in the community should be compared to what same-age peers without disabilities do. For example, walking to the corner pharmacy to pick up a prescription is more appropriate for an adult (i.e., over 18 years of age) than for a child. It is important to avoid age-inappropriate community activities (e.g., going to a children's museum, visiting a fire station) that lead to the stigmatization of older students and adults with disabilities.

3. Access to Environments and Activities

Increasing the number of environments and variety of activities may be a critical consideration in an individual's program. For example, some individuals with disabilities have limited exposure to their communities, only traveling between school or day program and home five days per week. Teaching a recreation skill (e.g., circuit training) at the local YMCA would add another place to which the individual goes during the week as well as increase opportunities for choosing other activities such as dressing or purchasing a soft drink.

4. Quality of Life

As stated in Chapter 1, quality of life is more likely to be improved when an individual learns skills related to the criterion of ultimate functioning (e.g., to balance a checkbook as opposed to copying math ditto sheets). All of the previously mentioned instructional considerations ultimately revolve around quality of life. When someone expresses an interest and has the opportunity to learn a new skill, her or his quality of life is enhanced in the quality of life domains.

The process of prioritization must include the individual and other stakeholders, such as family members, teachers, adult service providers, related service personnel, coworkers, and so on. Typically this would include the IEP team for school-age youth and a planning team from the service provider for adults. Person-centered planning activities (discussed in detail in Chapter 9) can be used to prioritize skills based on the individual's preferences and interests.

After the team identifies priority skills necessary for independent performance in current and future environments, an ecological inventory of possible training domains is conducted (*see* Chapter 2). Chapter 1 emphasized the importance of training functional skill sequences versus teaching isolated skills. Community-based instruction is an excellent example of this principle. For example, a special education teacher may implement a community skills curricular plan with several students that involves an in-class lesson on Monday that teaches menu planning, budgeting, and grocery item preferences. On Tuesday, students may learn travel skills to and from the grocery store and shopping skills out in the actual community sites. Food preparation, eating, and kitchen cleanup may be learned in a home economics class on Wednesday. In this example, grocery shopping is taught as part of a larger sequence of community living skills.

Key Point Question 6: How Is Systematic Instruction Used to Teach Travel/Mobility Skills?

Self-determination and self-control are important goals for all individuals with disabilities. The ability to travel independently or semi-independently in the community enhances the control a person has over his or her life. Travel/mobility training is often ignored because of concerns over safety. Indeed, moving independently throughout the community poses many challenges for individuals who require intensive supports. Even if total independence is not fully achieved, travel/mobility training may be an appropriate goal. The safety concerns associated with mobility and travel in community settings requires service providers and caretakers to allow individuals with disabilities the dignity that comes with taking risks (Perske, 1972). Social barriers (e.g., vulnerability to exploitation) fall into this category as well. Other concerns may include the accessibility of the physical environment (e.g., sidewalks and curbs) and public transportation (e.g., buses). What a person does when lost or dealing with strangers in the community are safety skills that are critical to mobility independence (Collins, Wolery, & Gast, 1992). Instruction is crucial to overcome physical and social barriers. Individuals with disabilities may need to be taught specific skills, such as how to use a cell phone to call for help or directions or to check directions through GPS.

Mobility training has long been a critical component of the curriculum for individuals with visual impairments. This training is equally important for individuals with other types of disabilities. Mobility skills include the use of public transit and pedestrian skills. Using public transit involves the ability to read bus schedules, purchase and/or pay fares, and board and exit at the appropriate stop. Pedestrian skills primarily involve safe street crossing and finding desired community sites (e.g., bank, fast food restaurant, etc.).

Most travel or mobility training requires individual or possibly small group instruction. The example of crossing the street safely demonstrates how general case programming can be used. For example, when Ms. Ramirez conducted an ecological inventory of the community in which Jackson would be walking, she noted that crossing the street required very different attention to stimuli and responses depending on the part of town, traffic, and signals. Busier streets in the middle of town had signals indicating "walk" and "don't walk." Other streets had marked crosswalks with no signals, and some streets did not have marked crosswalks. Additionally, some streets had crosswalks that were not located at or near intersections.

Ms. Ramirez taught Jackson to cross the street safely at crosswalks with and without signals and at streets without marked crosswalks. During the ecological inventory, Ms. Ramirez noted that all three types of streets were encountered when walking from the school to a nearby coffee shop. She taught Jackson using a task analysis of the street-crossing activity and time delay fading procedure with indirect verbal prompting.

Key Point Question 7: How Is Systematic Instruction Used to Teach a Functional Skill in Community Settings?

When a planning team decides to teach a functional skill in a community setting, several important instructional considerations must be addressed. There are many skills associated with the task analysis that must be considered by the instructor. As we discussed in Chapter 1, functional skills must be seen as lifestyle routines not isolated skills. For example, grocery shopping may include routines (with sets of other skills) that need to be taught, including planning healthy menus, getting to and from the grocery store, cutting coupons and matching them to the items, greeting patrons and store personnel, ordering items from the deli, and so on. If the learner typically uses public transportation to go grocery shopping, it may be necessary to shop for only the number of items that can be carried. Another example would be the necessity to inhibit impulse buying by teaching the individual the skill of preparing a shopping list in advance based on menu planning.

Teaching individuals to shop for groceries is an important community skill. It meets the immediate and future need criteria to be considered a functional skill and must be done by someone else if not performed by the individual. We will describe how grocery shopping can be taught using concurrent chaining. Total task (concurrent chaining) is useful because of the limited opportunities for teaching the skill (usually once a week) and also that it makes sense to teach all of the skills as part of the activity, rather than arbitrarily stopping at certain points in the instruction. For example, since Charles could not recognize sight words associated with the shopping task. Mr. Puchner taught Charles to use a pictorial shopping list. Charles and Mr. Puchner used Google Images to find pictures of specific items by brand. Charles pointed to the picture of his favorite food items (e.g., macaroni and cheese).

As stated before, Mr. Puchner chose concurrent chaining (see Task Analysis in Table 6.1) as the most efficient method for Charles to learn the steps of grocery shopping. The many natural cues and correction procedures (Falvey, Brown, Lyon, Baumgart, & Schroeder, 1980) associated with grocery shopping were highlighted by Mr. Puchner during training. These natural cues were noted along with praise for completing steps so that they became reinforcing (e.g., items checked off the list or placed in the cart). A least-to-most fading procedure was used to teach this task. For example, when Charles and Mr. Puchner got off the transit bus, they would walk toward the store entrance together. Mr. Puchner would say "What is the first thing to do in order to buy groceries" (an indirect verbal cue, the least prompt) and wait for Charles to enter the store. If there was no response, Mr. Puchner modeled walking toward the store entrance as a prompt (a modeling prompt, a greater prompt than the indirect verbal cue). If the Charles did not enter the store, Mr. Puchner would give a more intrusive prompt (e.g., gesturing by pointing at the entrance). A partial physical prompt, by touching Charles's elbow and slightly moving it toward the entrance, might be needed if Charles still did not respond. Prompting can be faded by systematically decreasing the level of prompt necessary to perform the entire task.

Key Point Question 8: How Is Systematic Instruction Used to Teach Recreation and Leisure Skills?

No other functional skill domain is driven by individual choice and preference more than the area of recreation and leisure skills. Some of these skills are learned and practiced in a person's home and others in the community. Leisure activities, such as watching a movie, may be enjoyed at home or in public theaters. Going to the movies in the com-

Table 6.1
TASK ANALYSIS DATA COLLECTION SHEET FOR GROCERY SHOPPING

		* = Mandatory											
Need to enter store.	Enter the grocery store.												
In store.	Get shopping cart.												
Have shopping cart.	Find item that matches picture on grocery list.												
Get item in hand.	Place item in shopping cart.												
Item in shopping cart.	Continue steps 3 and 4 until all items on list are found.												
All items on list in shopping cart.	Go to checkout.												
At checkout line.	Wait in line.												
At cashier.	Place items on conveyer.												
Items on conveyer.	Pay cashier.												
Items paid for.	Collect bag.												
Bag in hand.	Replace cart.												
Cart replaced.	Leave the store.												

munity requires many skills not demanded when viewing at home. The skills for going to the movies requires getting to the theater, purchasing a ticket, possibly purchasing snacks, locating seats, refraining from disruptive talking, leaving the theater, returning home. As stated before, the benefits of active community presence cannot be overstated. Although it may be easier (and cheaper) to limit recreation and leisure activities to the home, this leads to a lifestyle of isolation (Putnam, 2000).

Recreation and leisure activities performed in the community significantly increase the number of options and opportunities for social integration. Friendships are often initiated through common interests. Even though watching a movie at a theater requires the audience to refrain from talking during the feature, individuals who enjoy a specific genre of films may establish a relationship based on going to the first opportunity to view the latest release, forming a group to get together to discuss the files, and getting together at someone's home to view films of this genre.

Because of the importance of individual choice and the variety of skills needed in community settings, instructors and family must work together to determine the recreation and leisure preferences of the individual. Many learners may have communication skill deficits that make it difficult for others to identify their preferences. Person-centered planning (*see* Chapter 9) has been utilized to identify individual preferences. Reid, Everson, and Green (1999) suggest that systematic preference assessment may be necessary for some individuals to verify the accuracy of preferences. Especially in the area of leisure activities, it is necessary to observe the individual in the natural environment to determine preferences (Browder, Cooper, & Lim, 1998). Individuals with disabilities may have limited exposure to a variety of recreation and leisure opportunities. Segregated recreation activities, such as bowling sessions only for people with disabilities, and Special Olympics have too often been viewed as the sole opportunity in this domain (Storey, 2008). Although the value of these self-contained activities can be debated, it is reasonable to assume that they should not be the only avenues for recreation. The goal of trying new and different events can be valuable in the lives of people with and without disabilities. However, due to this lack of exposure to varied possibilities, individuals with disabilities may need to be observed in the actual event to determine if it is preferred and desirable for future participation.

For example, Sal's planning team believed that he would enjoy going to basketball games at the university in his hometown. Sal often watched basketball on television and enjoyed shooting hoops at home and at the local YMCA. Sal's community trainer, Carla, showed him a picture taken at a college basketball game and a picture of Sal and his roommate shooting hoops in the backyard. When asked which picture showed what he would like to do, Sal pointed to the picture of the college basketball game. Finally, to learn more about this preference, Carla took Sal to the arena to watch an exhibition game. Sal would not sit down to watch the game. He appeared upset when the horn sounded to begin the game and placed his fingers in his ears until they left the arena. A few days after the exhibition game, Carla presented Sal with the same pictures. This time he pushed the picture of the college game away. It was necessary for Sal to experience the stimulus conditions of the activity before making an informed choice.

To illustrate how a recreation and leisure skill can be taught once it is determined to be a personal preference, consider how a student with Down syndrome learned to participate in karate. Chris wanted to learn karate and expressed this interest to his teacher, Derrick Johnson. Mr. Johnson contacted Chris' parents to confirm that they would enroll him in karate classes at the local karate center and provide transportation. Mr. Johnson went to the karate club that Chris wanted to join, spoke with the owner/instructor about Chris, observed a class session, and conducted an ecological inventory of the setting and activities. The owner/instructor expressed a willingness to make any necessary accommodations for Chris to be successful. Mr. Johnson and the owner/instructor discussed the simulated training that would be provided at school and how appropriate models could be provided when Chris began attending classes.

The club consisted of four basic subenvironments: foyer, equipment storage area, open floor, and club store. Mr. Johnson determined that the critical skills for Chris to participate in the karate class were required in the foyer and the open area. The equipment storage area and club store subenvironments were less important and could be introduced later. The skills in these subenvironments could also be learned by Chris through modeling by other members. Mr. Johnson did a task analysis on entering the foyer, which involved (1) taking off shoes, (2) waiting in line behind classmates, (3) putting shoes on shelf, and (4) saluting Korean flag. Mr. Johnson simulated the foyer sub-environment in the locker room at school (simulated instruction) because he believed that Chris could generalize the skills to the karate club (the criterion environment). He taught Chris the four steps of the task analysis using a concurrent chaining procedure with least-to-most prompting. Chris demonstrated all steps independently after four trials at school.

The next necessary portion of training, in simulation, was entering the open floor area, lining up, and following leader directions. Mr. Johnson observed club members and identified the following steps: (1) find a place in the room at least arm's length from others; (2) perform warm-up stretching exercises; (3) when the leader says "line up," take a position at the end of the line to the right; and (4) perform motions as directed by the leader. Mr. Johnson enlisted the assistance of several students who were also interested in karate and worked with the physical education teacher to develop an introduction to karate activity in the gym. There was a video available of the motions performed by beginners. Mr. Johnson placed a television at the front of the gym so that Chris and the other interested students could perform each motion modeled on the video. Mr. Johnson provided least-to-most prompts for Chris to enter the gym area, stand arm's length from others, warm up, and line up. When everyone was in line, the video was turned on, and they performed the motions as led by the instructor. Chris demonstrated the ability to warm up, get in line, and approximate the motions of the leader on the tape after three trials.

The systematic instruction in simulation was only conducted for the week before Chris went to his first karate class. Mr. Johnson met with Chris and his parents to discuss participation in the class. Mr. Johnson had previously suggested that the owner/instructor provide specific verbal prompts for any steps of the task that might be problematic for Chris. The owner/instructor also asked for a volunteer (with Chris's permission) to help mentor Chris in following the directions from the leader (e.g., natural supports).

Key Point Question 9: How Is Systematic Instruction Used to Teach Financial Skills?

Control over one's finances is a major goal for self-determination. If people are not taught to develop a budget and choose what to purchase, a caretaker or guardian must do it for them. The inability to

budget properly and engagement in needless spending practices are
certainly not deficits restricted to individuals with disabilities. Totally
controlling another person's finances based on the assumption that he
or she will make bad decisions is an ethical dilemma frequently faced
by program planning teams. Banking is one skill routine that can be
learned by many people and can give them greater control over the
finances. Functional math skills (*see* Chapter 4) are closely associated
with financial skills. Many individuals with disabilities have limited
financial resources, and learning to monitor their income and spending is important.

The initial step to developing financial skills is to obtain a photo
identification card (which is of course important to have in many community settings). Many individuals with disabilities do not have a dri-
ver's license; however, identification cards are available through Department of Motor Vehicle offices. Once a person has a photo identification card, she or he may open a checking and/or savings account
and make deposits and withdrawals.

A critical financial skill in the community is the use of automatic
teller machines (ATMs). Both withdrawals and deposits can typically
be made at ATMs. These machines are found in multiple locations,
and users can access their accounts in a variety of settings. The instructor can do a task analysis of the steps to completing a transaction at an
ATM. There may be some minor variability from bank to bank. For
example, some banks may not allow deposits at their ATMs. Once an
individual opens an account with a bank and receives an ATM card,
community-based instruction can begin.

Table 6.2 describes a typical task analysis for making a withdrawal
or deposit. The instructor would assess how many of the steps of the
task analysis the learner can complete prior to instruction without
prompts. After these baseline data are collected, the instructor can systematically teach the steps to completing a transaction. This task has
the advantage of allowing for multiple trials at a single visit or possibly making a transaction at different machines on the same trip into
the community. For example, the learner could make a deposit at the
nearest ATM early in the day and later make a withdrawal at a
machine in the mall before shopping. The instructor would use task
analysis instruction and fading procedure to monitor the progress of
the learner.

Table 6.2
STEPS FOR USING AN ATM MACHINE

Developing a task analysis using these steps would require identifying the discriminative stimulus for each step.

Step 1   Insert your ATM Card into the machine.
Step 2   Enter your PIN (Personal Identification Number).
Step 3   Press Enter.
Step 4   Select a transaction.

Deposit money. If you want to put money into your account

Step 5   Enter the amount you will deposit.
Step 6   Confirm the amount.
Step 7   Insert the envelope into the deposit slot when the machine opens it.

With draw money. If you want to take money out of your account

Step 5   Select fixed amount of your choice.
Step 6   Take the cash when the door opens.
Step 7   Put it directly into your wallet.

For any transaction

Step 8   Choose whether to do an additional transaction. Select Yes or No.
Step 9   Choose whether you want a receipt, select Yes or No.
Step 10   Take the receipt if you requested it.
Step 11   Wait while the system processes your transaction(s).
Step 12   When the machine beeps, take your card and receipt (if applicable).
Step 13   Make sure that you have both your cash and your card.
Step 14   Use the receipt to record the transaction in your check register or passbook.

BEST PRACTICE RECOMMENDATIONS

1. Teach community skills in the natural settings where they will be used in the future.
2. If using simulated environments for increased trial opportunities, they should be as closely similar to the natural setting as possible.
3. Always assess mastery in the natural environments.
4. Individual safety and the "dignity of risk" must be considered and balanced when identifying meaningful goals for community settings.

FUTURE RESEARCH ISSUES

1. How can the Smartphone and other handheld devices increase independence in community settings for individuals with significant disabilities?
2. How can systematic instruction be provided with the least intrusiveness in the community?
3. How can greater implementation of universal design principles support community inclusion of individuals with disabilities?

DISCUSSION QUESTIONS

1. How would you decide if an individual with a disability can travel independently in the community?
2. What are the problems with group instruction in the community? Brainstorm ways to overcome these problems.
3. What are the accessibility barriers for individuals with disabilities in the community in which you live and/or teach?

SCHOOL AND COMMUNITY-BASED ACTIVITY SUGGESTIONS

1. Write a letter to your administrator requesting funding for community-based training. Provide a rationale for the benefits to the program and to learners.
2. Identify and analyze a community site. Complete the following steps: (a) select a community domain, (b) identify the environments within the chosen domain, (c) identify the subenvironments, (d) identify the activities within one subdomain, and (e) identify the skill steps and write a task analysis for one skill within one of the activities.
3. Go to your personal bank and ask for a list of ATM locations. Consider how convenient ATM access would be for an individual with a disability who may need to use public transportation or walk when moving about in the community.

REFERENCES

Browder, D. M., Cooper, K., & Lim, L. (1998). Teaching adults with severe disabilities to express their choice of settings for leisure activities. *Education and Training in Mental Retardation and Developmental Disabilities, 33,* 226–236.

Brown, L., Nietupski, J., & Hamre-Nitupski, S. (1976). Criterion of ultimate functioning. In M.A. Thomas (Ed.), *Hey, don't forget about me!* (pp. 2–15). Reston, VA: Council for Exceptional Children.

Carter, E. W., & Hughes, C. (2007). Social interaction interventions: Promoting socially supportive environments and teaching new skills. In S. L. Odom, R. H. Horner, M. E. Snell, & J. Blacher (Eds.), *Handbook of developmental disabilities* (pp. 310–329). New York: Guilford.

Collins, B. C., Wolery, M., & Gast, D. L. (1992). A national survey of safety concerns for students with special needs. *Journal of Developmental and Physical Disabilities, 4,* 263–276.

Falvey, M., Brown, L., Lyon, S., Baumgart, D., & Schroeder, J. (1980).Curricular strategies for teaching severely handicapped students to acquire and perform chronological age appropriate functional skills in response to naturally occurring cues and correction procedures. In W. Sailor, B. Wilcox & L. Brown (Eds), *Instructional design for the severely handicapped* (pp. 109–134). Baltimore, MD: Brookes.

Lipsitt, P., Groden, G., Baron, M. G., & Groden, J. (2006). *Stress and coping in autism.* Cambridge, MA: Oxford University Press.

Nietupski, J., Hamre-Nietupski, S., Clancy, P. L., & Veerhusen, K. (1986). Guidelines for making simulation and effective adjunct to in-vivo community instruction. *Journal of the Association for Persons with Severe Handicaps, 11,* 12–18.

Perske, R. (1972). The dignity of risk and the mentally retarded. *Mental Retardation, 10,* 24–27.

Putnam, R. D. (2000). *Bowling alone: The collapse and revival of American community.* New York: Simon and Schuster.

Reid, D. H., Everson, J. M., & Green, C. W. (1999). A systematic evaluation of preferences identified through person-centered planning for people with profound multiple disabilities. *Journal of Applied Behavior Analysis, 32,* 367–477.

Snell, M. E., & Browder, D. M. (1986). Community-referenced instruction: Research and issues. *Journal of the Association for Persons with Severe Handicaps, 11,* 1–11.

Storey, K. (2008). The more things change, the more they are the same: Continuing concerns with the Special Olympics. *Research and Practice for Persons with Severe Disabilities, 3,* 134–142.

Chapter 7

FUNCTIONAL SKILLS IN RESIDENTIAL SETTINGS

Keypoint Questions

1. What are different models of residential settings for people with disabilities?
2. What skills do individuals need to be independent at home?
3. Why are residential living skills important?
4. What are domestic skills?
5. What are personal care and hygiene skills?
6. What are health and safty skills?
7. How is systematic instruction used to teach functional skills in residential settings?

Window to the World Case Study One

Kim is an eight-year-old with autism. Her parents have expressed concern that Kim's list of food she will eat is extremely restricted. She mainly eats only cinnamon rolls or Lucky Charms cereal for breakfast, chicken noodle soup with the chicken pieces picked out for lunch, and macaroni and cheese or hamburgers for dinner. No amount of coaxing could get her to try new foods. She thought everything "looked gross" or would state emphatically that she had tasted it in the past and did not like it. If the family goes out to eat, they must go to a restaurant that has hamburgers (always plain) or Kim becomes quite upset.

The planning team at school brainstormed and suggested that Kim learn to plan and prepare supper each day with Mom. Kim was willing to try to fix new recipes as long as they did not contain ingredients that she believed she would not like. It was a natural consequence for Kim to try a dish that she agreed to prepare, such as beef and noodles. When she was involved in the menu planning and participated in adding the ingredients into the dish during preparation, she always tasted the finished product. Kim found that she liked many other kinds of food items when she selected the dish and was actively involved in its preparation.

Window to the World Case Study Two

Tian is twenty-six years old with an intellectual disability who requires extensive support across all domains. He has lived with his parents all of his life. He receives supported employment services to maintain his employment at a car dealer (where he works prepping cars for going into the showroom). His parents had believed that he should continue to live with them for as long as they were capable of taking care of him. Tian dresses himself and is independent in toileting. Most of the other personal care skills, such as shaving and tooth brushing, have been done for him by his mother. Tian did not perform any domestic skills in his parents' home.

Tian's job coach talked to his parents about finding a supported living arrangement for Tian, and he hooked them up with an agency that provides supported living services. After meeting with the agency and visiting several supported living situations, they came to realize that it is natural for Tian to move out of his parents' home and into a place of his own. After several months of planning, Tian moved into an apartment and has a roommate, Kevin, who does not have a disability. Kevin does not pay rent and in return has agreed to help provide support to Tian in their home. Kevin coordinates his services with those of the agency providing supported living services to Tian.

Supported living staff are helping to teach Tian how to brush his teeth and shave with an electric razor. Tian is also learning to load and unload the dishwasher, do laundry, and vacuum the carpet. Kevin and Tian plan meals, go grocery shopping, and cook meals together. (Kevin agreed to these supports because he works as a chef and thus has many skills in these areas.) Although Kevin's instruction is informal, Tian is learning skills in these areas as well. Tian is a contributing member to the household and a good roommate.

Key Point Question 1: What Are Different Models of Residential Settings for People With Disabilities?

Individuals with disabilities live in a wide variety of settings from owning their own home to being in a state institution. Historically, many individuals, especially those with developmental disabilities, were served in large residential state institutions with thousands of residents. Exposés of the terrible conditions in those settings in the 1960s and 1970s led to the downsizing and closing of many of those institutions in a process called deinstitutionalization, in which individuals were moved out of institutions into community settings (Blatt & Kaplan, 1966; Johnson & Traustadottir, 2005; Rothman, 1984). Unfortunately, many of those individuals ended up living in nursing homes or large group homes. Lately, independent living and supported living services in which the individual is provided whatever supports are necessary to live successfully in the residence of their choosinghave been seen as best practices. The idea is that the individual lives in his or her home, not in a "facility" (Taylor, 2006).

With supported living services, individuals are provided with supports up to twenty-four hours a day, seven days a week. These supports could include dressing, feeding, bathing, medical, or whatever supports the person needs to be able to live in his or her residence. For individuals with more mild support needs, the concept of independent living services has been successfully developed to support individuals. Independent living services are more limited than are supported living services in both the amount and type of support that the individual receives, and supports are often focused on specific living skills such as food preparation or budgeting/money management. Table 7.1 provides a description of various residential services that are used to support individuals with disabilities.

Boles, Horner, and Bellamy (1988) make the important point that quality in supported living is evidenced by the current lives of the individuals receiving services, not in the potential future as implied by skill development. In other words, what is most important is how individuals are living their lives now. IQ scores, adaptive behavior scale scores, type or severity of disability do *not* predict community success. In other words, accurate assessment of "potential" is not possible. Given adequate support, people with the most severe disabilities have been successful living in the community. Table 7.2 provides a list of

Table 7.1
CONTINUUM OF RESIDENTIAL SERVICES

Program	Description
Nursing Homes	Congregate care facility designed to provide 24-hour-a-day medical care. Little emphasis is placed on providing training that would lead to independent living.
Intermediate Care	Designed to provide 24-hour care to participants. The size of the facility can vary significantly from small group homes to large institutions. These programs are required by federal law to provide "active treatment" based on an individualized assessment of the participant's habilitative needs.
Group Homes	Designed to provide habilitative programming that will lead to independent living. The size ranges from small community residences to large congregate care facilities.
Foster Care	Provides services to individuals in their own home or in the home of another family. These programs provide basic room and board; however, some specialized foster care programs may also provide habilitative programming.
Board and Supervision Facilities	Provides room and board to the participant. Typically, the program provides no training or supervision.
Semi-Independent Living Programs	Designed to provide the participant with training that will lead to independent living. Participants live in their own residences. Staff are located nearby to provide necessary training and supervision.
Supported Living	Persons with disabilities living where and with whom they want, for as long as they want, with the ongoing support needed to sustain that choice. • Accountability for lifestyle outcomes • Diversity of residential options • Individually determined support • Broad technology of residential support

factors that influence the positive outcomes of residential services. Table 7.3 lists factors to consider in assessing residential situations.

In this chapter we discuss functional skills as they relate to individuals living in their homes such as a house or apartment. We also want to stress that not being able to independently perform a skill (such as getting dressed) or a series of skills (such as preparing food and cleaning up afterward) does not preclude individuals from living in their own residences. Although this chapter is focused on how to teach res-

Table 7.2
FACTORS THAT INFLUENCE THE POSITIVE
OUTCOMES OF RESIDENTIAL SERVICES

1. The physical environment
2. Regular patterns of activities
3. Availability of community opportunities
4. Network of social support
5. Quality of training and support available
6. Focus on lifestyle outcomes
7. Choices are based upon personal preferences
8. Services are controlled by the individual
9. The use of appropriate technological supports

Source: Adapted from Evolution of a new service paradigm, by V. J. Bradley (pp. 11–32), in *Creating Individual Supports for People With Developmental Disabilities: A Mandate for Change at Many Levels,* V. J. Bradley, J. W. Ashbaugh, and B. C. Blaney (Eds.), 1994, Baltimore, MD: Paul Brookes; Supported living for people with profound disabilities and severe problem behaviors, by R. H. Horner, D. W. Close, H. D. Fredericks, R. E. O'Neill, Albin, J. R.. Sprague, C. H. Kennedy, K. B. Flannery, and L. T. Heathfield (pp. 209–240), in People With Disabilities Who Challenge the System, D. H. Lehr and F. Brown (Eds.), 1996, Baltimore, MD: Paul Brookes; and *The Illustrated Guide in Assistive Technology and Devices: Tools and Gadgets for Living Independently,* by S. Robitaille, 2010, New York: Demos Medical Publishing; and Taylor (2006).

Table 7.3
FACTORS TO CONSIDER IN ASSESSING RESIDENTIAL SITUATIONS

1. How satisfied is the person?
2. What activities does the person do?
3. What help is provided in selecting activities?
4. What types of supports are provided in performing activities?
5. How are independence and activity varieties tracked?

idential living skills, a variety of supports may be brought in to support the individual, often through what are known as personal assistance services. These involve hired personnel or roommates to provide supports to an individual who cannot independently perform a skill. For example, if a person cannot get dressed alone because of physical mobility issues, an attendant could come in the mornings to help the individual get dressed. Local centers for independent living can provide many resources for individuals, their families, teachers, and support providers. Support needs must be based on individual needs, not upon the type or severity of the disability. Table 7.4 provides a matrix for analyzing support needs in residential settings.

Table 7.4
RESIDENTIAL SUPPORTS PLANNING MATRIX

Skill Area	Supports From Family, Roommate, Friends, etc.	Paid Supports	Modifications and Adaptations	Technological Supports	Skills to be Taught
Domestic					
Personal Care					
Health and Safety					
Money Management					
Home Maintenance					
Food Management					
Time Management					
Morning and Evening Routine					
Home Leisure					

Key Point Question 2: What Skills Do Individuals Need to Be Independent at Home?

Generally speaking, individuals need to be able to complete daily living routines (also known as activities of daily living) such as bathing, dressing, preparing food, cleaning, doing laundry, and recreating in the home setting. The skills required in a person's home can be broadly categorized as domestic, personal care and hygiene, and health and safety skills. Typical daily routine involves many tasks that must be completed in one's home. Most people have a routine they follow on mornings when they are preparing to go to work or school. However, weekend and nonworkday routines usually differ. For example, getting to work on time typically requires finishing the morning routine and leaving home by the same time each day, but the days that they do not have to work many people like to "sleep in."

Halpern, Close, and Nelson (1986) found that individuals receiving independent living services stated that the four hardest things about living independently were money management, social networking, home maintenance, and food management. Bosch (1994) points out that time management skills (such as prioritizing daily and weekly schedules) are often critical for success in residential settings. Chapter 10 covers self-management strategies, and provides a variety of skills that individuals can use in this area.

Although independence in living skills may be a goal, it may be better analyzed as "interdependent." Very few people live alone and do everything for themselves. In fact, an individual's quality of life may be negatively affected without areas of mutual dependence. Furthermore, many skills in home settings are performed for the benefit of others as well as oneself. For example, taking out the trash, cleaning the bathroom, and other tasks benefit everyone who lives in a residence. The contributions thus become interdependent and if people are not skilled in one area (such as cooking) they can balance living outcomes by contributing in different areas in which they are skilled (such as being good at cleaning) so that through collective effort the household tasks are completed.

Skill needs for residential settings can be conducted using an ecological inventory (*see* Chapter 2) to assess the individual's performance on skills, provide a basis for systematic instruction for unlearned skills, and identify accommodations/adaptations to support independence. Skills in residential settings may not have the same contextual demands as those demanded in the community or work. For example, how well a bed should be made, how often one cleans or vacuums, or even how often one cooks varies from household to household and involves varying standards of acceptability.

Key Point Question 3: Why Are Residential Living Skills Important?

As individuals get older (from child to adult), there is an expectation of greater autonomy or independence in making decisions that most affect their life. Most people desire a home of their own whether it is a house that they purchase or an apartment that they lease. A great deal of satisfaction is associated with having a place to call your home (whether you live individually or with others). This expectation of autonomy has not always been viewed as critical for individuals with disabilities because they often require significant and ongoing support in their daily lives. The fulfillment of greater control over one's daily living activities is just as important for these individuals, and all these necessary skills should be performed by the person if possible, although it is important to remember that control is the key concept. For example, even if individuals cannot dress themselves they can still control who dresses them and what clothes they wear.

In the discussion about Key Point Question 2, the household standards for acceptability for skills, such as bed making, dishwashing, vacuuming, and so on, are personally defined. Some individuals may not believe it necessary to make their bed every day; some do. The importance of making your bed if someone is coming over and may want to see your bedroom is something that may need to be taught to an individual with a disability. There is general agreement as to the necessity of washing dirty dishes; however, there is less agreement whether or not those dishes can sit overnight, or possibly longer, before being washed. The importance of keeping a clean home is an important concept to be taught for health and welfare purposes as well as social acceptance of visitors.

The traditional residential living model has been a continuum from large congregate living (such as a group home with twelve people living there) to small group or individual living arrangements. Deinstitutionalization has resulted in increased quality of life for individuals (McVilly & Rawlinson, 1998), but the more skills people have, the more benefit they experience from community living outcomes (Perry & Felce, 2003). For example, individuals living in supported living arrangements have experienced an increase in preferred and varied community activities (Howe, Horner, & Newton, 1998). Although the value of supported living should not exclude community living for individuals needing intensive supports, it does drive the need to teach people to carry out residential living tasks or to partially participate in the task completion (Ferguson & Baumgart, 1991).

Key Point Question 4: What Are Domestic Skills?

Domestic skills are those that are needed to maintain a home environment. These skills include, but are not limited to, cleaning, laundry, dishwashing, cooking, and home repair and maintenance, including exterior maintenance such as lawn care. For the purposes of this discussion, we will differentiate between these skills and those necessary to maintain personal appearance and well-being. However, there is a great degree of overlap among domestic, personal care, and health and safety skills. For example, cooking increases the possibility of injury due to accidents when using knives, stoves, and other appliances and materials. Thus, teaching domestic skills must also consider safety issues. Good health also involves household cleaning skills as well as personal care skills.

Many people see food preparation as being an important skill to have whether for wellness (e.g., cooking healthy meals), for socializing (having friends over for dinner), or as a recreational activity (reading cookbooks and preparing meals). These skills can be taught and practiced in one's home setting as well as in other settings, such as school or a cooking class at a community college or adult school.

Cellular phones have almost become a universal tool for communication. Traditionally, telephone usage was a skill that was targeted for home environments. As stressed in Chapter 6 on Smartphone uses in community settings, the cell phone has become a valuable device across multiple, if not all, settings. Many American homes no longer have landlines. Unfortunately, limited access of individuals with disabilities and—when they have access—primarily use of noncommunicative functions (e.g., games) have limited the possibilities of these devices (Durkin, Whitehouse, Jaquet, Ziatas, & Walker, 2010). Thus, it is important to consider the use of Smartphones for both communication (such as keeping in touch with family and friends) and supporting individuals in their homes. For example, an individual can receive communication (regarding time management or remembering schedules or routines) through calls, texts, or "tweets" as well as by programming the Smartphone for prompts in these areas. Consequently, instruction for individuals on how to best use smart phone technology can be very important in residential as well as in other settings.

Just as Smartphones have revolutionized how communication occurs, smart houses have revolutionized how we live in our homes (Helal, Mokhtari, & Abdulrazak, 2008; Mann, 2005). Table 7.5 provides an overview of the concepts and technological applications of a smart house. As with all supports, what is important is to analyze what smart house technologies are appropriate for supporting individuals in their homes. In addition, it may be important to teach the individual how to use and respond to the smart house technology; one cannot assume that just because the technology is in place that the individual

Table 7.5
COMPONENTS OF SMART HOUSE FUNCTIONS

1. Basic communications (telephone, e-mail, world wide web)
2. Responds to simple commands (turn on/off lights, lock doors)
3. Automates household functions (lights on/off at certain times, temperature)
4. Tracks location, behavior, and health indicators of individual (sleep patterns, vital signs)
5. Analyzes data, makes decisions, and takes actions (door is unlocked, stove is on, alert care provider, adjusts temperature)
6. Provides information, reminders, and prompts for tasks (medication reminder, hygiene, social contacts)
7. Answers questions (have I taken my medication, what time is it)
8. Make household arrangements (schedule maintenance visits, prepare grocery lists and send to grocer)
9. Provides timely information (medication has not been taken, vital signs of individual) as well as reports (how often and what times has the person left the house) to relevant others

Source: Adapted from Helal, Mokhtari, and Abdulirazak (2008) and Mann (2005).

will use it or respond to it correctly. As with all universal design procedures, they benefit all of us.

Technological advances have also made it easier for individuals to operate home appliances and consumer electronics through the use of electronic control devices (environmental control units [ECUs]) or interface devices. ECUs may be controlled through voice activation systems, remote controls, switches, and/or the use of Smartphone applications (Nichols & Myers, 2006; Robitaille, 2010). The ECUs then control the appliances through the use of infrared or other technology. For example, ECUs can be programmed to control lights, televisions, thermostats, electric beds, and so on, which makes an individual more independent and less dependent on support providers or others. Obviously individuals must be taught how to use both the ECUs and the interface system, and they must be adapted to the needs and living environment of the individual. For example, a person with very limited physical mobility can have a Smartphone programmed for voice activation, which then allows the use of the Smartphone to control appliances in the residential setting.

Key Point Question 5: What Are Personal Care and Hygiene Skills?

The skills necessary to take care of oneself are easily identified as being functional. If you cannot feed yourself, get dressed, use the bathroom, shave, or shower, someone would have to do it for you. These highly individualized and personal skills affect a person's acceptance when interacting with people in the community, at school, or at work. Typical personal care and hygiene skills include, but are not limited to, eating, toileting, showering, toothbrushing, and dressing. Some personal care skills may be gender specific, such as menstrual care, or closely associated with maturity, such as shaving.

The desirability of interdependence discussed in the Key Point Question 2 section has less application to personal care and hygiene skills. Individuals may need assistance from parents, caregivers, or roommates in performing these skills, which can be intrusive and undesirable for all involved, so teaching individuals to perform these skills is very important. As with other residential skills, the frequency and acceptable quality of these skills is a very personal decision. Parents and other caregivers quickly recognize that good hygiene is an important aspect to social acceptance. For example, good dental hygiene (e.g., toothbrushing and using mouthwash) can prevent breath odor that may negatively effect social interactions.

Partial participation may be of utmost importance in the area of personal care and hygiene skills. Some degree of control on the part of the individual can make these daily routines more pleasant for everyone. For example, the adverse feeling of toothbrushing has been lessened for many individuals with hand over hand guidance, allowing for greater predictability and sensory feedback. Another example of the benefit of partial participation could be the ability to pull one's pants down and sit on the toilet before toileting even though assistance may be needed in unbuckling and unzipping pants. The partial independence of completing that toileting task may provide a degree of privacy and dignity.

This greater emphasis on independence and/or partial participation promotes consideration of modifications that may be made in the home environment (such as a roll in shower), the use of low-technology supports (such as the Independent Tools' PocketDresser for opening and closing zippers or buttons), or the use of high-technology supports (such as the use of an automated feeder that only requires head movement to eat independently). Assistive technology devices can compensate for the lack of skills in many areas of daily living. The previous example of hand over hand guidance for toothbrushing can be further supported by an adapted toothbrush with a large handle for grasping and designed to prevent the toothbrush from being inserted too far into the mouth.

Key Point Question 6: What Are Health and Safety Skills?

Health and safety skills require careful analysis as to independence and autonomy. Caregivers and others in the lives of individuals with disabilities continuously balance the need for safety and healthy living with an individual's personal choice. It is easy to identify an individual without a disability who makes choices that are unhealthy (e.g., lack of exercise or overeating), but similar choices may not be supported by parents or guardians or other caregivers for an individual with a disability. It is clear that there is a direct relation between personal care skill of eating and one's health. Eating involves the selection and amount of food one consumes. Thus individuals must not only be taught how to select and prepare food but also how to make healthy choices in their eating habits.

For individuals who must take medication, keeping track of the times, dosage and needs for refills are important skills to learn and independently perform. For example, John is a twenty-nine year old with a seizure disorder as well as cerebral palsy and a mild intellectual disability who lives in his own apartment and is supported through independent living services. He takes an anticonvulsant twice a day, morning and evening. John uses a weekly organizer and reminder to take his medication each day. In addition, he uses a pill organizer that has rows corresponding to daily doses and dispenses one pill at a time so that he cannot accidentally overmedicate himself. The pill organizer also has an alarm that reminds John when to take the medication. His pill organizer is also a MD.2 device that monitors the dispenser and alerts John's independent living counselor by phone if medications are not dispensed (Pigat, Bauchet, & Giroux, 2008). His Smartphone also cues John to call the pharmacy and request refills. John's ability to administer his own medication improves his health and allows him greater independence at home and in the community.

Of course, the issue of safety goes far beyond health concerns. The bathroom has been identified as the room in the home in which the most accidents occur. The discussion of Key Point Question 4 included the need for safety awareness when cooking and completing other tasks in the kitchen. A house fire would require evacuation and could occur at anytime. The possible safety concerns in a home are endless. The safety of individuals with disabilities is critical in decisions of independence versus the need for support and supervision. What someone will do in case of an emergency cannot be fully predicted and addressed through instruction. Individuals without disabilities have made bad decisions, such as entering their home during a fire to retrieve belongings. Teaching safety skills, such as how to use a knife properly and emergency evacuation in case of fire, must be part of any instruction in residential skills. When these skills are not mastered at a socially acceptable level, supports must be in place.

Key Point Question 7: How Is Systematic Instruction Used to Teach Functional Skills in Residential Settings?

Many schools, community colleges, adult schools, and adult programs have simulated settings, such as kitchens and bedrooms. Simulation can be especially useful when teaching safety skills to provide mass trials without putting the individual at unnecessary risk. For example, in learning how to prepare grilled cheese sandwiches it could be natural to use massed trials by preparing sandwiches for peers in a class. As with any learning situation in which generalization is important and the use of similar materials (pots, pans, utensils, food items, etc.) can help facilitate that generalization.

Skills may be taught in the criterion environment or in a similar type environment. For instance, for students in school settings, in addition to school instruction, instruction could also take place in student homes, the teacher's home, or an apartment that the school rents for instructional purposes. Older students might also spend some nights or weekends in a residential setting for instructional purposes (Freagon et al., 1983). As always with any simulated instruction, generalization becomes a concern. For example, if students are successful in learning vacuuming skills in a classroom setting can they then vacuum in an apartment (generalization across settings) with a different vacuum cleaner, a different room setup, and a different level of cleanliness (generalization across behaviors).

The systematic approach of breaking down a task into its component steps (task analysis), selecting a chaining procedure, providing cues/prompts, delivering reinforcement, and fading are effective in teaching skills that must be performed in residential settings effective with individuals with disabilities (Singh, Oswald, Ellis, & Singh, 1995). Because residential living tasks often consist of complex chains of behaviors, the sequence for teaching the steps of the chains (forward chaining, concurrent chaining, or backward chaining) must be carefully selected. Wehman, Renzaglia, and Bates (1985) recommend that if the learner has already acquired some of the steps of the task or if the task consists of steps that are repeated, then the use of a concurrent chain may be most efficient. For tasks that are new to the learner, the use of backward chaining may be most appropriate. For tasks that are very long or involve many different subtasks (such as cleaning an apartment, for which the individual has to dust, vacuum, clean sinks, mop the kitchen floor, etc.) it may be beneficial to teach the subtasks separately and once they are mastered to then combine them in instructional situations.

In residential settings it is important to collaborate with family members and caregivers. Parents of children with moderate/severe/ profound disabilities generally recognize the importance of functional life skills (Hamre-Nietupski, Nietupski, & Strather, 1992). Enlisting their support in teaching these skills will greatly help the child learn the tasks through repeated practice over time and before he or she leaves home as an adult.

Teaching with technology can be very useful for teaching residential skills. The use of videos for which a competent model is viewed completing the task has been found to be an effective instructional intervention, especially for individuals with autism spectrum disorders (Van Laarhoven, Zurita, Johnson, Grider, & Grider, 2009). Hybrid instruction involving in person and video prompting can increase both skill acquisition and generalization (Sigafoos et al., 2005). Video modeling can also be used for error correction, in which the individual has to analyze mistakes that were made in the video (Goodson, Sigafoos, O'Reilly, Cannella, & Lancioni, 2007). Video modeling allows individuals to use their visual strengths when learning new skills by allowing them to focus on a particular behavior being taught, much like the camera itself. Video modeling allows the individual to watch the video repeatedly in order to maximize the likelihood for skill acquisition and success. For example, Cathy is a high-school senior with autism spectrum disorders. She is planning on moving into an independent living residence after high school and attending the local community college. She has been learning how to perform residential living skills at her home with her parents as well as at school, although her enthusiasm for these tasks is limited. Cathy enjoys watching videos as a recreational activity, so her teacher and parents decided to try video modeling as an instructional strategy. Her teacher taped both Cathy and her family members performing household chores. In addition, Cathy is planning to move into an apartment that her friend Joyce (who is a year older and attending the community college) lives in. The teacher also video-taped Joyce doing household tasks in her apartment. Cathy enjoys watching the videos with her teacher, Joyce, and her parents and discussing them. This has led to an increase in her wanting to learn how to perform these tasks as well as her ability to generalize the skills to the apartment that she and Joyce will share (the criterion environment).

BEST PRACTICE RECOMMENDATIONS

1. Continually assess the living preferences of the individual because they may change over time.
2. Skill independence may not be as important as appropriate supports in residential settings.
3. Do not allow lack of independence to keep someone from living in his or her preferred situation.

FUTURE RESEARCH ISSUES

1. How can technological advances be used to assist people in residential settings?
2. How do you best train staff to support individuals?
3. How can staff turnover be reduced in residential settings?

DISCUSSION QUESTIONS

1. How do preferences for living environments change over time?
2. Can all people, no matter how severe their disability, be successful in community living settings with appropriate supports?
3. How do residential support needs vary from person to person? Are support needs driven by the type of disability that the individual has or the skills that they have or need?

4. How do long-term safety and security issues influence residential choices and supports?
5. How can individuals and their support providers best stay current with advances in technology for residential settings?

SCHOOL AND COMMUNITY-BASED ACTIVITY SUGGESTIONS

1. Write down your morning routine. Identify the crucial activities and those that could be omitted. Ask a friend to write out his or her routine and compare with your own.
2. Analyze your morning routine to determine if there are different ways you could achieve the functional outcome.
3. Make a list of activities that you perform in your home. For each activity, list multiple ways in which you use or could use technology to assist in performing the task.

REFERENCES

Blatt, B., & Kaplan, F. (1966). *Christmas in purgatory: A photographic essay on mental retardation.* Boston, MA: Allyn & Bacon.

Boles, S., Horner, R. H., & Bellamy, G. T. (1988). Implementing transition programs for supported living. In B. L. Ludlow, A. P. Turnbull, & R. Luckasson (Eds.), *Transitions to adult life for people with mental retardation—Principles and practices* (pp. 101–117). Baltimore, MD: Paul Brookes.

Bosch, H. K. (1994). Independent living services and programs: Integration into the community. In C. A. Michaels (Ed.), *Transition strategies for persons with learning disabilities* (pp. 213–237). San Diego, CA: Singular.

Durkin, K., Whitehouse, A., Jaquet, E., Ziatas, K., & Walker, A. J. (2010). Cell phone use by adolescents with Asperger Syndrome. *Research in Autism Spectrum Disorders, 4,* 314–318.

Ferguson, D. L., & Baumgart, D. (1991). Partial participation revisited. *Journal of the Association for Persons with Severe Handicaps, 16,* 218–227.

Freagon, S., Wheeler, J., Hill, L., Brankin, G., Costello, D., & Peters, W. (1983). A domestic training environment for students who are severely handicapped. *Journal of the Association for Persons with Severe Handicaps, 8,* 49–61.

Goodson, J., Sigafoos, J., O'Reilly, M., Cannella, H., & Lancioni, G. E. (2007). Evaluation of a video-based error correction procedure for teaching a domestic skill to individuals with developmental disabilities. *Research in Developmental Disabilities, 28,* 458–467.

Halpern, A. S., Close, D. W., & Nelson, D. J. (1986). *On my own: The impact of semi-*

independent living programs for adults with mental retardation. Baltimore, MD: Paul Brookes.

Hamre-Nietupski, S., Nietupski, J., & Strather, M. (1992). Functional life skills, academic skills, and friendship/social relationship development: What do parents of students with moderate/severe/profound disabilities value? *Journal of the Association for Persons with Severe Handicaps, 17,* 53–58.

Helal, A., Mokhtari, M., & Abdulrazak, B. (2008). *The engineering handbook of smart technology for aging, disability, and independence.* Hoboken, NJ: Wiley.

Howe, J., Horner, R., & Newton, S. (1998). Comparison of supported living and traditional residential services in the state of Oregon. *Mental Retardation, 36,* 1–11.

Johnson, K., & Traustadottir, R. (2005). *Deinstitutionalization and people with intellectual disabilities: In and out of institutions.* Philadelphia, PA: Jessica Kingsley.

Mann, W. C. (2005). *Smart technology for aging, disability, and independence: The state of the science.* Hoboken, NJ: Wiley-Interscience.

McVilly, K. R., & Rawlinson, R. B. (1998). Quality of life issues in development and evaluation of services for people with intellectual disabilities. *Journal of Intellectual and Developmental Disability, 23,* 199–219.

Nichols, J., & Myers, B. A. (2006). Controlling home and office appliances with smart phones. *IEEE Pervasive Computing, 5,* 60–67.

Perry, P., & Felce, D. (2003). Quality of life outcomes for people with intellectual disabilities living in staffed community housing services: A stratified random sample of statutory, voluntary and private agency provision. *Journal of Applied Research in Intellectual Disabilities, 16,* 11–28.

Pigat, H., Bauchet, J., & Giroux, S. (2008). Assistive devices for people with cognitive impairments. In A. Helal, M. Mokhtari, & B. Abdulrazak. (Eds.), *The engineering handbook of smart technology for aging, disability, and independence* (pp. 217–236). Hoboken, NJ: Wiley.

Robitaille, S. (2010). *The illustrated guide to assistive technology and devices: Tools and gadgets for living independently.* New York: Demos Medical Pub.

Rothman, D. J. (1984). *The willowbrook wars.* New York: Harper and Row.

Sigafoos, J., O'Reilly, M., Cannella, H., Upadhyaya, M., Edrishinha, C., Lancioni, G. E., Hundley, A., Andrews, A., Garver, C., & Young, D. (2005). Computer-presented video prompting for teaching microwave oven use to three adults with Developmental Disabilities. *Journal of Behavioral Education, 14,* 189–201.

Singh, N. N., Oswald, D. P., Ellis, C. R., & Singh, S. D. (1995). Community-based instruction for independent meal preparation by adults with profound mental retardation. *Journal of Behavioral Education, 5,* 77–92.

Taylor, S. J. (2006). Supporting adults to live in the community: Beyond the continuum. In S. M. Pueschel (Ed.), *Adults with Down syndrome* (pp. 173–182). Baltimore, MD: Paul Brookes.

Van Laarhoven, T., Zurita, L. M., Johnson, J. W., Grider, K. M., & Grider, K. L. (2009). Comparison of self, other, and subjective video models for teaching daily living skills to individuals with developmental disabilities. *Education and Training in Developmental Disabilities, 44,* 509–522.

Wehman, P., Renzaglia, A., & Bates, P. (1985). *Functional living skills for moderately and severely handicapped individuals.* Austin, TX: Pro-Ed.

Chapter 8

TEACHING SOCIAL SKILLS

Keypoint Questions

1. What are social skills?
2. What is the difference between social skill and social competence?
3. Why are social skills and social competence important?
4. How do you best assess social skills?
5. How do you teach social skills?
6. What are some difficulties with social skills instruction?

Window to the World Case Study One

Theodore is a fifth-grade student with a mild intellectual disability who has difficulty conversing about age-appropriate topics with peers during recess, lunch times, and so on. He often brings up topics that others are not interested in (e.g., TV shows about Thomas the Tank Engine, etc.) and gets teased by his peers. He does not seem to mind the teasing as long as he is getting peer attention.

His inclusion teacher takes several steps to improve his social interactions with his nondisabled peers. First, she does an informal survey of what topics they most like to talk about. At the beginning of recess and lunch she has five-minute teaching sessions with Theodore in an unused classroom. She first sets the stage for the instruction by describing why it is important to discuss age-appropriate topics that others are interested in. Because of the interest survey, she knows the top three areas of discussion among his peers during lunch and recess (baseball, music, and YouTube videos), which allows her to specify the skills components (e.g., the topics). Next she models the skill for Theodore

141

(When sitting down at lunch I say to the group, "Hey, did anyone catch the White Sox game last night?"). She then has Theodore engage in cognitive rehearsal during which he imitates the modeled skill and verbally describes what to do ("When I sit down at lunch I ask the group about the baseball game on TV last night"). Next, she does behavioral rehearsal, and Theodore does the behavior. She acts as the group of peers and gives him feedback on how he did. She then sends him out to the criterion setting (the lunchroom) where Theodore is successful in using his newly learned social skills.

Window to the World Case Study Two

Sally was a twenty-two-year-old woman with a learning disability who was working in the admissions office in a hospital. She was very shy but really wanted to be liked by her coworkers in the office. Unfortunately, Sally had trouble reading social cues and would often interrupt her coworkers in the middle of an interaction and, not knowing what to say, would often blurt out inappropriate questions and then would get embarrassed and leave the area.

Fortunately, Sally was a member of a job club for individuals with learning disabilities run by the DSPS at the local community college. The group leader often worked on social skills instruction and decided on instruction for asking question for Sally.

This intervention involved role playing a series of question-asking conversational exchanges appropriate to conversational context (Chadsey-Rusch, Karlan, Riva, & Rusch, 1984; Haring, Roger, Lee, Breen, & Gaylord-Ross, 1986). Question-asking was taught by (1) giving a rationale for asking questions, (2) modeling examples of different questions using socially validated topics, (3) practicing asking questions by role-playing and corrective feedback, (4) prompting question asking during training conversations, and (5) reinforcement of appropriate behavior. Sally was instructed to ask initiating or expansion questions of coworkers or to make a response statement and to make a terminating statement at the end of the interaction. Initially, initiation behaviors and topics of conversation were modeled. Expansion training (Haring et al., 1986) was also used. This training involved producing a response that expanded on the statement or interaction that just occurred. Sally was asked to covertly take data on what topics coworkers talked about during breaks. Using socially validated topics during role-playing sessions, Sally was prompted to ask questions that would initiate a new topic or expand the current topic. After several role-playing sessions with other members of the job club Sally was able to successfully generalize the skills learned to the work site.

Key Point Question 1: What Are Social Skills?

Various definitions of social skills have been offered in the literature. Basically, what they refer to is that the individual engages in specific positive skills or behaviors when interacting with one or more people, and those people find those interactions reinforcing. For example, Combs and Slaby (1977, p. 163) define social skill as "the ability to interact with others in a given social context in specific ways that are socially acceptable or valued and at the same time personally beneficial, mutually beneficial, or beneficial primarily to others." In other words, social skills involve the person interacting appropriately with others from the perspective of the other people. Obviously, social skill can be complex, and there are several dimensions of social skills to consider for instructional purposes.

Gresham, Sugai, and Horner have identified five dimensions of social skills: (1) peer relational skills (getting along with others), (2) self-management skills (controlling one's own behavior), (3) academic skills (social behaviors related to academics such as listening to the teacher), (4) compliance skills (following directions), and (5) assertion skills (using skills learned with others) (2001, pp. 333–334).

There are several important parameters or dimensions of analysis that appear across definitions that are important for understanding social skills instruction.

INTERPERSONAL BEHAVIOR EMITTED BY THE INTERACTOR. These are specific social behaviors that the person engages in, such as looking at others, shaking their hand, standing an appropriate distance from the other person, and so on. These are important skills for the individual to have, but it is also important for the person to know when to use the skills and when not to. For instance, in some situations it may be appropriate to shake another person's hand (e.g., when greeting the person interviewing you for a job) and in other situations it may not be (e.g., when greeting a person of a different gender, culture, and/or religion). Discriminating between the appropriate discriminative stimulus and other situations is critical to other aspects of social skills. For example, you may greet a person the first time you pass them in the hall, just nod or smile the second time, and try to avoid eye contact the third time!

THE SITUATIONAL AND INTERPERSONAL ANTECEDENTS OF THESE INTERPERSONAL BEHAVIORS. There are situational and antecedents between the person and one or more others who are engaging in the social interaction that have an important influence on what interpersonal behaviors are appropriate in that specific situation. For instance, if a student is waiting in line for going on the slide on the playground there are situational antecedents, such as other students before and/or after the person, that need to be taken into account in a social interaction, such as a peer asking to can cut in the line ahead of the student (probably not to be looked on favorably by others behind the student). Then there are interpersonal antecedents to consider. For instance, what if the peer wanting to cut in line had asked the student in line before our student and had been turned down for a cut? How should that then influence the social behavior of our student? The student should probably turn down the cut in line as well in order to follow the informal rules of playground behavior and to avoid antagonizing peers in line.

CHARACTERISTICS OF THE INTERACTORS. There are a variety of characteristics of the individuals involved in the interaction that influence the appropriateness of different social skills, such as their ages (same or different such as two first graders or a first grader interacting with a teacher), gender, ethnicity, and so on. For instance, a high-school student greeting peers in the quad may use specific phrases (e.g., "hey bro") and handshakes (e.g., the bump) that are appropriate with peers but would not be appropriate in other instances, such as when being called into the vice principal's office to be quizzed about a violation of school rules.

QUALITATIVE OUTCOME OF BEHAVIOR WITHIN THE GIVEN SITUATION. Qualitative outcome by definition implies that a value judgment is made regarding the social interaction; that is, that an individual (such as employer, friend, etc.) or group of individuals (such as peers, teachers, etc.) defines a response to be good, skillful, or acceptable according to some criterion. For example, in an interview the panel may rate the quality of the social responses of the person being interviewed on a one to ten scale.

IMPORTANCE OF RECIPROCITY. There is an expected "norm of reciprocity" in social interactions whereby prosocial responses induce a cyclic pattern of positive responding among the interactors. For instance, if an individual is talking with a friend, then each will expect the other to continue to engage in prosocial behaviors (such as staying on topic, responding to comments, etc.) as the interaction continues.

All of these dimensions are important to consider due to the complexity of social interactions. If one of these components is not taken into consideration when teaching social skills, then it may negate the positive effect of the skills being used.

Key Point Question 2: What Is the Difference Between Social Skill and Social Competence?

Social competence is how good the person is at interacting with others, and social skill refers to specific skills needed in specific social situations. Gresham and coworkers define social competence as "the degree to which students are able to establish and maintain satisfactory interpersonal relationships, gain peer acceptance, establish and maintain friendships, and terminate negative or pernicious interpersonal relationships" (2001, p. 331). For instance, one may have social skills that are useful in one situation, such as when hanging out with friends, but inappropriate in other situations, such as a job interview. Thus, one may have social skills that lead to competence in one situation but not in another. Part of social competence is being able to decide on which social skills are appropriate to the social situation at hand.

It is important to highlight the difference between a skill deficit and a performance deficit. If a student has a skill deficit (the student does not know how to act productively in a specific social situation), then it is necessary to teach the specific social skills to that student to give the student the necessary skills. For example, many high-school students have never had a job interview and thus may not know how to greet an interviewer appropriately (a skill deficit). Thus, it would be important for a teacher to teach specific social skills for this instance. The teacher, Ms. Seibert, might teach her student June appropriate greeting skills by describing expected social behavior, showing video clips of appropriate and inappropriate greeting skills with an interviewer, having June and other students verbally rate the performances in the videos, role-playing with June and other students, and giving feedback and reinforcement to June.

If the student has a performance deficit (has the social skills but does not use them), then he or she needs positive reinforcement or other supports (such as self-management strategies) for using those skills in appropriate situations.

Key Point Question 3: Why Are Social Skills and Social Competence Important?

We often underestimate just how much social behavior can affect individuals' success in school, the community, and work. In integrated settings, individuals with disabilities must interact appropriately with others, including authority figures such as teachers or bosses, in addition to performing specific tasks. Attending a movie, purchasing grocery items, eating at a restaurant are community activities that all involve the need for appropriate social interactions. For example, at a restaurant, one must greet the hostess, request a table, greet and give an order to the waitress, and pay the cashier. Deficits in any of these interactions can negatively impact the quality of service or even being able to receive any service at all.

In community and work settings, the social skills of the person may be the critical component in how competent others believe them to be and how well they achieve quality of life outcomes. For example, in employment settings, the worker may be exemplary in performing the work tasks but have difficulties on the job because of problems in interacting with others (the supervisor, coworkers, customers). Many research studies have found that lack of appropriate social skills is one of the main reasons for job termination for people with disabilities (Martin, Rusch, Lagomarcino, & Chadsey-Rusch, 1986).

You may have had a coworker who had very good social skills but perhaps not the best ability in performing job tasks who was nonetheless considered a valuable worker by others whereas a different coworker who was very competent in performing job tasks but lacked good social skills was seen as not being a valuable worker. This reflects Gold's competence/deviance hypothesis discussed in Chapter 1; the person's social competence may outweigh his or her job task deviance (or vice versa).

There is a clear body of research documenting that the mere placement of persons with disabilities in proximity to persons without disabilities does not necessarily lead to social integration (Storey &

Horner, 1991). The more socially skilled the person with a disability is, the more likely it is that he or she will develop friendships and social networks with peers. We often mistakenly assume that just because the individual is physically integrated social integration will occur and that it should occur "naturally," without formal interventions such as social skills instruction (Amado, 2004).

A person's ability to get along with others and to engage in prosocial behaviors determines popularity among peers and with teachers, parents, and other significant adults. Thus, an individual who does not engage in prosocial behaviors (lack of appropriate social skills) or engages in negative social behaviors (the use of inappropriate social skills) is less likely to be popular and have friends and will be less valued by adults (such as teachers or employers).

Social skills deficits have been a defining characteristic of intellectual disabilities and autism spectrum disorders and have long been viewed as problematic for individuals with other types of disabilities. For instance, individuals with learning disabilities often have difficulty with social skills (see Table 8.1 for a listing).

Table 8.1
DIFFICULTIES THAT INDIVIDUALS WITH LEARNING
DISABILITIES OFTEN HAVE SOCIALLY

1. Choosing socially unacceptable behavior for use in social situations
2. Less able than peers without disabilities to solve social problems and predict consequences for their social behavior
3. Often misinterpret social cues associated with nonverbal communication
4. Have difficulty demonstrating empathy
5. Often have difficulty assessing their own social position in relation to others
6. Are often poorly accepted and are often rejected or neglected by classmates
7. Social skills problems persist as students grow older. This contradicts the common myth that students will "outgrow" social skills problems.
8. As adolescents, rarely participate in organized activities either in or out of school
9. Perform significantly less effectively than nondisabled peers do in a variety of specific social skill areas such as giving and accepting negative feedback, giving positive feedback, conversational skills, negotiation, and resisting peer pressure
10. Are invited out by peers less frequently than others who are low achievers but have no learning disability

continued

Table 8.1—*Continued*

11. As adolescents, interact just as frequently as others but the nature and/or quality of the social interactions tend to be more negative

12. Social problems, such as talking or acting out, shyness, frustration, lack of difficulty controlling emotions, continue into adulthood

13. For adults, the majority of whom are single, social relationships and skills are the major area of concern

14. In one study of 500 adults with learning disabilities, the most frequently mentioned need for assistance was social skills training (Cheslar, 1982).

15. Poor social skills, associated with higher incidence of dropping out of school, juvenile delinquency, mental health problems, and unsatisfactory employment adjustment

Source: Adapted from Helping young adults understand their learning disabilities, by A. J. Roffman, J. E. Herzog, and P. M. Wershba-Gershon, *Journal of Learning Disabilities, 27,* 413–419, 1994.

Key Point Question 4: How Do You Best Assess Social Skills?

There are a variety of ways to assess the social skills of individuals. What follows is a description of different strategies that may be effective for different individuals in different situations. There is no one method that is best for all individuals in all situations, and it is possible to use a combination of these methods.

SELF-MONITORING. Individuals record their own social behavior (see description of self-monitoring procedures in Chapter 10). This is often an overlooked method, but it helps to tie assessment with self-monitoring for teaching purposes. For example, if the individual can self-monitor his or her social behavior, such as the number of times that he or she greets others, then the teaching of skills can be specific to the behavior being self-monitored. Thus, the teacher could directly teach greeting behaviors and then reinforce the occurrence of those behaviors in the natural setting.

DIRECT OBSERVATION. A specific behavior is assessed to see if it actually occurs in a given setting. Direct observations may include methods such as frequency counts (the number of times that someone does a behavior), duration recording (the length of time for each occurrence of the target behavior within a predefined observation period (such as ten minutes, one hour, etc.), and interval recording (brief observations at specific times).

Direct observation procedures can be time consuming but if done correctly can provide accurate data and be especially useful in assessing changes in behavior. Direct observation has often been favored because (1) it uses clearly defined codes, (2) is less biased, (3) is more objective, and (4) is more sensitive to treatment effects. There are also three major limitations concerning direct observation that need to be considered as well: (1) it usually only addresses a small number of specific behaviors, (2) it requires a lot of training to execute properly, and (3) as mentioned previously, it can be a time-intensive approach to assessment.

NORMATIVE BEHAVIOR. It is important to consider what is "typical" behavior of peers. For example, how do peers greet one another, say goodbye, stand, and so on? There is not one level of appropriate behavior but a band or range of appropriate behavior. What is normative behavior for one group of peers (friends hanging out socially) may be quite different from what is normative behavior for another group (coworkers during work times).

FORMAL TESTING. There are a number of formal tests available, and these usually depend upon either a verbal or a written response. Formal tests can be useful in getting a measure of overall social development or for comparing social development in two or more persons. The major problem with tests of this type is that they do not usually assess individual skills in specific situations. In short, they are not specific enough for planning instruction.

SELF-REPORT. With self-report, the person is interviewed about his or her behavior and the problems being experienced. This can be a useful assessment procedure but depends on (1) the skill of the interviewer, (2) the appropriateness of the questions, and (3) the accuracy of the responses given.

SELF-RATING. Here the person is often asked to use a numeric rating to estimate how often he or she exhibits the behavior, or an alternative is to supply descriptions of various social situations. The person then selects from a set of choices provided under each item. Self-rating can only be used with persons who have sufficient reading skill to complete the scale independently. Unfortunately self-rating scales often correlate poorly with peer and teacher ratings. In other words, self-ratings are often biased by social desirability and to yield the lowest estimate of deviance. This may be an important strategy for instruction; increased awareness of social skills deficits.

INFORMANT REPORTS/RATINGS BY SIGNIFICANT OTHERS. The viewpoint of important others, such as peers, family members, teachers, and employers, can also be an important way to rate the social skills of the individuals. The assessment strategies described in this chapter can often be easily used by one or more significant others. Informant reports are often interviews with someone who is knowledgeable about the person, such as a teacher, friend, supervisor at work, and so on. This can be an informal interview (e.g., "How is Alma doing in getting along with her peers these days?") or more structured with specific situations to be covered (e.g., "How is Alma doing in greeting her peers in the lunch line at school? How about when going out to recess? How about greeting her different teachers?"). An advantage is that a large number of specific behaviors of interest can be assessed in a short time.

Key Point Question 5: How Do You Teach Social Skills?

Social skills can be taught similarly to any other behavior using the systematic instructional procedures outlined in Chapter 3. There are some teaching procedures that have often been used specifically for teaching social skills, and these are discussed here. These procedures are not presented in a specific order, and instructors may choose one or a combination of these procedures that would be most effective for a specific learner in a specific social situation. Research has shown that the components discussed in the following were most effective when used in conjunction with other components, rather than using one component in isolation. It is also important to consider individual versus group applications of intervention components and contingencies.

Modeling or Demonstration

Modeling involves having an individual (teacher, peer, etc.) engage in the social skills for the learner in a specific instructional context. There are two generic types of modeling for social skills:

MASTERY MODEL. This is someone who has mastered the skill to be taught and provides a flawless demonstration of it (without any mistakes or errors).

COPING MODEL. With the coping method you do not want the model to provide an error-free demonstration. This is because you want to show the learner the difference between positive and negative examples because showing the learner the differences helps to rule out possible misinterpretation on their part (Engleman & Carnine, 1982). Students may have trouble imitating the mastery model because they may not know about certain common mistakes that they make. The purpose of the coping model is to incorporate additional instruction into the initial modeling performance so that students can see the difference between correct and incorrect performances.

Advantages to the coping model include that (1) it alerts the learner to difficult components and focuses attention on those components, (2) reduces errors by providing instruction on how to deal with the difficult components, and (3) saves time, in the long run, because it reduces the amount of time reteaching a skill that the student learns incorrectly. You want to use the coping model for teaching skills that you have good reason to believe will give the learner problems (such as known previous instances when the learner has not used appropriate social skills or upcoming situations such as a job interview when you can predict that the person will have difficulty).

With the coping method you want to

1. Stop after mistakes are made and correct the error.
2. Point out what the error was and why it was made.
3. Provide instruction on how to avoid the error
4. Demonstrate the strategy used to avoid the mistake.

Table 8.2 provides examples of mastery and coping models.

Table 8.2
EXAMPLES OF MASTERY AND COPING MODEL

MASTERY MODEL
1. Model dials phone number and waits for an answer.
2. Call is answered with "Hello."
3. Model says, "Hello, this is Harry, May I speak to Bob?"

COPING MODEL
1. Model dials phone number and waits for an answer.
2. Call is answered with "Hello."
3. Model says, "May I speak to Bob?"
4. Model says, "No! That isn't correct. I goofed. I have to remember the person on the line can't see me, so they don't know who is speaking. Many people find it irritating to talk with an unidentified person on the phone. They may also have doubts about what information they should give out to an unidentified caller. I should have identified myself first, before asking to speak to Bob."
5. Model says, "Hello, this is Harry. May I speak to Bob?"

VIDEOTAPE MODELING. There is an increasing body of research indicating that many individuals with disabilities, especially those with autism spectrum disorders, can learn social and community skills by observing models on videotapes. Video modeling allows individuals to use their visual strengths when learning new skills by allowing them to focus on a particular behavior being taught much like the camera itself.

Two types of video modeling are video self-modeling (VSM) and video peer modeling (VPM). VPM is when any peer or adult is used as the model in the tape; VSM incorporates the individual himself or herself as the model. Specific target behaviors are presented to the individual as a form of observational learning so that the individual will imitate and generalize the particular skill or behavior. In VSM the person watches his or her own performance on the videotape. One advantage of VSM rather than using others as models is the immediate feedback and reinforcement when individuals see themselves completing tasks (Mechling, Pridgen, & Cronin, 2005). Table 8.3 provides an overview of ten steps necessary for effective video modeling as discussed by Banda, Matuszny, and Turkan (2007).

There are many theories about why video modeling is effective. One explanation for positive results is that by eliminating the necessity for eye contact with the instructor and prompts from the instructor, individuals are better able to focus and emulate the new skill when watching the video. Furthermore, video modeling allows the individual to watch the video repeatedly in order to maximize the likelihood for skill acquisition and success.

Video technology has been shown to be an effective medium by creating an environment that closely models a individual's natural environment, allowing for feedback and repetition. Most agree that video may be automatically reinforcing for some individuals, thereby increasing their motivation to learn the task being presented. In addition, by using video, the camera is able to zoom in on relevant discriminative stimuli, which may help individuals with autism focus on the task being taught rather than on irrelevant stimuli.

There appear to be many benefits for individuals and parents as well as educators when using video modeling. The convenience of being able to video, and then edit in order to target specific skills makes video modeling a practical intervention. In addition, videotapes are seen as advantageous because individuals can view antecedents as

Table 8.3
TEN STEPS NECESSARY FOR EFFECTIVE VIDEO MODELING AS DISCUSSED
IN BANDA, MATUSZNY, AND TURKAN (2007)

1. Identify and select target behaviors. (Target behaviors need to be observable and measurable).

2. Assessment should be made to find out if the individual is even interested in watching videos. Not all individuals with a disability have interest in watching videos.

3. Select and train models. It is important to choose models that will consistently and correctly act out the target behavior.

4. Prepare equipment and setting. Keep in mind that the ability for the individual to use the videos at home as well as at school or employment site could be important.

5. Record target behaviors. Make more than one video depicting the same behavior or activity in order to pick up the one that most closely resembles the behavior expected.

6. Edit the video. Editing may be the most important step in using video modeling. The tape should look as close as possible to the real-life behavior being demonstrated. It is possible to use a task analysis to break down the demonstration into small steps. Timing and the length of the video as well as the speed in which the target behavior is exhibited are also crucial.

7. Collect baseline data. Establishing the current skill performance status of the individual is important in order to show the effectiveness or ineffectiveness of the intervention or needed change in the intervention.

8. Show video. Show the video while being careful to minimize distractions such as noises or other individuals in the room that could affect the individual's ability to focus solely on the video and the behavior presented.

9. Collect data. After viewing the video, the individual should attempt to perform the behavior. Based on the performance, reinforce if the individual performed the behavior correctly or reinforce approximations if appropriate. If necessary, the tape can be reshown as many times as needed. In addition, if particular steps are not being performed correctly, showing only those steps may help the individual to learn the steps being performed incorrectly.

10. Generalization and maintenance. It is important to have the individual practice generalization by having him or her perform target behavior across various individuals, behaviors, settings, and/or times. Maintenance involves the individual's continuing to be able to display the desired behaviors after the intervention is successful and has been terminated. It may be beneficial to have the individual periodically review videos even though she or he is using the behaviors that she or he has learned.

well as consequences both before and after performing a behavior (Bernard-Ripoll, 2007). Another benefit is cost, ecause the tapes can be used repeatedly and shared with parents and other educators throughout multiple learning environments.

For example, Haring, Kennedy, Adams, and Pitts-Conway (1987) used videotapes of competent models purchasing items in community stores. The high-school students with autism were able to successfully generalize the skills for purchasing items in stores in the community (the social skills involved behaviors such as waiting in line and paying for items).

IMPORTANT MODEL CHARACTERISTICS. There are important characteristics to take into consideration when selecting role models. These include the following:

1. Age of the model. Similarity in age is particularly important when teaching children and youth. Generally speaking, the younger the learner the more important it is that the model be of a similar age.
2. Gender of the model. Same gender models are more effective than opposite models are.
3. Like ability of the model. Models who are personable are more effective.
4. Similarity of the model. Models the observer can identify with are more effective.
5. Status of the model. Competent models with social status are more effective.
6. Observed consequences to a model affect learning in observers. In other words, does the model get reinforced for the appropriate social behavior?
7. Competency of the role model. The more competent the better.

ROLE-PLAY PRACTICE AND REHEARSAL. The learner or a group of learners practice using the social skills in a role-playing situation (socially competent peers can also be a part of this group). Research has found role-playing and rehearsal to be a very effective intervention for teaching social skills and probably the key component to include in an intervention. For instance, the Skillstreaming curriculum (McGinnis & Goldstein, 1997) has nine teaching steps (*see* Table 8.4).

Advantages for role playing include (1) flexibility in presenting a wide range of potentially relevant situations that cannot be easily replicated in the natural environment; (2) control over the places, persons, and environments with which the person is presented; and (3) greater accuracy in monitoring and measuring precise social skill components.

There are also potential disadvantages for role-playing. Role-play situations are often highly structured, and there may be little correspondence between a role-play test and the naturalistic interaction.

Table 8.4
NINE TEACHING STEPS OF THE SKILLSSTREAMING CURRICULUM

1. Define the skill
2. Model the skill
3. Establish student skill need
4. Select role-player
5. Set up the role-play
6. Conduct the role-play
7. Provide performance feedback
8. Assign skill homework
9. Select next role-player

This lack of correspondence may produce poor generalization for the social skills learned. Thus, it may be helpful to conduct the role-playing sessions as close to the actual situation as possible (a break room next to the work area where the social skills are to be used), as close to the actual time as possible (right before going into the work area), and perhaps with a coworker from the work area.

FEEDBACK AND CONTINGENT REINFORCEMENT. Often overlooked in social skills instruction is the importance of feedback to the learner (what was correct as well as what was incorrect). Reinforcement of the learner (and others in the group) for appropriate social skills is critical so that the learner is more likely to use the social skills learned in the future. All of the strategies discussed earlier are more effective when feedback is provided after the individual performance. Of course, it is critical to reinforce the appropriate use of desired social skills.

The timing of instructor intervention—that is, whether it is contingent on appropriate or on inappropriate behaviors—is a critical and often overlooked determinant of the consequences of any intervention.

Reinforcement from peers for appropriate and/or inappropriate behavior can be critical in the use of the social skills that have been learned. Peers may provide naturally occurring reinforcement in the social context (such as laughing at a joke or continuing to hang out socially with the person), or they may be used as confederates to provide specific reinforcement when the learner displays desired social behavior (such as initiating an appropriate greeting with the peer).

INSTRUCTION OF SOCIAL SKILLS

1. Setting the State
   A. Introduce the skill to be taught through discussion, stories, or film. Purpose is to
      a. Communicate to learners what the nature of the skill is
      b. Explain why it is the preferred way of behaving
      c. Show how it can be useful to the person (person is more motivated to learn when the personal relevance of the skills is clear)
2. Specifying the Skills Components: Works like an advance organizer or task analysis for observing the demonstration and attending to the components included (*see* Table 8.5 for example).
3. Modeling the Skill
   A. Model should have been through the modeling strategy with you previously so that everything is clear.
   B. Need to have a role-playing situation to provide the context for the demonstration.
   C. Should have more than one role-playing situation ready so that the demonstration can be repeated if necessary.
4. Cognitive Rehearsal
   A. Before the learner imitates the modeled skill, have that person verbally describe the specific components in the skill.
   B. If the learner makes errors in the verbal description, go back over the components with the learner, referring to the demonstration for illustrative purposes.

Table 8.5
SPECIFICATION OF SKILL COMPONENTS

Example: for assertiveness skill of saying no.

1. Look directly at the person and make eye contact.
2. In a calm, normal voice say, "No! I don't want to do that."
3. Suggest an appropriate alternative.
4. If the alternative is declined and the original suggestion is repeated, in a calm, normal voice, say "No! I don't want to do that."
5. If the No statement is still not accepted, in a calm, normal voice, say "I'm sorry, I've got to go now. I'll see you later."
6. Walk away.

C. Have the learner describe the skill components until they can be given in their entirety without any errors or prompting.

5. Behavioral Rehearsal

A. The learner is given a role-playing situation in which to practice the skill.

B. Learner should get practice with different situations before the behavioral rehearsal phase is over.

C. Give the learner feedback on his or her performance. If you give criticism, sandwich it between positive feedback.

D. If the learner has made errors, give additional practice opportunities, so your feedback can be used to correct mistakes. If the mistakes were serious enough, repeat the modeling phase before giving additional practice.

E. Videotapes can be extremely useful for providing feedback because the people can directly observe their own performance, and if they performed incorrectly then the situation can be replayed as often as necessary until they understand what social skill they need to use in that situation.

6. Evaluation of Performance: May use checklist or rating scale (*see* McGinnis & Goldstein [1997] for specific examples) that may be used by the individual, peers, and/or the teacher.

7. Generalization

A. This is the most important step in successful social behavior and unfortunately the most difficult for many learners.

B. It may be helpful to use a contract with the learner to try out the skill in a new situation.

C. It may require a detailed verbal report of the situation in which the skill was used and how it was used. The instructor may also want input from the other person involved in the interaction.

D. Collaboration with family/caregivers to practice and evaluate may also be very important in facilitating generalization.

8. Steps to Developing Social Skills Curricula

A. Describe the students' difficulties in terms of the skills and actions they must perform to improve their behavior, rather than in terms of the failures they experience.

B. Categorize social situations into structured situations and unstructured situations.

C. Understand explicit and implicit demands in social situations.

TEACH PERSON WITH DISABILITIES AND/OR PERSON WITHOUT DISABILITIES. The individual with a disability can greatly benefit from direct instruction of social skills; teaching nondisabled peers how to interact appropriately with the person with a disability may increase effectiveness of social skills for both (Hughes & Carter, 2006). Teaching individuals with disabilities social skills in isolation may not result in development of friendships and social networks, partly because isolated formal instruction may limit "natural" interactions and the ability of learners to generalize skills learned.

PEER-MEDIATED INTERVENTION STRATEGIES. There is a large body of research indicating that peers without disabilities can be effective instructors for social skills for individuals with disabilities. Peers can provide prompting and reinforcement. It is also possible for the instructor to reinforce peers (vicarious reinforcement) so that the student sees peers getting reinforcement for appropriate social skills.

Peer modeling can also alleviate the problem of the learner becoming dependent on the instructor. If the instructor is doing all cueing, then the student may focus on the instructor and not the natural discriminative stimulus. Peer modeling can also help in facilitating generalization because the learner is likely to interact with peers in a variety of settings where the social skills can be used.

ROLE OF COMMUNICATION. The learner must have the means to communicate different social functions (greeting, requesting, calling, commenting), otherwise these skills must be taught before or in conjunction with the social skills. Communication skills may be best taught in integrated settings at the same time that social skills are being taught so that both are being taught in the criterion environment with natural reinforcement most likely to occur.

Key Point Question 6: What Are Some Difficulties With Social Skills Instruction?

Trower (1984) provides an overview of several difficult issues in social skills instruction (*see* Table 8.6). The most important ones for our discussion here are that social skills do not generalize well or maintain well. In other words, the learner may not use the skills outside of the instructional setting (poor generalization) and may not continue to use the skills learned (poor maintenance). Generalization strategies are discussed in Chapter 3.

Table 8.6
PROBLEMS WITH SOCIAL SKILLS TRAINING

1. There is no agreed-upon definition of social skills, even though we all seem to "know what social skills are intuitively." This makes it difficult to carry out research, assessment, or training in any systematic way.
2. There is no consensus or standard by which to define social skills deficits. This makes it difficult to know what to measure and what to change.
3. There is no standard objective source for guiding the selection of any skills. This creates problems for selecting clear training targets.
4. Assessment instruments and procedures are of doubtful validity an reliability. Role-play tests may be too artificial (low ecological validity) for either assessment or training. Global measures are unreliable and subjective.
5. Trained behaviors do not maintain well.
6. Trained behaviors do not transfer (generalize well) to situations outside the training setting.

Source: Adapted from Trower, 1984.

THINGS THAT AFFECT MAINTENANCE. Maintenance of skills has often been a problem for people with disabilities, as well as for individuals without disabilities. For instance, how many of us have made New Year's resolutions to exercise regularly and did so for a while but then gradually stopped exercising over time. Clearly, we know how to engage in the behavior (exercising) but for some reason fail to do so. There are several ways to analyze why behavior maintains or fails to maintain over time.

LEVEL OF STIMULUS CONTROL. Does the individual barely know how to do the behavior or really know how to do it?

FLUENCY. Fluency refers to the rate and ease at which the learner performs the appropriate behavior. As we learn new skills we are often tentative or unsure performing them (remember the first time that you drove a car), but as we perform the skills correctly many times then it becomes more "natural" and can often be performed with little thought. It is important to also realize that procedures that maximize response acquisition and response maintenance may not be identical.

LEVEL OF REINFORCEMENT. Skinner (1953) distinguished between responses that are not maintained because they have been extinguished (i.e., lack of reinforcement) and responses that are "forgotten" (i.e., lost due to a low rate of opportunity).

For maintenance, a number of strategies may be useful. These include self-management strategies (*see* Chapter 10), booster sessions, and contingency contracting (written agreement between teacher and student about the goal that the student wants to achieve and the reinforcement for achieving that goal).

PROBLEMS IN ACHIEVING SOCIAL COMPETENCE

1. Students may not have the requisite skills to interact or to do so successfully.
2. Students may not be able to match their behavior with the ongoing demands of the situation.
3. Students may misinterpret or not understand the outcomes of their behavior and its potential effects.
4. Students may be unable or unwilling to value conventional outcomes.
5. Students may not respond well to the activities or circumstances in which social interactions occur.
6. Students may be reluctant to interact because they fear or expect negative outcomes.

BEST PRACTICE RECOMMENDATIONS

1. Social skills must be directly taught to individuals with skill deficits in this area just as with any skill need (e.g., reading, math, vocational, etc.).
2. The integration of individuals with disabilities can have positive impact on their social skills by having role models who may be more capable of displaying appropriate social behaviors.
3. Instructors must plan carefully for generalization (*see* Chapter 3 for a discussion of generalization) of social skills because learners often have difficulty generalizing these skills.

FUTURE RESEARCH ISSUES

1. What are the best ways to increase the generalization of social skills?
2. Does the type of disability influence how social skills should be taught?
3. What are the best ways to increase the maintenance of social skills?

DISCUSSION QUESTIONS

1. How do different cultures view what are appropriate social behaviors, and how does this influence what social skills should be taught?
2. How do appropriate social behaviors change as the individual gets older (e.g., at age fifteen versus age fifty-five)?
3. How do the specifics of the social situation influence what social skills should be used (e.g., having lunch with friends, coworkers, or a boss)?
4. Review the social skills programs that are commercially available (*see* Table 8.7) to see which program is best for teaching the individuals that you support.

Table 8.7
SOCIAL SKILLS PROGRAMS COMMERCIALLY AVAILABLE

Program and Reference

ACCEPTS
Walker, H. M., McConnell, S., Holmes, D., Todis, B., Walker, J., & Golden N. (1988). *The Walker social skills curriculum: The ACCEPTS program.* Austin, TX: Pro-Ed.

ACCESS
Walker, H. M., Todis, B., Holes, D., & Horton, G. (1988). *The ACCESS program: Adolescent curriculum for communication and effective social skills.* Austin, TX: Pro-Ed.

Life Skills Activities for Secondary Students with Special Needs
Mannix, D. S. (1998). *Social skills activities for secondary students with special needs.* West Nyack, NJ: Center for Applied Research in Education.

The PREPARE Curriculum
Goldstein, A. P. (1999). *The PREPARE curriculum: Teaching prosocial competencies.* Champaign, IL: Research Press.

Skillstreaming the Adolescent
McGinnis, E., & Goldstein, A. P. (1997). *Skillstreaming the elementary school child: New strategies and perspectives for teaching prosocial skills* (2nd ed.). Champaign, IL: Research Press.

Social Skills for Daily Living
Schumaker, J. B., Hazel, J. S., & Pederson, C. S. (1988). *Social skills for daily living.* Circle Pine, MN: American Guidance Service.

The Waksman Social Skills Curriculum
Waksman, S. A., & Waksman, D. D. (1998). *The Waksman social skills curriculum.* Austin, TX: Pro-Ed.

SCHOOL AND COMMUNITY-BASED
ACTIVITY SUGGESTIONS

1. Go to a variety of community settings (sporting event, grocery store, playground) and observe the different social skills needed to be successful in those environments. What are the common social skills, and which social skills are specific to that situation?

2. Related to the activity in Suggestion 1, what social behaviors would be inappropriate in those settings? Analyze how the individual would judge what social skills would be appropriate or inappropriate in those situations?

3. Ask employers what social skills they look for in employees at their work site. Compare this with social behaviors that you see high-school students or others displaying. How might differences influence the ability of the students to be successfully employed?

REFERENCES

Amado, A. (2004). Lessons learned about promoting friendships. *TASH Connections, 30,* 8–12.

Banda, D. R., Matuszny, R. M., & Turkan, S. (2007). Video modeling strategies to enhance appropriate behaviors in children with Autism Spectrum Disorders. *Teaching Exceptional Children, 39,* 47–52.

Bernard-Ripoll, S. (2007). Using a self-as-model video combined with social stories to help a child with Asperger syndrome understand emotions. *Focus on Autism and Other Developmental Disabilities, 22,* 100–106.

Chadsey-Rusch, J., Karlan, G. R., Riva, M., & Rusch, F. R. (1984). Competitive employment: Teaching conversation skills to adults who are mentally retarded. *Mental Retardation, 22,* 218–225.

Combs, M. L. & Slaby, D. A. (1977). Social skills training with children. In B. B. Lahey & A. E. Kazdin (Eds.), *Advances in clinical child psychology* (Vol. 1) (pp. 161–201). New York: Plenum Press.

Engelmann, S., & Carnine, D. (1982). *Theory of instruction: Principles and applications.* New York: Irvington Publishers.

Gresham, F. M., Sugai, G., & Horner, R. H. (2001). Interpreting outcomes of social skills training for students with high-incidence disabilities. *Exceptional Children, 67,* 331–344.

Haring, T. G., Roger, B., Lee, M., Breen, C., & Gaylord-Ross, R. (1986). Teaching social language to moderately handicapped students. *Journal of Applied Behavior Analysis, 19,* 159–171.

Haring, T. G., Kennedy, C. H., Adams, M. J., & Pitts-Conway, V. (1987). Teaching generalization of purchasing skills across community settings to autistic youth using videotape modeling. Journal of Applied Behavior Analysis, 20, 89-96.

Hughes, C., & Carter, E. W. (2006). *Success for all students: Promoting inclusion in secondary schools through peer buddy programs.* Boston: Allyn and Bacon.

Martin, J. E., Rusch, F. R., Lagomarcino, T., & Chadsey-Rusch, J. (1986). Comparison between workers who are nonhandicapped and mentally retarded: Why they lose their jobs. *Applied Research in Mental Retardation, 7*, 415–430.

McGinnis, E., & Goldstein, A. P. (1997). *Skillstreaming the elementary school child: New strategies and perspectives for teaching prosocial skills* (2nd ed.). Research Press: Champaign, IL.

Mechling, L. C., Pridgen, L. S., & Cronin, B. A. (2005). Computer-based video instruction to teach students with intellectual disabilities to verbally respond to questions and make purchases in fast food restaurants. *Education and Training in Developmental Disabilities, 40*, 47–59.

Skinner, B. F. (1953). *Science and human behavior.* New York: The Free Press.

Storey, K., & Horner, R. H. (1991). Social interactions in three supported employment options: A comparative analysis. *Journal of Applied Behavior Analysis, 24*, 349–360.

Trower, P. (1984). A radical critique and reformulation: From organism to agent. In P. Trower (Ed.), *Radical approaches to social skills training* (pp. 48–88). New York: Methuen, Inc.

Chapter 9

SELF-DETERMINATION AND SELF-ADVOCACY SKILLS

Keypoint Questions

1. What is self-determination?
2. What is self-advocacy?
3. At what age should individuals learn self-determination skills?
4. Who teaches self-determination skills?
5. How do you teach choice making skills?
6. What is person-centered planning?
7. How do you conduct person-centered planning?
8. How do you teach individuals to direct their own planning meetings?

Window to the World Case Study One

Jennifer is a sixteen-year-old young woman with a severe intellectual disability who does not communicate in traditional ways. In addition to being able to answer yes or no questions accurately, Jennifer smiles and frowns to indicate a preference for items, activities, and people. The school staff and Jennifer's parents all agree that she clearly communicates her preferences.

At her first individual transition plan meeting (since she just turned 16) it was decided that Jennifer needs to be able to make informed choices about what she wants to do, especially regarding possible careers. The team thought that it would be a good idea to have Jennifer initially do some job shadowing, during which she would spend a half day to a full day in a variety of work situations. Jennifer is very social and likes being around a lot of people. Thus, it was decided to look for job shadowing experiences that involved jobs with a lot of social interactions. It was decided to start with a wide variety of situations (e.g., indoor/outdoor, physically active/nonactive, loud/quiet, etc.) and to videotape Jennifer in those situations. Then the team could watch the video clips with Jennifer and get her reaction (e.g., did you like this job, would you like to try it again, how about a similar job, etc.) so that the choices could then be narrowed down. Jennifer could then work a variety of jobs in these areas for several weeks and then up to a semester. This would allow Jennifer and the team to make informed choices and also to have Jennifer working in a job when she is twenty-one and would continue in as she exits the public school system. This would also allow a thorough job analysis of that job and time to teach Jennifer skills for that job and also to develop appropriate supports for her in the job.

Window to the World Case Study Two

Juan is a twenty-seven-year-old man with autism spectrum disorders who was not taught self-determination skills when he was in school. He never attended any of his IEP meetings because the team thought it would be inappropriate. He has struggled to maintain jobs as an adult and has been on his own after graduating from high school, living in a variety of situations that were less than desirable.

Juan joined a support group for adults with autism spectrum disorders and learned that the Department of Rehabilitation offers services for adults with autism spectrum disorders. (Neither Juan nor his family had been told about this service when he was in high school.) Juan went through the Department of Rehabilitation assessment process, and it was determined that he was eligible for services. He was assigned a counselor, Ms. Wong, who met with him and realized that he had few self-determination skills. She took several steps to help him in this area. First, he joined a job club for people with autism spectrum disorders where Ms. Wong directly taught self-determination skills to individuals in the club. At the club she went over setting goals, making choices, solving problems, making decisions, self-regulation, and self-advocacy. Ms. Wong also met individually with Juan to provide additional teaching of skills in these areas as well as to plan with him.

From this process, Juan decided that his occupational goal was to become a social worker and help individuals with autism spectrum disorders and their families so that they could avoid some of the problems he encountered. Juan decided to enroll in the local community college for two years and then transfer to a university for his B.A. in Social Work. Ms. Wong went with Juan to meet Gayther Plummer at the DSPS at the community college. There the three of them planned the classes that Juan would take and the supports that he would need to be successful (e.g., a tutor, joining a support group, and weekly check-in meetings with Mr. Plummer). With these supports in place, Juan was successful in becoming a social worker, and he always made sure that the students with autism spectrum disorders that he worked with were taught self-determination skills (especially regarding how to run their own IEP meetings) while in the school system.

Key Point Question 1: What Is Self-Determination?

Although there are many definitions of self-determination proposed throughout the literature, the term can be defined simply as having control in one's life. The concept is simple; the implementation of the concept is extremely complex (Wehmeyer, 1999). Teaching someone to be self-determined is a long-term, ongoing goal, but the outcomes can clearly be observed. For example, during her transition planning meeting, a young woman named Judy told her parents that she wanted to live on her own with a friend. Judy's parents always expected that she would continue to live with them after she graduated from high school. Based on Judy's expressed preference for living with a roommate, she was taught specific skills pertaining to finding an apartment, obtaining support, and choosing a roommate. One year after graduating from high school, Judy and a friend, Amy, moved into a supported living apartment.

Self-determination is the capacity to choose and act on the basis of those choices (Wehmeyer, Lance, & Bashinski, 2002). Self-determination can be viewed as empowerment and involves not only choice but also control over one's changing life, major issues such as where and with whom to live, career decisions, and leisure preferences. In other words, people with self-determination know how to choose, know what they want, and know how to get it (Martin & Marshall, 1995). This is a complex process with tough issues that must be addressed. As individuals get older, they must make choices and decisions that involve taking risks. Caregivers, parents, teachers, and other service providers must balance the responsibility for caring for an individual with the right of the individual with a disability to make personal decisions. It is certainly common for everyone (with or without a disability) to sometimes make poor decisions and hopefully to learn from those poor decisions so as to be able to make better decisions in the future. What makes self-determination so important is that it can have a positive impact on school and adult quality-of-life outcomes for individuals with disabilities. In other words, it can have an immediate impact on a person's life as well as positively influencing long-term outcomes (Wehmeyer, Gragoudas, & Shogren, 2006).

Key Point Question 2: What Is Self-Advocacy?

Self-advocacy can be viewed as a critical component to self-determination and may be simply defined as advocating or speaking up for oneself (Dybwad & Bersani, 1996; Tufail & Lyon, 2007). Self-advocacy is essential to becoming self-determined; individuals cannot self-advocate if they do not have self-determination skills. In other words, you have to know what you want in order to know how to get it. As children reach adolescence, the need for self-advocating increases. They must learn to answer questions posed by teachers, employers, and service providers about their support needs, express their strengths, and assert their rights. The earlier example of Judy's transition planning meeting illustrates the relationship between self-determination and self-advocacy. At the beginning of the meeting, the team discussed postschool goals. Judy's parents stated that Judy would live with them after high school, and the teacher recorded that goal on the transition section of the IEP. Judy spoke up and said she wanted to live with a friend in her own apartment and that she did not agree with that goal. At first, her parents did not take the comment seriously and restated their position. Judy emphatically restated her desire to live on her own with a roommate whom she would choose. The team realized that this was an important choice for Judy and changed the goal on the IEP.

Key Point Question 3: At What Age Should Individuals Learn Self-Determination Skills?

Self-determination must be promoted starting in early childhood education and continued throughout an individual's life. Like many skills for individuals with disabilities, when teaching self-determination skills, the earlier the better. The specific skills that are taught may change, but starting to teach self-determination when an individual is young prepares him or her to be more autonomous later in life. For example, an early childhood special education teacher may target making choices, initiating tasks, expressing preferences, and other skills that will lead to a more self-determined individual in the future (Brown & Cohen, 1996). These skills lay the foundation for having self-advocacy skills and being able to use them in school and other settings. Self-advocacy skills are very important in educational settings, whether elementary school or graduate school. Students with disabilities need to know what their legal rights are (whether under IDEA, Americans with Disabilities Act, or Section 504 of the Rehabilitation Act of 1973), be able to state them, and know what to ask for under these laws. For example, Betty, a high-school student with a learning disability, understands that her IEP indicates that she is eligible for note-taking services in classes as an accommodation. When at the beginning of the semester Mr. O'Connor, her high school biology teacher, said that he was not willing to provide a note-taker for her, Betty showed him a copy of her IEP and stated that she was entitled to this accommodation for her to be academically successful in his class. Mr. O'Connor realized that she was right and set up the note-taker for her.

Self-determination is especially crucial for successful transition from school to adult life. Students need to be aware of their capabilities and interests, be aware of the choices available (e.g., going to college or getting a job), and have the skills to make informed choices. All too often individuals with disabilities are told what jobs they will hold, where they will live, with whom they will live, and when and where they will recreate. This leads to passivity and a poor quality of life.

Key Point Question 4: Who Teaches Self-Determination Skills?

The most common instructor of self-determination skills is a special education teacher. It is critical that teachers/instructors/trainers believe that individuals can become self-determined and that they can teach these skills (Soto & Goetz, 1998). Self-determination is often viewed as a necessary skill for those making the transition from school to adult life. Some high schools offer specific courses in self-determination for students with disabilities, whereas others may infuse the content into existing coursework. Self-advocacy mentors, school psychologists, or private counselors may provide assistance in coming to terms with the presence of a disability and how it affects an individual's life. Unfortunately, many individuals did not acquire self-determination skills during their school career, so it is necessary for adult service providers to address them as well. In addition, family/caregiver involvement is critical to the acquisition of self-determination skills (Turnbull & Turnbull, 2001).

Parents may need information about self-determination in order to "let go" and allow the child with a disability to become more autonomous. Parents sometimes also need outside help to assist them with issues of letting go. When a child with disabilities is nearing the time for leaving home and becoming less dependent on parents, the parents themselves may suffer some "withdrawal pangs." Taking care of a child with disabilities can be an enormous responsibility. The tendency on the part of some parents is to be protective or even overprotective. When letting go must take place, parents may need emotional support themselves to weather this significant change in their lives. Peer supports for parents can be very important in this area.

Key Point Question 5: How Do You Teach Choice Making Skills?

Although making informed choices is a critical component of self-determination, they are only one component of this complex process. It is clear that all individuals make choices. They choose to refuse or comply with many demands, directions, or other stimuli in their environment. Individuals with the most challenging behaviors have been described as communicating their choices in inappropriate or undesirable ways.

In school settings, there are specific steps that teachers can take to teach skills for making choices. It is important to remember that if you give a student a choice, you must then respect that choice.

STEP ONE. Analyze a student's schedule and potential choices.

STEP TWO. Present two options to the student. It may be one preferred option and one nonpreferred (e.g., do math or play a game) or two preferred options (e.g., play a game or go to the library to check out a book).

STEP THREE. Deliver the chosen item/activity. If the student does not want what he or she has chosen, remove it immediately. The student should not be forced to eat something or engage in an activity that he or she does not want.

STEP FOUR. Identify as many choice making opportunities as are feasible for the student throughout the day and repeat Steps One through Three.

STEP FIVE. Increase the number and variety of options as well as the number of opportunities to make a choice.

Key Point Question 6: What Is Person-Centered Planning?

Individuals with disabilities, their families, and service providers may have difficulty setting personal goals due to past experience with the deficits approach to planning (e.g., the need to eliminate undesirable behaviors rather than increasing desirable skills). Thus, their vision of the future may be limited to what they have seen others with disabilities achieve. The outcomes experienced by other individuals with disabilities may have been based on availability of services, such as congregate living, sheltered workshops, and segregated recreation and leisure opportunities. Teaching individuals to set personal goals based on a challenging vision of the future requires overcoming deficits orientation and lack of knowledge regarding what individuals may be able to achieve.

Person-centered planning encourages a positive view of the future based on strengths and preferences (Miner & Bates, 1997). Adolescents must begin to ask such questions as: After high school, where will I live? What kind of job would I like to have? What will I do for fun? The transition planning process promotes the discussion of these questions before school exit, officially starting at age sixteen with the Individual Transition Plan.

Person-centered planning may also be conducted before the age of sixteen and this should be encouraged. The vision of postschool life may be unclear, but person-centered long-term goals may be developed. Goals to be attained over the next five years may focus on such questions as: "How will I participate in daily living activities at home? What will I be doing in school? What will I do for fun?"

The process of person-centered planning consists of four components: (1) a personal profile that promotes a positive view of the individual, (2) a challenging vision of the future, (3) action steps leading to the attainment of the desirable future lifestyle, and (4) any necessary changes to the current support system (i.e., school or adult services).

Key Point Question 7: How Do You Conduct Person-Centered Planning?

The major purpose of person-centered planning is to clearly describe long-term goals based on an individual's strengths, talents, and preferences. The following description of conducting person-centered planning relates to an adolescent in the transition planning process. If the student is in early childhood or elementary school, the activities would be the same but long-term goals would be identified for "five years in the future" instead of after high school. This would also be the case for an adult who is no longer in school. Adult goals could be related to the perspective of five years from now.

PERSONAL PROFILE. Who is this person? What are his or her strengths, preferences, and support needs?

CIRCLE OF SUPPORT. The facilitator asks the student, family, and other members to think about the people who are important in the student's life. The diagram in Figure 9.1 has four concentric circles, each being progressively larger. Using an example, the facilitator describes the relationships and corresponding circles. Inside the innermost circle the student's name is written. The participants should be asked to name the people closest and most important to the student. The names of these individuals are written around the inner circle. The student and participants are then asked to name the people who are close to the student but not quite as close as those in the inner circle. The names of these individuals are written on the diagram around the second circle. Next, the participants are asked to name those people in the individual's life who are associated through situations or places, such as church, sports teams, or clubs. The facilitator writes the names of these individuals around the third circle from the center. Finally, the participants are asked to name the people who are paid to be in the individual's life, for example, teachers, bus drivers, doctors, and so on. The names of these people are written around the outer circle. This provides an illustrative view of the focus person's important relationships.

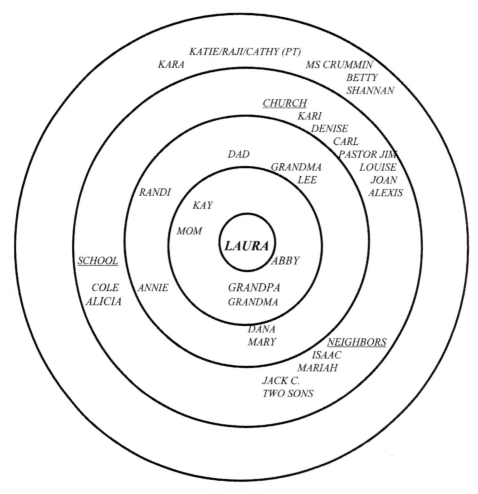

Figure 9.1

The student's circle of support is examined and the possibility of including people from the support map in future lifestyle planning is discussed. People who are important in the student's life can be helpful in finding jobs, developing natural supports, and making other community connections. Many people who have a stake in the student's future may only need the invitation to become more involved in planning for a desirable future.

Whenever there are few people identified for the two inner circles, there is an apparent need to develop more close relationships. When the people involved in the focus person's life are primarily paid providers, it is desirable that they approach support from a person-centered perspective.

COMMUNITY PRESENCE. The number and variety of places that an individual goes frequently or occasionally also can be used as an indicator of current lifestyle status. The community presence map provides a measure of an individual's lifestyle through the graphic display of places and frequency. The desirability of community presence should be measured by the individual's choice and preferences.

After conducting the circle of support activity, the facilitator asks the student and participants to think about the community settings that the student uses daily, weekly, or occasionally. The student's community presence map is recorded by writing the names of places at the end of arrows pointing away from the graphic of the student's home (Figure 9.2). The student and participants are asked to consider ways that the student could increase choice and competence in community participation.

The number of places, variety, and frequency are all considered when evaluating community presence. Individual preference is important when assessing the quality of the student's community participation. When creating a desirable future lifestyle with the student, consideration of increasing choice in community presence may be necessary.

PREFERENCES. Preferences can be communicated in many ways. People with disabilities who do not communicate in traditional ways say a great deal about their preferences through their behavior. People who know the student well are needed to identify preferences based on experience in many situations. The preferences list can be used in conjunction with the community presence map to evaluate the individual's quality of choice.

COMMUNITY PRESENCE MAP

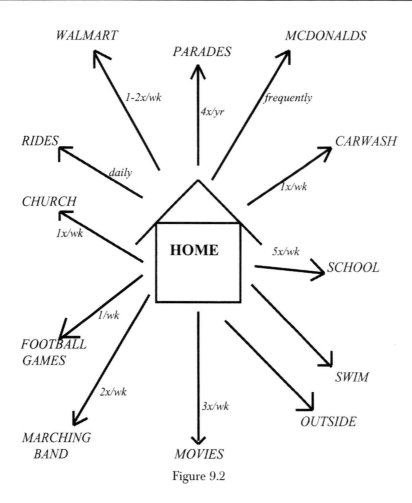

WALMART   PARADES   MCDONALDS

1-2x/wk   4x/yr   frequently

RIDES   CARWASH

daily   1x/wk

CHURCH

1x/wk   **HOME**   5x/wk → SCHOOL

1/wk

FOOTBALL
GAMES   SWIM

2x/wk   3x/wk   OUTSIDE

MARCHING
BAND   MOVIES

Figure 9.2

The next step in the personal profile development is to list the student's preferences of things that "work" and "don't work" in her or his life. A sample preference list for an individual with disabilities may be displayed to provide a perspective of the relationship between a student and her or his preferences (Figure 9.3). The student's reactions to service provision should be discussed within the context of preferences. The facilitator emphasizes the concept that system-centered planning and service provisions do not usually address individual preference. The participants are asked to think about the things that work and the things that do not work in supporting the student. The facili-

PREFERENCES	
THINGS THAT "WORK" FOR LAURA	**THINGS THAT "DON'T WORK" FOR LAURA**
• *MUSIC* • *CHEWING ON TOWEL* • *CHOCOLATE PUDDING* • *GO OUTSIDE* • *STANDER* • *SOCIAL TALK* • *PIZZA/PASTA* • *ICE CREAM* • *SITTING CLOSE TO MOM* • *LIGHTED TOYS* • *ROCKING/SWING* • *DOGS* • *FEET RUBBED* • • • •	• *TOUCHING HER FACE* • *FURRY THINGS* • *VEGETABLES/FRUIT* • *FACE WASHED* • *TOOTHBRUSHING* • *HEAT OR COLD/RAPID CHANGES IN TEMP* • *WIND IN HER FACE* • *LAYING ON HER STOMACH* • •

Figure 9.3

tator lists these preferences and concludes with a summary of the importance of personal preferences being reflected in identifying necessary supports.

The preferences list can be used as a basis for creating and evaluating a desirable lifestyle. The things that work in a person's life should be a major part of everyday life. When choosing a job, a place to live, or a recreation activity, matching can be done by comparing what occurs in the environment to the preferences list. Similarly, the things that do not work should be avoided whenever possible. For example, if being in large crowds is identified as something that does not work for an individual, then going to concerts may not be a desirable leisure activity.

The importance of including preferred activities in a typical daily schedule cannot be overemphasized. Most people make career choices, develop significant relationships, and decide on weekend activities based on their personal preferences.

GIFTS AND CAPACITIES. When parents brag about their children they tend to ignore faults and shortcomings. Individuals with disabilities have extensive records pertaining to their deficits and weaknesses. The strengths listed on a typical IEP may not promote the awareness of a student's unique qualities. "Knows his activities of daily living (ADLs)" may not lead to high expectations on the part of those who support a student.

The final step in the development of the personal profile is to list the student's gifts and capacities. The facilitator begins this step by writing down the descriptors that participants provide when asked what people who like the individual say about her or him. This list is similar to the list of things a parent says about her or his child when bragging to friends. The facilitator prompts contributions by encouraging the identification of unique skills and emphasizing the importance of valued community roles (e.g., club member) as positive attributes. For example, participants in a student's person-centered planning meeting may identify gifts and capacities such as honest, a person with a good sense of humor, loving, compassionate, and so on (Figure 9.4).

GIFTS AND CAPACITIES LIST
LAURA IS:
⇨ *HAPPY*
⇨ *SOCIAL*
⇨ *WILLING TO PARTICIPATE/TRY THINGS*
⇨ *CUTE (AND KNOWS IT)*
⇨ *EASY TO GET ALONG WITH*
⇨ *GOOD NATURED*
⇨ *FUN*
⇨ *HONEST*
⇨ *FRIENDLY*
⇨
⇨
⇨

Figure 9.4

This component of person-centered planning provides the perspective from which a desired future lifestyle should be viewed. Each individual is unique, possessing talents and skills that contribute to the home and community. Such talents have often been overshadowed by deficits. This list is an initial step in the development of a positive view of the individual with a disability. With this positive perspective, expectations of a meaningful lifestyle are raised.

Future Lifestyle

CREATING A CHALLENGING VISION OF THE FUTURE. Regardless of disability, each individual has the right to an enviable life (e.g., someone who has a very good quality of life). Too often expectations of an enviable life are thought to be unrealistic because of a disability. When creating a challenging vision of a desirable future, teams should refrain from making judgments as to what is realistic. Identify the hopes and dreams of the student and provide experience that will teach the student what is realistic.

With the personal profile fresh in the minds of participants, a challenging vision of the future should be described. Dreams of the future should be exciting in order to be worth working toward. A common vision of a desirable future lifestyle is necessary for the level of commitment required if participants are going to take action on behalf of the individual with a disability.

Describe the lifestyle that Joe and his team developed. Point out that this is only the initial description of Joe's future and will be expanded and changed over time.

After the personal profile is completed, the facilitator should ask the student and participants to describe a desirable future for the student by answering the following questions:

1. What is our image of a desired lifestyle for the student?
2. Where will she or he live in this desired future (e.g., own home, with family, supported apartment, etc.)?
3. What will she or he do during the day and where will she or he do it (work, volunteer, etc.)?
4. What will she or he do for fun and recreation?
5. With whom will she or he participate in recreation and leisure activities?

DESIRED FUTURE LIFESTYLE

After graduation . . .

Where will the Laura live?

Laura will live in a small group home with one or two other people. They will have a small dog. Laura will need continuous support from people who work <u>for</u> her. Family and friends will come see her regularly.

What will Laura do during the day and where will she do it?

Laura will attend an adult program where she can socialize. The future vision for this part of her lifestyle needs further exploration. Laura could be a fashion model for disability-related products such as United Access. Whatever she does during the day, it should be consistent with her preferences and interests.

What will the Laura do for fun and recreation?

In the future, Laura will continue going to church, swimming, and going to the movies. Laura will lead an active social life with lots of trips outside of her home.

Figure 9.5

In completing this activity, the facilitator should encourage the creation of a vision based on the student's desired future (including systems change if needed) rather than on the limits of an individual's disability. To evaluate the desired future, the facilitator asks the team to consider whether or not an individual without an identified disability would find the proposed lifestyle goals desirable (Figure 9.5).

Action Steps

NEGOTIATING ACTION STEPS AND RESPONSIBLE PARTIES. No personal profile or vision of the future is worthwhile without action towards making the vision come true. When a few short-term tasks can be realized, the possibility of a desirable lifestyle is enhanced. Early successful completion of action steps can ignite a support circle in their efforts.

With the student's desired future as a focal point, the facilitator discusses activities, supports, and responsible parties for attaining these future goals. The facilitator asks the participants to identify three to

ACTION STEPS AND RESPONSIBLE PARTIES	
"ACTIVITIES"	**"WHO"**
PRESENT INFORMATION AT UPCOMING IEP MEETING	LAURA/MS. CRUMMIN
PURSUE INFORMATION ABOUT THE LEGAL ASPECTS OF THE FUTURE	MOM/LAURA WITH HELP FROM SANDY/ANGIE
TALK TO OTHERS ABOUT RESIDENTIAL AND DAY PROGRAM OPTIONS	MOM/LAURA

Figure 9.6

five activities that should be undertaken to provide immediate movement toward the focus person's desired lifestyle. The facilitator lists responses under the "activities" column. Individuals responsible for performing an activity or overseeing its performance are identified and listed under the "who" column. Whenever possible the student should be encouraged to take responsibility or coresponsibility for seeing that an activity is completed. No one should be coerced into accepting responsibility for an action step. Voluntary commitment is important. A typical example of an action step would be for the student to lead his or her subsequent IEP meeting utilizing the information gathered in the person-centered planning meeting. The person responsible would be the student and the parent or teacher may be jointly responsible to provide support for the process (Figure 9.6).

The action steps should include some activities that have immediate benefit to the individual. This will encourage future activity due to the immediate success. This success will also promote a greater willingness to dream of what might be, instead of settling for what is available.

Necessary Systems Change

IDENTIFYING NECESSARY CHANGES IN THE CURRENT SERVICE SYSTEM IS IMPORTANT. If people with disabilities are going to realize

NECESSARY CHANGES IN SERVICE SYSTEM
1. *FUND ADULT SERVICES*
2. *INCREASE "OWN YOUR HOME" OPTIONS*

Figure 9.7

their desired future, the way services have traditionally been provided may have to change. In other words, just because things have always been done a certain way does not mean that they are a good way to do things or that other ways might be better (Albin, 1992; Dileo, 2007).

The facilitator asks participants to develop a statement of any necessary changes in the capability of the service system. Statements are identified by circle members and listed by the facilitator. Too many identified changes will be overwhelming to the system. Each support circle should be encouraged to list up to three statements of necessary change (Figure 9.7).

Share the necessary changes identified during the preliminary planning meeting with appropriate administrators of local services and supports. Tell other community members, such as ministers, teachers, politicians, and business owners, about the changes that need to occur for the attainment of the individual's desired lifestyle. If possible, the individual with a disability should be actively involved in relating this information to service providers and community members. This promotes self-advocacy skills on the part of the individual and listening skills on the part of others.

This is a process that is highly sensitive to student and individual direction; this approach promotes a person-centered perspective in individualized education or service program development.

Key Point Question 8: How Do You Teach Individuals to Direct Their Own Planning Meetings?

The discussion on Key Question 7 described how individuals with disabilities can set personal goals. There is still a need to relate those goals to others and attain them. When special education services were federally mandated in 1975, extensive efforts went towards providing a quality education to all students with disabilities. IEPs were developed and reviewed annually, often without involvement from the student. In the late 1980s and into the 1990s, the need to involve students in planning for transition from school to adult life gained significant attention. It quickly became apparent that students with disabilities were not prepared to take on the role of active participant in the transition planning process. High schools may offer courses in self-determination training or incorporate self-determination skills into coursework. Public speaking or mass communications courses fit well with the goal of teaching students to speak for themselves. A natural context for this skill is the IEP meeting for students in kindergarten through twelfth grade (K–12) school settings and the individual service planning meeting for adults.

Bates and Miner (2005) developed the *10 Step Guide to the Student-Directed IEP* adapted from the components of the self-directed IEP by Martin, Marshall, Maxson, and Jerman (1997). Once the manuscript is completed, it can be used to lead a subsequent planning meeting (Table 9.1).

Students can learn to participate and present their information at the meeting in a variety of ways. Graduated guidance of physical prompts can systematically teach students the motor skills of advancing slides with the use of an alternative mouse or adaptive switch. Teachers can utilize VSM, role-playing, and rehearsal to provide opportunities for additional practice and feedback (Torgerson, Miner, & Shen, 2004).

There are many ways for a student or adult to actively participate in a planning meeting. In many cases, this may take the form of partial participation. Table 9.2 provides a list of possible strategies for this participation. For example, Laura was able to communicate a yes and no response during her person-centered planning meeting. After all of the information was gathered, Laura, her mom, and her teacher Ms. Crummin developed slides to be used to lead her upcoming IEP meeting (*see* Table 9.3). A student without disabilities the same age as Laura narrated the presentation. Laura pushed a large single switch to advance the slides during her meeting.

Table 9.1

TEN STEPS TO THE STUDENT-DIRECTED IEP

Welcome!

Welcome to my IEP.
Today we're going to plan my
program for the next year.

Introductions

My name is Laura Blakemore
and I am a student at King
Middle School in Ms.
Crummin's class.

Would everyone please
introduce yourselves.

My Future

When I finish school, I want to live in a home with one or two
other people. We will have a small dog. I will need lots of
support from people who work for me. I want my family and
friends to come by and see me regularly.
I want to go somewhere during the day where I can socialize.
I need more experience to know what I want to do in the
future. Maybe I could be a fashion model for United Access.
I want to continue going to church, swimming, and going to
the movies for fun. I expect to have an active social life with
lots of trips in the community.

Would anyone like to comment?

This Year…

Things that have worked well for me this
 year are using my PECs book to make
 choices, standing up from my
 wheelchair, and helping feed myself.
Things that haven't worked very well for
 me are standing up from the floor,
 using my walker, and eating too fast
(I just can't get enough pizza.)

Comments?

Does anyone want to
comment on how I've been
doing in school this year?

Next Year…

Next year I want to participate in
new activities, especially fun
stuff. I will work on
communication by choosing
favorite foods and activities by
pointing to pictures.
Any comments or questions?

Support

To be successful in school next year,
I need help from my speech,
occupational, and physical
therapists. I need my teachers to pay
attention when I'm asking for
something.

Any comments or questions?

Summary of Goals

In summary, my future plans are
to have a home, do something I
enjoy during the day, and have
an active social life.

For me to make progress toward
these goals, I will need to try new
things and work on my
communication.

Support Needs Review

The things that need to be in my
program to help me succeed
are understanding therapists
and others who will listen to
me.

Does anyone have anything
they want to say about my
program?

Conclusion

Thank you all for coming to
my meeting and believing in
me.

I appreciate all you do.

Table 9.2
STUDENT-DIRECTED IEP STRATEGIES

Student verbally leads meeting
Student leads meeting utilizing AAC
Student may perform selected steps
Student utilizes presentation software
Pointing to poster/materials prepared for meeting
Student's response validates or vetoes (supported by someone who knows student well)
Activating video
Passing around pictures
Digital storytelling
Introduce student in terms of gifts and capacities

Table 9.3
LAURA BLAKEMORE'S IEP SLIDES

1. Begin by greeting everyone and stating purpose of the meeting.
2. Introduce yourself and others.
3. Identify your postschool goals (or long-term, 5-year goals for younger students).
4. Review how you have been doing in school.
5. Request input from other participants in the meeting.
6. Identify your goals for this year.
7. Identify the supports you need to be successful.
8. Summarize your goals.
9. Review support needs and finalize program.
10. Conclude meeting.

BEST PRACTICE RECOMMENDATIONS

1. Teach choice-making skills starting in early childhood settings and continue as the student gets older. Young children with disabilities should learn to make choices and express preferences in effective ways.
2. Self-advocacy and self-determination involve specific skills that need to be directly taught to individuals.
3. Individuals need to practice and use the self-advocacy and self-determination skills that they have learned.
4. Teach students to use information gathered during person-centered planning meetings in student-directed IEP meetings.

FUTURE RESEARCH ISSUES

1. What are the skills needed by facilitators to successfully conduct person-centered plans?
2. How should person-centered plans vary depending on the setting (school, college, adult life)?
3. What should be done if the service delivery system is incapable of implementing desired lifestyle outcomes that individuals have identified through their person-centered plan?

DISCUSSION QUESTIONS

1. Are some individuals "too disabled" to make choices and be self-determined?
2. What should family members and/or service providers do if they do not agree with the choice that an individual makes?
3. Can self-determination be used against an individual (e.g., we should have sheltered workshops because people are choosing to be there)?
4. What is the role of informed choice in self-determination?

SCHOOL AND COMMUNITY-BASED ACTIVITY SUGGESTIONS

1. Conduct a person-centered plan on yourself involving family members, friends, and so on.
2. Conduct a person-centered plan on a friend.
3. Videotape an IEP that is led by a teacher and one that is led by the student with a disability and analyze differences between the two IEPs.
4. Interview some adults with disabilities. Ask them about how they are self-determined and what they wish that they had been taught in school regarding self-determination.

REFERENCES

Albin, J. M. (1992). *Quality improvement in employment and other human services: Managing for quality through change.* Baltimore, MD: Paul Brookes.

Bates, P. E., & Miner, C. A. (2005). *The 10 step guide to the student-directed IEP.* Unpublished manuscript. Carbondale, IL: Southern Illinois University.

Brown, F., & Cohen, S. (1996). Self-determination and young children. *Journal of the Association for Persons with Severe Handicaps, 21,* 22–30.

Dileo, D. (2007). *Raymond's room: Ending the segregation of people with disabilities.* St. Augustine, FL: Training Resources Network.

Dybwad, G., & Bersani, H. (1996). *New voices: Self-advocacy by people with disabilities.* Cambridge, MA: Brookline Books.

Martin, J. E., & Marshall, L. H. (1995). Choicemaker: A comprehensive self-determination transition program. *Intervention in School and Clinic, 30,* 147–156.

Martin, J. E., Marshall, L. H., Maxson, L. M., & Jerman, P. L. (1997). *The self directed IEP.* Longmont, CO: Sopris West.

Miner, C. A., & Bates, P. E. (1997). The effects of person centered planning activities on the IEP/transition planning process. *Education and Training in Mental Retardation and Developmental Disabilities, 32,* 105–112.

Soto, G., & Goetz, L. (1998). Self-efficacy beliefs and the education of students with severe disabilities. *Journal of the Association for Persons with Severe Handicaps, 23,* 134–143.

Torgerson, C. W., Miner, C. A., & Shen, H. (2004). Developing student competence in self-directed IEPs. *Intervention in School and Clinic, 39,* 162–167.

Tufail, J., & Lyon, K. (2007). *Introducing advocacy: The first book of speaking up: A plain text guide to advocacy.* Philadelphia, PA: Jessica Kingsley.

Turnbull, A., & Turnbull, R. (2001). Self-determination for individuals with significant cognitive disabilities and their families. *Journal of the Association for persons with Severe Handicaps, 26,* 56–62.

Wehmeyer, M. (1999). A functional model of self-determination: Describing development and implementing instruction. *Focus on Autism and Other Developmental Disabilities, 14,* 53–62.

Wehmeyer, M. L., Gragoudas, S., & Shogren, K. A. (2006). Self-determination, student involvement, and leadership development. In P. Wehman (Ed.), *Life beyond the classroom: Transition strategies for young people with disabilities* (4th ed.) (pp. 41–69). Baltimore, MD: Paul Brookes.

Wehmeyer, M. L., Lance, G. D., & Bashinski, S. (2002). Promoting access to the general curriculum for students with mental retardation: A multi-level model. *Education and Training in Mental Retardation and Developmental Disabilities, 37,* 223–234.

Chapter 10

SELF-MANAGEMENT SKILLS

Keypoint Questions

1. What is self-management?
2. Why are self-management strategies important?
3. What are antecedent cue regulation strategies?
4. What are self-monitoring strategies?
5. What are self-determined consequences?
6. What are self-punishment strategies?
7. How do you best teach self-management skills?

Window to the World Case Study One

Gayther was a young man with Down syndrome who worked at a coffee company packaging bags of coffee. He was often off task (more than 50% of the time), even with a job coach present most of the time to prompt him to focus on his work. The employer was concerned with his productivity and had approached the supported employment director that he might be fired soon. It was decided that auditory prompting procedures might be appropriate to help his on-task behavior and thus his productivity. The supported employment director and Gayther made some MP3 selections with some of his favorite music on it and every sixty seconds there was a self-selected phrase inserted by Gayther ("work hard," "earn lots of money") to keep him on task. Gayther then wore headphones attached to his MP3 player, which he listened to as he worked. There was a immediate and remarkable increase in his on-task behavior and productivity. Within two days his on-task behavior was close to 100 percent and his productivity was no longer a concern to his employer.

Window to the World Case Study Two

Alma is a high-school student with a physical disability. Throughout elementary and middle school she had a "one-on-one aide," but it was becoming obvious to all concerned that Alma was growing increasingly dependent on the aide for prompts about what to do and feedback and reinforcement when she completed tasks. So it was decided to eliminate the aide and that self-recruited feedback would be a very valuable skill for Alma to have, especially when she graduated from school and went to work.

Alma had been performing most classroom tasks and assignments at an acceptable level of quality; however, she was used to getting immediate feedback and reinforcement from the aide on her performance and also to determine what to do next and to elicit a response regarding the task she just completed. A checklist was created for Alma that listed all the tasks she needed to perform in each class (e.g., materials ready, assignments turned in, class notes taken, etc.). Alma gets the checklist ready the night before for each class, and after she completes each task, she checks off the task she just completed, then at the end of class she shows it to the teacher. The teacher reviews the work and indicates his or her rating of Alma's performance on the checklist. The teacher then tells Alma if any tasks are missing or need to be completed next. This self-management system accomplished three things for Alma: (1) she is now provided feedback and verbal reinforcement from each teacher on tasks she completes for each class; (2) Alma records when she completes a task, which provides documentation of her performance; and (3) the teacher cues Alma as to which missing or new tasks need to be completed next.

Key Point Question 1: What Is Self-Management?

Self-management may be broadly construed as giving people skills and specific strategies to control or modify their own behavior. Both philosophically and in practice, it is important that people with disabilities be given as much control as possible over their own lives, whether it be major lifestyle decisions such as where they live or work or such daily decisions as what shirt to wear, what to each for lunch, and so on. Although none of us can control *all* aspects of our lives (we are all interdependent with others to varying degrees), we all want to have as much control or "say so" as possible. The self-management procedures that are outlined in this chapter are designed to increase the amount of control that people with disabilities have in their own lives and to help them live more independently. We also want to stress that self-management strategies are not an either-or process and that these strategies can easily be used in conjunction with other strategies outlined in this book. The overall goal of self-management strategies is to help individuals function more effectively and independently (Gross & Drabman, 1982).

Self-management procedures are effective with people with all types of disabilities. Do not get caught up in the belief that because people have a certain label (i.e., severe disabilities, visually impaired) they cannot use self-management procedures. There are many examples in the literature clearly demonstrating that even people with severe intellectual disabilities can learn to use self-management procedures effectively (Browder & Shapiro, 1985).

Self-management techniques include the use of antecedent cue regulation, self-monitoring, self-determined consequences, self-punishment, or a combination of any of these techniques (Buckley & Mank, 1989; Storey, 2007). The application of these techniques has been used to increase acquisition, maintenance, and generalization of skills.

In this chapter we will use the term self-management to refer to the procedures outlined by Baer (1984). However, terms such as self-regulation, self-control, self-observation, or self-assessment are often used interchangeably with self-management, although technically there are differences among these terms (Karoly & Kanfer, 1982).

Baer (1984) has outlined that self-management ideally involves

(a) *recognizing one's own problem*
   For example, if a person at work wants to have friends but does not have any friends and does not interact socially with anyone, it could be a problem.
(b) *translating problems into behaviors to be changed*
   As discussed in Chapter 3, you can only change people's behavior. Thus we could take the problem of lack of social interactions at work and target specific greeting skills as a behavior that could occur and potentially improve the problem.

(c) *finding natural contingencies or contriving them to support change*
Because the worker may not find it reinforcing to interact with coworkers, it would then be necessary to contrive contingencies to occur so that interactions are reinforced.

(d) *arranging the contingencies for change to occur*
In this example, it would be possible for the worker to pay himself a quarter each time that he initiates a greeting with a coworker (he could subtly transfer a quarter from one pocket to another) and then buy a reinforcer at the end of the day with the money that he earned (self-delivery of a back-up reinforcer).

Key Point Question 2: Why Are Self-Management Strategies Important?

Self-management can be especially useful when an individual has become dependent on an external prompt (from a teacher, job coach, or other support person) or external reinforcement or needs to avoid these dependencies in the first place. Self-management strategies can be very effective methods of transferring that external prompt or reinforcement to a self-delivered prompt or self-delivered reinforcement. Self-management procedures have also been implemented when an individual has not acquired skills with the external prompts or has trouble responding to appropriate stimuli in the environment. Self-management strategies can be added to the task to provide additional stimuli, which can become a permanent part of the task. For example, a supported employee may have difficulty learning in what order to perform tasks. A picture cue book could be made up to cue the employee to perform the task. The booklet can be kept as a permanent part of the job, and there may be no reason to fade the self-management strategy.

Too often persons with disabilities become dependent on others to tell them what to do. This is known as learned helplessness. With self-management procedures, behaviors may come under the control of naturally occurring stimuli more easily. For instance, if a worker needs to change job tasks at certain times during the day but has trouble telling time, he or she maydepend on a job coach or coworker to tell when it is time to change tasks. If the worker has a watch timer set to those times and a picture book indicating what task is next, then he or she is not dependent on somebody else telling when to change tasks.

The following four sections discuss types of self-management procedures.

Key Point Question 3: What Are Antecedent Procedures?

Antecedent refers to information or stimuli provided before the behavior is to occur. The logic here is that you are providing information to individuals beforehand so that they do not not have to receive a prompt from others about what they should do, thus increasing their independence (e.g., their ability to respond appropriately to discriminative stimuli in their environment). There are several types of antecedent procedures that can be used, such as auditory prompts, self-instruction, and self-determined criteria. Different applications providing visual and other prompts can be downloaded into phones and other devices for learners (www.iprompts.com).

AUDITORY PROMPTS. A barrier to successful employment for individuals with autism is dependence on others for acceptable task completion (Smith, Belcher, & Juhrs, 1995). The need for ongoing step-by-step instructions and prompting to accurately complete a task is a critical problem. For teachers and other support providers (such as job coaches) of individuals with a disability, the attainment and mastery of these basic skills can be tentative because these students often have difficulty sustaining focus, remembering task steps in a chained sequence, and/or generalizing a learned skill (Koegel & Koegel, 2005). With any one of these difficulties in mastering a skill, repetitive instruction and ongoing supervision by a teacher or a job coach is necessary. Unfortunately, the result of this dependence on a teacher/job coach is that the individual is often incapable of independent performance in employment settings.

Extending competence requires the use of procedures that promote independence, productivity, acceptable behavior, and self-direction without the continuous supervision of others. One type of procedure is the use of auditory prompting. Auditory prompting is a self-management strategy that gives an antecedent cue to increase the probability of a desired behavioral outcome. Auditory prompts are defined as prerecorded antecedent cues to increase the probability of a desired behavioral outcome. These digitally recorded auditory prompt systems consist of prerecorded prompts of step-by-step instructions guiding the student to complete a task and/or consist of prerecorded prompts encouraging a student to focus and stay on task (Post, Montgomery, & Storey, 2009). These prerecordings are listened to through the use of headsets attached to playback devices such as MP3 players. Recorded auditory prompts are considered a strategy for a self-management system that enables the person with disabilities to self-initiate, self-maintain, and self-monitor her or his own performance.

Advantages to using auditory prompting procedures include

1. Increased generalization
2. Increased independence
3. Decrease in off-task behavior
4. Increase in self-management
5. Increase in task acquisition
6. Maintenance of learned tasks

Table 10.1 provides information on developing an auditory training program for task completion. Post, Storey, and Karabin (2002) provide an example of a supported employment worker who needed assistance staying on task for his job labeling bags and bagging coffee beans. The worker listened to music on headphones with self-selected phrases ("make lots of money"). These auditory prompts were combined with self-monitoring and self-recruited feedback strategies. These combined strategies increased his on-task behavior from a mean of 35 percent to 94 percent.

SELF-INSTRUCTION. Self-instruction involves delivering instructions or cues to oneself as opposed to receiving those cues externally (from a teacher or job coach). For example, using a picture cue book to signal what task is to be performed next would be providing an antecedent cue to the learner before the task. An employee with a disability could perform a task and when that task is completed, refer to the picture notebook and turn the page to see what task is cued (i.e., next). The employee could then return the notebook to his or her pocket and refer to it again when completing the task at hand. Instructions can be delivered by various means, using a Walkman with a tape that has prerecorded instructions (Davis, Williams, Brady, & Burta, 1992); using a checklist that has the instructions either written or illustrated (Wheeler, Bates, Marshall, & Miller, 1988); or using a cell

MONDAY	PUT PLUS MARK WHEN CHECKED
1. Look in mirror after eating lunch.	
2. Check face, mustache, shirt, and tie for food.	
3. If there is food on face or mustache, wet washcloth.	
4. Use wet washcloth to wash all food off face and/or mustache.	
5. Brush any crumbs off shirt and tie.	

Adapted from Garff and Storey (1998).

Figure 10.1. Workplace Hygiene Self-Evaluation Checklist.

phone, personal digital assistant (PDA), or other electronic device on which cues are programmed (e.g., programming a cell phone to give a signal and say "time to go to lunch" at noon and then signal and say "time to get back to work" at 12:30). Garff and Storey (1998) used a self-management checklist in conjunction with other procedures to increase the appropriate hygiene skills of three adults with disabilities. The intervention consisted of (1) the development of a check-list (task analysis) with the steps necessary to address their particular hygiene issue, (2) modeling the steps to each participant, (3) providing praise and feedback as each participant completed the steps and learned to do all of them independently, and (4) teaching the participants to self-reinforce for correct performance. Figure 10.1 provides an example of a checklist used by a supported employment worker to check his hygiene before leaving for work (Garff & Storey, 1998).

Self-instruction can be used to help persons with disabilities perform tasks, such as in a work setting, as well as academic material in a school setting. Self-instruction involves teaching individuals to provide their own verbal cues prior to when the target behavior needs to occur. Agran, King-Sears, Wehmeyer, & Copeland (2003) describe four self-instruction steps:

1. Identify the problem (e.g., need to open program on computer)
2. State a solution (e.g., click on the icon)
3. Evaluate the action (e.g., the program opened)

4. Reinforce self (e.g., I did a good job)

For example, Rusch, McKee, Chadsey-Rusch, and Renzaglia (1988) taught a student with severe disabilities to request materials at his job site through self-instructional strategies. The sequence of instruction was as follows:

1. Providing rationale for self-instruction
2. Teaching the self-instruction skills and requesting skills through modeling and prompting
3. Providing feedback, correction, and praise
4. Teaching the student to tap a picture to begin the self-instruction
5. Teaching self-reinforcement strategy (paying of money) for use of self-instruction strategy

SELF-DETERMINED CRITERIA. A third antecedent procedure involves an individual setting goals for herself or himself. This procedure is often combined with a consequence procedure such as self-monitoring or self-reinforcement. With self-determined criteria, individuals are taught to set their own goals based on either other people's performance or their own performance. An example of this procedure combined with a self-evaluation procedure is when a worker sets a production goal for himself or herself based on the previous morning's production. When that person reaches the set goal, he or she takes a break. For example, Oma has been diagnosed as having Asperger's syndrome, and she works for an electronics company writing user manuals that accompany DVD players and other electronic devices. Oma's work requires her to focus on both her writing and how the devices work. When Oma completes a draft of a section of a manual, she makes sure that she takes a break during which she makes sure that she reinforces herself for her productivity (by having a juice drink or a small snack).

Key Point Question 4: What Are Self-Monitoring Strategies?

Consequence Procedures

SELF-MONITORING/SELF-RECORDING. Self-monitoring and self-recording are generally used in combination with self-observation

When the timer sounds, place a + beside the number if you were on task and a 0 beside the number if you were not on task.

Monday	Tuesday	Wednesday	Thursday	Friday
1	1	1	1	1
2	2	2	2	2
3	3	3	3	3
4	4	4	4	4
5	5	5	5	5
6	6	6	6	6
7	7	7	7	7
8	8	8	8	8
9	9	9	9	9
10	10	10	10	10

Figure 10.2. Self-Monitoring Example for a Classroom Setting.

(Browder & Shapiro, 1985). Self-monitoring consists of setting up a monitoring system that can be used independently by oneself. Two steps are usually involved in self-monitoring: an individual (1) must observe his or her own behavior and (2) then record that behavior. For instance, Mank and Horner (1987) had workers with severe disabilities use a stopwatch to self-monitor the number of minutes worked and the number of units completed.

Self-monitoring and self-recording can also be used to help individuals perform tasks. For example, in a classroom setting it is important that students are on task (e.g., focused on their work). A teacher could set the time (or have it prerecorded) when it goes off on a variable schedule (so that students cannot predict when it goes off). A variable interval schedule is in other words, time based, and the opportunity for reinforcement varies (e.g., the interval varies). For instance, the teacher could set the timer to go off after two minutes, then after ten minutes, then six minutes, then eleven minutes, and so on. The teacher would set a mean (say five minutes) and then vary the time. Figure 10.2 provides an example of a self-monitoring chart.

SELF-EVALUATION. Self-evaluation is comparing performance with a criteria and evaluating that performance. This is another method that is often used in combination with other self-management procedures (self-observation, self-reinforcement). People must observe their own behavior and then evaluate that behavior. Grossi and Heward (1998) taught four adults with mild mental retardation to self-evaluate their productivity by using a self-monitoring form, adjusting their performance from data on their self-monitoring form, and verbalizing if they met the performance criteria or not.

Key Point Question 5: What Are Self-Determined Consequences?

SELF-RECRUITED FEEDBACK. One way to involve people to a greater extent in their own intervention is through self-recruited feedback procedures. Self-recruited feedback involves three components: (1) self-monitoring of the target behavior, (2) self-evaluation of performance against a predefined criterion, and (3) recruitment of contingent feedback from the external environment (Mank & Horner, 1987). An example of self-recruited feedback is when a worker completes a specific task, such as finishing all the dishes in the kitchen, self-evaluating and scoring the behavior (e.g., did he or she complete the dishes correctly and on time?) and then going to the supervisor to obtain feedback and reinforcement ("good work" or "take a break now"). This self-recruitment nnot only provides feedback and reinforcement to the individual with a disability but also involves the supervisor who otherwise might not provide the feedback and reinforcement in a timely manner. It also provides feedback to the supervisor on the employee's work performance.

SELF-REINFORCEMENT. Self-reinforcement is when learners deliver reinforcers to themselves following a specific behavior. For example, if Heinrich prepares a pre-specified number of lunch boxes at the airport eatery where he works, then he could eat a mint from the small container that he keeps in his pocket.

Self-reinforcement must always be combined with another method, such as self-evaluation or self-monitoring (Browder & Shapiro, 1985). For example, Christian and Poling (1997) taught two adults with mild mental retardation to self-monitor their productivity and to self-select a reinforcer (lunch with supervisor, restaurant "money") for completing a task before a prespecified time period ended.

Key Point Question 6: What Are Self-Punishment Strategies?

Self-management procedures can be used not only to increase behaviors but they can also be used to punish or decrease behaviors.

Punishment is the presentation or removal of an event after a response that decreases the frequency of the response. In other words, following a behavior that the individual did not want to occur or in the absence of a behavior that he or she wanted to occur, the individual punishes himself or herself so that the behavior is less likely to occur in the future. It is important to emphasize that the use of self-punishment alone is generally a poor idea and, if used, it needs to be incorporated with other strategies, especially the use of positive reinforcement (because punishment does not increase or build behaviors, it only decreases them). In addition, people tend to avoid punishing themselves, even if their plan calls for the punishment (Worthington, 1979).

Self-punishment strategies have generally used response cost procedures. Response cost is when points, tokens, privileges, or other reinforcers already given to an individual are removed contingent upon instances of a specific behavior or behaviors. For example, Carlos, a young man with Down syndrome was overweight, and he and his family were concerned about his health because of his weight. Carlos and Tamy, his independent living coordinator, came up with a plan that used self-punishment in conjunction with other strategies. First, Carlos joined an aerobics class at the local health club that he went to three days a week. Second, he self-monitored his caloric intake using an online program. Third, he weighed himself every Friday and if he lost one pound or more that week he put $5 into a jar so that he could save for going to the state People First conference where he wanted to present on his efforts to lose weight. Fourth, if he did not lose at least one pound at the Friday weigh in he fined himself $5 from his fund for the conference (self-punishment). Fifth, he self-graphed the amount of money he had in his travel fund so that he could monitor and receive visual feedback on his progress.

Key Point Question 7: How Do You Best Teach Self-Management Skills?

It is important to emphasize that self-management skills, as with any skill, must be directly taught; it cannot be assumed that the learner will be able to use the skills without adequate instruction (Mithaug, 2002). The strategies provided in Chapter 3 can be used for teaching self-management skills in the same manner as any other skill.

Koegel, Koegel, and Parks (1992) have identified the following steps for implementing a self-management program:

A. Getting Ready
   a. Define behaviors
   b. Measure behaviors
   c. Choose a reinforcer
   d. Select an initial goal
B. Teaching Self-Management
   a. Get materials
   b. Teach identification of the behavior
   c. Record the behavior
   d. Reinforce self-management
C. Creating Independence
   a. Increase the amount of time the individual self-manages behavior
   b. Fade reliance on prompts
   c. Increase the number of responses necessary for a reinforcer
   d. Fade the presence of the treatment provider

For example, Mr. Hasenwinkle wants to teach Emma, a first grader with autism in his general education class, to increase her compliance to his instructions.

First he defined what he meant by compliance ("engaging in requested behavior within ten seconds of a given request" from Ellingson, Miltenberger, Stricker, Galensky, & Garlinghouse, 2000). He then decided that he would measure the behavior by frequency counts of compliance and noncompliance. For reinforcing the compliance, he decided to use a token economy where Emma could choose from a variety of reinforcers on a daily and weekly (on Fridays) basis based on the number points that she earned daily and weekly.

He then taught Emma how to use the self-management system (an index card was placed on her desk so that she could make hash marks each time that she complied with a direction) through modeling, rolplaying, feedback, and praise. He did this in short time periods three times a day for a week. He then decided to continue teaching Emma how to use the self-management system in small groups, and he rotated nondisabled peers through the groups so that he could then use the same system with all of the students in the class because it was not only

Emma who was having problems with following directions. He initial-ly reinforced Emma both for the use of the self-management system (through praise and bonus points) and for her compliance.

Once the self-management system was in place and working well, Mr. Hasenwinkle slowly increased the number of points necessary for reinforcers. Because the system was working so well, he did not want to entirely phase out the system. He wanted to continue to make sure that students were getting reinforced for following directions so that they would continue to do so. He could then also expand the system to other behaviors such as turning in homework, being nice to others, and so on.

BEST PRACTICE RECOMMENDATIONS

1. When developing an instructional package, consideration should be given to including a self-management component from the beginning. If a person's instructional history indicates that self-management may be warranted to allow for acquisition or maintenance of skills, then the self-management system can be developed at the beginning of instruction. Often, however, self-management procedures are instituted with the fading of instructional procedures.

2. When developing a management package, careful consideration must be given to the environment in which the procedure will be used. The self-management "device" (checklist, cell phone, picture board, etc.) must be created so that it can be used with-out drawing undue negative attention to the user. The environ-ment should first be surveyed to assess whether there are any existing systems in place that can be adapted for use. For exam-ple, it is not unusual to see "recipe" picture cards on the wall of a preparation table in a restaurant kitchen. These cards typical-ly indicate exactly which materials are to be used, in what quan-tities, and in what order they should be prepared. Implementing a self-management program that is similar to what may already exist for persons without disabilities will lessen the possibility of negative attention focusing on the person with a disability.

FUTURE RESEARCH ISSUES

1. How can recent electronic developments (e.g., handheld planners, cell phones, etc.) best be incorporated with self-management strategies?
2. How can peers at school or work sites be involved in supporting individuals using self-management strategies?

DISCUSSION QUESTIONS

1. Is it better to use self-management strategies to increase new behaviors or to change undesirable behaviors?
2. What is the best way to increase generalization of skills using self-management strategies?
3. How do you decide what type of self-management strategy is most appropriate for an individual?
4. How do you avoid potential stigmatization of the individual using the self-management procedure?
5. Should you fade the use of the self-management procedure or keep it in place if the procedures are effective for the individual?

SCHOOL AND COMMUNITY-BASED ACTIVITY SUGGESTIONS

1. Observe and/or ask how high school students without disabilities use self-management strategies? How might these strategies be similar or different than for students with disabilities?
2. Related to the previous suggestion, go to several different work sites. Observe and/or ask how workers without disabilities use self-management strategies? How might these strategies be similar or different than for workers with disabilities?
3. Develop and implement a self-management procedure for yourself. What type of data will you collect to determine if the procedure was effective or not?

REFERENCES

Agran, M., King-Sears, M.E., Wehmeyer, M.L., & Copeland, S.R. (2003). *Student-directed learning.* Baltimore, MD: Paul Brookes.

Baer, D. M. (1984). Does research on self-control need more control? *Analysis and Intervention in Developmental Disabilities, 4,* 211–218.

Browder, D. M., & Shapiro, E. S. (1985). Applications of self-management to individuals with severe handicaps: A review. *Journal of the Association for Persons with Severe Handicaps, 10,* 200–208.

Buckley, J., & Mank, D. M. (1989). Self-management programming for supported employment. In P. M. Ferguson & D. Olson (Eds.), *Supported community life: Connecting policy to practice in disability research* (pp. 41–61). Eugene, OR: Specialized Training Program, University of Oregon.

Christian, L., & Poling, A. (1997). Using self-management procedures to improve the productivity of adults with developmental disabilities in a competitive employment setting. *Journal of Applied Behavior Analysis, 30,* 169–172.

Davis, C. A., Williams, R. E., Brady, M. P., & Burta, M. (1992). The effects of self-operated auditory prompting tapes on the performance fluency of persons with severe mental retardation. *Education and Training in Mental Retardation, 27,* 39–50.

Ellingson, S. A., Miltenberger, R. G., Stricker, J., Galensky, T. L., & Garlinghouse, M. (2000). Functional assessment and intervention for challenging behaviors in the classroom by general classroom teachers. *Journal of Positive Behavior Interventions, 2,* 85–97.

Garff, J. T., & Storey, K. (1998). The use of self-management strategies for increasing the hygiene of persons with disabilities in supported employment settings. *Education and Training in Mental Retardation and Developmental Disabilities, 33,* 179–188.

Gross, A. M., & Drabman, R. S. (1982). Teaching self-recording, self-evaluation, and self-reward to nonclinic children and adolescent. In P. Karoly & F. H. Kanfer (Eds.), *Self-management and behavior change: From theory to practice* (p. 285–314). New York: Pergamon Press.

Grossi, T. A., & Heward, W. L. (1998). Using self-evaluation to improve the work productivity of trainees in a community-based restaurant training program. *Education and Training in Mental Retardation and Developmental Disabilities, 33,* 248–263.

Karoly, P., & Kanfer, F. H. (1982). *Self-management and behavior change: From theory to practice.* New York: Pergamon Press.

Koegel, R. L., & Koegel, L. K. (2005). *Pivotal response treatments for autism: Communication, social, and academic development.* Baltimore, MD: Brookes Publishing.

Koegel, L. K., Koegel, R. L., & Parks, D. R. (1992). *How to teach self-management to people with severe disabilities: A training manual.* Santa Barbara, CA: University of California, Santa Barbara.

Mank, D. M., & Horner, R. H. (1987). Self-recruited feedback: A cost-effective procedure for maintaining behavior. *Research in Developmental Disabilities, 8,* 91–112.

Mithaug, D. K. (2002). "Yes" means success: Teaching children with multiple disabilities to self-regulate during independent work. *Teaching Exceptional Children, 35,* 22–27.

Post, M., Montgomery, J., & Storey, K. (2009). A decision tree for the use of auditory prompting strategies. *Journal of Vocational Rehabilitation, 31,* 51–54.

Post, M., Storey, K., & Karabin, M. (2002). Cool headphone for effective prompts: Supporting students and adults in work and community environments. *Teaching Exceptional Children, 34,* 60–65.

Rusch, F. R., McKee, M., Chadsey-Rusch, J., & Renzaglia, A. (1988). Teaching a student with severe handicaps to self instruct: A brief report. *Education and Training in Mental Retardation, 23,* 51–58.

Smith, M. D., Belcher, R. G., & Juhrs, P. D. (1995). *A guide to successful employment for individuals with autism.* Baltimore, MD: Paul Brookes.

Storey, K. (2007). Review of research on self-management interventions in supported employment settings for workers with disabilities. *Career Development for Exceptional Individuals, 30,* 27–34.

Wheeler, J. J., Bates, P., Marshall, K. J., & Miller, S. R. (1988). Teaching appropriate social behaviors to a young man with moderate mental retardation in a supported competitive employment setting. *Education and Training in Mental Retardation, 23,* 105–116.

Worthington, E. L. (1979). Behavioral self-control and the contract problem. *Teaching of Psychology, 6,* 91–94.

Appendix

JOURNALS AND RESOURCES

It is important to join professional organizations, read professional journals, and visit web sites. Here is a list of suggestions. Joining an organization will help you in your professional development and assist you in staying current in the field.

GENERAL, PUBLIC POLICY AND LEGAL

Journals

Disability and Society
Disability Studies Quarterly
Education and Treatment of Children
Educational Evaluation and Policy Analysis
Educational Forum
Educational Horizons
Educational Policy
Evaluation and Program Planning
Evaluation Review
Exceptional Children
Exceptional Education Quarterly
Exceptionality
Journal of Disability Policy Studies
Journal of International Special Needs Education
Journal of Social Issues
Journal of Special Education
Journal of Special Education Leadership
Mouth Magazine
Ragged Edge, The

Remedial and Special Education
Rural Special Education Quarterly Journal
Social Policy
Teacher Education and Special Education

Resources

Council for Exceptional Children
1110 North Glebe Road, Suite 300
Arlington, VA 22201
800/224-6830
service@cec.sped.org
www.cec.sped.org

National Disability Rights Network
National Association of Protection and Advocacy Systems
900 Second Street, NE, Suite 211
Washington, DC 20002
202/408-9514
www.napas.org
info@ndrn.org

National Council on Disability
1331 F Street, NW, Suite 850
Washington, DC 20004
202/272-2004
www.ncd.gov
ncd@ncd.gov

American Council on Rural Special Education
Montana Center on Disabilities/MSU-B
1500 University Drive
Billings, MT 59101
888/866-3822
www.acres-sped.org

Association on Higher Education and Disability
107 Commerce Center Drive, Suite 204
Huntersville, NC 28078
704/947-7779
ahead@ahead.org
www.ahead.org

Society for Disability Studies
The City University of New York
101 West 31st Street (12th floor)
New York, NY 10001
212/652-2005
www.disstudies.org

Disability Rights Education and Defense Fund
2212 Sixth Street
Berkeley, CA 94710
510/644-2555
dredf@dredf.org
www.dredf.org

National Dissemination Center for Children with Disabilities
1825 Connecticut Avenue, NW, Suite 700
Washington, DC 20009
800/695-0285
www.nichcy.org
nichcy@aed.org

National Organization on Disability
888 Sixteenth Street, NW, Suite 800
Washington, DC 20006
202/293-5960
www.nod.org
ability@nod.org

National Association of State Directors of Special Education
1800 Diagonal Road, Suite 320
King Street Station 1
Alexandria, VA 22314
703/519-3800
www.nasdse.org

Bazelon Center for Mental Health Law
1101 Fifteenth Street, NW, Suite 1212
Washington, DC 20005-5002
202/467-5730
www.bazelon.org
info@bazelon.org

World Institute on Disability
510 Sixteenth Street, Suite 100
Oakland, CA 94612
510/763-4100
www.wid.org
wid@wid.org

VISUAL IMPAIRMENTS

Journals

Journal of Visual Impairment and Blindness

Resources

American Council of the Blind
2200 Wilson Boulevard, Suite 650
Arlington, VA 22201
800/424-8666
www.acb.org
info@acb.org

National Federation of the Blind
200 East Wells Street
Baltimore, MD 21230
410/659-9314
www.nfb.org
nfb@nfb.org

American Foundation for the Blind
11 Penn Plaza, Suite 300
New York, NY 10001
800/232-5463
www.afb.org
afbinfo@afb.net

National Association for the Visually Handicapped
22 West 21st Street, 6th Floor
New York, NY 10010
212/889-3141
www.navh.org
navh@navh.org

LEARNING DISABILITIES

Journals

Journal of Direct Instruction
Journal of Learning Disabilities
Journal of Precision Teaching
Journal of Reading, Writing, and Learning Disabilities
Learning Disabilities Forum
Learning Disabilities Quarterly
Learning Disabilities Research and Practice
Reading and Writing Quarterly: Overcoming Learning Difficulties

Resources

Learning Disabilities Association of America
4156 Library Road
Pittsburgh, PA 15234-1349
412/341-1515
www.ldanatl.org
info@LDAAmerica.org

International Dyslexia Association
40 York Road, 4th Floor
Baltimore, MD 21204
410/296-0232
www.interdys.org

The Council for Learning Disabilities
11184 Antioch Road
Box 405
Overland Park, KS 66210
913/491-1011
www.cldinternational.org
CLDInfo@ie-events.com

All Kinds of Minds
2800 Meridian Parkway, Suite 100
Durham, NC 27713
888/956-4637
www.allkindsofminds.org

Children and Adults with Attention Deficit Disorders (CHADD)
8181 Professional Plaza, Suite 150
Landover, MD 20785
800/233-4050
www.chadd.org

Attention Deficit Disorder Association
P.O. Box 7557
Wilmington, DE 19803-9997
800/939-1019
info@add.org
www.add.org

National Center for Learning Disabilities
318 Park Avenue, South, Suite 1401
New York, NY 10016
888/575-7373
www.ncld.org

COMMUNICATION DISORDERS

Journals

American Journal of Speech Language Pathology
Augmentative and Alternative Communication
Communication Education
Human Communication Research
Journal of Child Language
Journal of Childhood Communication Disorders
Journal of Communication
Journal of Communication Disorders
Journal of Fluency Disorders
Journal of Speech and Hearing Disorders
Journal of Speech and Hearing Research
Language
Language and Communication
Language and Speech
Language, Speech and Hearing Services in the Schools
Seminars in Child Language
Seminars in Speech and Language
Speech Communication Teacher

Speech and Hearing Services in the Schools
Topics in Language Disorders

Resources

American Speech, Language, and Hearing Association
2200 Research Boulevard
Rockville, MD 20850-3289
800/638-8255
www.asha.org

Stuttering Foundation of America
P.O. Box 11749
Memphis, TN 38111-0749
800/992-9392
www.stutteringhelp.org
info@stutteringhelp.org

BEHAVIOR DISORDERS/EMOTIONAL DISTURBANCE

Journals

Behavior Modification
Behavior Therapy
Behavioral Disorders
Journal of Applied Behavior Analysis
Journal of Emotional and Behavioral Disorders
Journal of Positive Behavior Interventions

Resources

The Association for Behavior Analysis
550 West Centre Avenue, Suite 1
Portage, MI 49024
269/492-9310
www.abainternational.org
mail@abainternational.org

National Alliance for the Mentally Ill
3803 North Fairfax Drive, Suite 100
Arlington, VA 22203
800/950-6264
www.nami.org

National Mental Health Association
2000 North Beauregard Street, 6th Floor
Alexandria, VA 22311
800/969-6642
www.nmha.org

Cambridge Center for Behavioral Studies
550 Newtown Road, Suite 700
Littleton, MA 01460
978/369-2227
www.behavior.org

The Association of Positive Behavior Support
P.O. Box 328
Bloomsburg, PA 17815
570/389-4081
www.apbs.org
tknoster@bloomu.edu

DEAF CULTURE/HEARING IMPAIRMENTS

Journals

American Annals of the Deaf
Audiology
British Journal of Audiology
Journal of the American Deafness and Rehabilitation Association
Journal of the British Association of Teachers of the Deaf
Perspectives for Teachers of the Hearing Impaired
Sign Language Studies
Silent News
Teaching English to Deaf and Second Language Students

Resources

National Association of the Deaf
8630 Fenton Street, Suite 820
Silver Spring, MD 20910-3876
301/587-1788
www.nad.org
NADinfo@nad.org

COMPUTERS AND TECHNOLOGY

Journals

Classroom Computer Learning
Computers and Education
Computers in Human Behavior
Computers in Human Services
Computers in the Schools
Journal of Computer Assisted Learning
Journal of Computer-Based Education
Journal of Special Education Technology
Teaching and Computers
Technology and Disability

Resources

Center for Applied Special Technology
40 Harvard Mills Square, Suite 3
Wakefield, MA 01880-3233
781/245-2212
www.cast.org
cast@cast.org

PHYSICAL DISABILITIES

Journals

American Journal of Occupational Therapy
Adapted Physical Activity Quarterly
Canadian Journal of Occupational Therapy
Journal of Developmental and Physical Disabilities

Mainstream: Magazine of the Able-Disabled
Physical and Occupational Therapy in Pediatrics
Physical Disabilities: Education and Related Services
Physical Therapy
Physical Therapy Practice

Resources

American Disabled for Attendant Programs Today (ADAPT)
201 South Cherokee
Denver, CO 80233
303/733-9324
www.adapt.org

United Cerebral Palsy
1660 L Street, NW, Suite 700
Washington, DC 20036
800/872-5827
www.ucp.org
info@ucp.org

TRANSITION AND EMPLOYMENT

Journals

American Rehabilitation
Canadian Journal of Rehabilitation
Career Development for Exceptional Individuals
Career Development Quarterly
Cognitive Rehabilitation
Disability and Rehabilitation
International Journal of Rehabilitation Research
Journal for Vocational Educational Special Needs Education
Journal of Applied Rehabilitation Counseling
Journal of Back and Musculoskeletal Rehabilitation
Journal of Career Development
Journal of Employment Counseling
Journal of Head Trauma Rehabilitation
Journal of Occupational Rehabilitation
Journal of Rehabilitation
Journal of Rehabilitation Administration

Journal of Rehabilitation Research and Development
Journal of Vocational Behavior
Journal of Vocational Education Research
Journal of Vocational Rehabilitation
NeuroRehabilitation: An Interdisciplinary Journal
Psychosocial Rehabilitation Journal
Rehabilitation Counseling Bulletin
Rehabilitation Education
Rehabilitation Psychology
Rehabilitation World
Vocational Education Journal
Vocational Evaluation and Word Adjustment Bulletin
Work: A Journal of Prevention, Assessment and Rehabilitation
Worklife

Resources

The Association for Persons in Supported Employment
451 Hungerford Drive, Suite 700
Rockville, MD 20850
1627 Monument Avenue, Room 301
804/278-9187
www.apse.org
apse@apse.org

Office of Disability Employment Policy
U.S. Department of Labor
200 Constitution Avenue, NW
Washington, DC 20210
866/633-7365
www.dol.gov/odep

Virginia Commonwealth University Rehabilitation Research
and Training Center on Workplace Supports and Job Retention
1314 West Main Street
Richmond, VA 23284-2011
804/828-1851
www.worksupport.com

Abledata
National Rehabilitation Information Center
8630 Fenton Street, Suite 930
Silver Spring, MD 20910
800/227-0216
www.abledata.com
abledata@orcmacro.com

National Clearinghouse on Postsecondary Education
for Individuals with Disabilities
The George Washington University
HEATH Resource Center
2134 G Street, NW
Washington, DC 20052-0001
800/544-3284
www.heath.gwu.edu
askheath@gwu.edu

Job Accommodation Network
West Virginia University
P.O. Box 6080
Morgantown, WV 26506-6080
800/526-7234
www.jan.wvu.edu
jan@jan.wvu.edu

National Rehabilitation Information Center
8201 Corporate Drive, Suite 600
Lanham, MD 20785
800/346-2742
www.naric.com
naricinfo@heitechservices.com

National Rehabilitation Association
633 South Washington Street
Alexandria, VA 22314
703/836-0850
www.nationalrehab.org
info@nationalrehab.org

National Business and Disability Council
201 I.U. Willets Road
Albertson, NY 11507
516/465-1516
www.nbdc.com

DEVELOPMENTAL DISABILITIES/
INTELLECTUAL DISABILITIES

Journals

American Journal on Intellectual and Developmental Disabilities
Applied Research in Intellectual Disabilities
Education and Training in Developmental Disabilities
Intellectual and Developmental Disabilities
Journal of Intellectual & Developmental Disability
Journal of Intellectual Disabilities Research
Journal of Policy and Practice in Intellectual Disabilities
Research and Practice for Persons with Severe Disabilities
Research in Developmental Disabilities

Resources

TASH
1025 Vermont Avenue, NW, Suite 300
Washington, DC 20005
202/263-5600
www.tash.org

American Association on Intellectual and Developmental Disabilities
501 3rd Street, NW, Suite 200
Washington, DC 20001
800/424-3688
wwww.aaidd.org

National Association for Down Syndrome
P.O. Box 206
Wilmette, IL 60091
630/325-9112
www.nads.org
info@nads.org

The Arc of the United States
1010 Wayne Avenue, Suite 650
Silver Spring, MD 20910
301/565-3842
www.thearc.org
info@thearc.org

National Down Syndrome Society
666 Broadway
New York, NY 10012
800/221-4602
www.ndss.org
info@ndss.org

International Association for the Scientific Study of Intellectual Disabilities
IASSID Member Affairs Office
Box 671, URMC
601 Elmwood Avenue
Rochester, NY 14642
www.iassid.org

PARENTS/FAMILIES

Journals

Child and Family Behavior Therapy
Child and Youth Services
Child Study Journal
Contemporary Family Therapy
Exceptional Parent, The
Families in Society
Family Process
Journal of Child and Family Studies
Journal of Divorce and Remarriage
Journal of Family History
Journal of Family Practice
Journal of Family Psychology
Journal of Family Violence
Journal of Marriage and the Family
Parent

Resources

Parent Advocacy Coalition for Education Rights
8161 Normandale Boulevard
Minneapolis, MN 55437
952/838-9000
www.pacer.org
pacer@pacer.org

Beach Center on Family and Disability
University of Kansas
Haworth Hall
1200 Sunnyside Avenue, Room 3136
Lawrence, KS 66045-7534
785/864-7600
www.beachcenter.org
beachcenter@ku.edu

AUTISM SPECTRUM DISORDERS

Journals

Autism Advocate
Autism Research Review International
Focus on Autism and Other Developmental Disabilities
Good Autism Practice Journal
Journal of Autism and Developmental Disorders
Research in Autism Spectrum Disorders

Resources

Autism Society of America
4340 East-West Highway, Suite 350
Bethesda, MD 20814
800/328-8476
www.autism-society.org

UC Davis M.I.N.D. Institute
2825 50th Street
Sacramento, CA 95817
916/703-0280
www.ucdmc.ucdavis.edu/mindinstitute

National Autism Association
1330 West Schatz Lane
Nixa, MO 65714
877/622-2884
www.nationalautismassociation.org/
naa@nationalautism.org

Autism Speaks
2 Park Avenue, 11th Floor
New York, NY 10016
212/252-8584
www.autismspeaks.org
contactus@autismspeaks.org

MISCELLANEOUS

Epilepsy Foundation of America
8301 Professional Place
Landover, MD 20785-7223
800/332-1000
www.epilepsyfoundation.org

Tourette Syndrome Association, Inc.
42-40 Bell Boulevard
Bayside, NY 11361
718/224-2999
www.tsa-usa.org

Anxiety Disorders Association of America
8730 Georgia Avenue, Suite 600
Silver Spring, MD 20910
www.adaa.org

Self-Advocate Leadership Network
Human Services Research Institute
7420 SW Bridgeport Road, Suite #210
Portland, OR 97224
503/924-3783
www.hsri.org/leaders

American Therapeutic Recreation Association
629 North Main Street
Hattiesburg, MS 39401
601/450-2872
www.atra-online.com

B. F. Skinner Foundation
12 Arrow Street, Suite 200
Cambridge, MA 02138
617/661-9209
www.bfskinner.org
info@bfskinner.org

Association for Direct Instruction
P.O. Box 10252
Eugene, OR 97440
541/485-1293
www.adihome.org
info@adihome.org

National Association for the Dually Diagnosed
132 Fair Street
Kingston, NY 12401
845/331-4336
www.thenadd.org
info@thenadd.org

EDUCATIONAL/GENERAL

Journals

Academic Computing
Academic Exchange Quarterly
Academic Therapy
Action in Teacher Education
Adult Basic Education
Adult Education and Development
Adult Education Quarterly
Adult Learning
Adult Literacy and Basic Education
Adults Learning

Advanced Skills Teacher
American Education
American Educational Research Journal
American Educator
American Journal of Distance Education
American Journal of Education
American Secondary Education
American Teacher
Applied Measurement in Education
Art Education
Arts and Activities
Australian Journal of Adult and Community Education
Australian Journal of Education
Australian Journal of Educational Technology
Australian Journal of Language and Literacy
Australian Journal of Reading
Basic Education
Better Teaching: Tips and Techniques
British Educational Research Journal
British Journal of Educational Studies
British Journal of Educational Technology
British Journal of Sociology of Education
Child Education
Child Language Teaching and Therapy
Child Life
Child Study Journal
Childhood Education
Classroom: The Magazine for Teachers
Cognition and Instruction
Comparative Education
Contemporary Education
Creative Child and Adult Quarterly
Creative Classroom
Creative Kids
Curriculum Inquiry
Curriculum Review
Discourse: The Australian Journal of Educational Studies
Distance Education
East/West Education
Educating At-Risk Youth
Education
Education and Urban Society

Education Canada
Education Digest
Education USA
Education Week
Educational Assessment
Educational Communication and Technology
Educational Considerations
Educational Forum
Educational Foundations
Educational Gerontology
Educational Horizons
Educational Leadership
Educational Management and Administration
Educational Measurement: Issues and Practices
Educational Philosophy and Theory
Educational Policy
Educational Record
Educational Research
Educational Research Quarterly
Educational Researcher
Educational Review
Educational Technology
Educational Theory
Effective School Report
Electronic Learning
Elementary School Guidance and Counseling
Elementary School Journal
English Education
English in Education
Equity and Excellence
Equity and Excellence in Education
European Education
European Journal of Education
Feminist Teacher
Focus on Learning Problems in Math
Forum for Reading
Forum of Education
Gifted Child Quarterly
Harvard Educational Review
High School Journal
High School Magazine
History of Education Quarterly

Independent School
Innovations in Education and Training International
Instructional Science
Instructor, The
Instructor Magazine
Integrated Education
International Education
International Journal of Educational Reform
International Journal of Educational Research
Intervention in School and Clinic
Issues in Education
It Starts in the Classroom
Journal of Adolescent and Adult Literacy
Journal of Adult Education
Journal of Artificial Intelligence in Education
Journal of Classroom Interaction
Journal of Cooperative Education
Journal of Correctional Education
Journal of Creative Behavior
Journal of Curriculum and Supervision
Journal of Curriculum Studies
Journal of Critical Analysis
Journal of Developmental Education
Journal of Education
Journal of Education for Teaching
Journal of Education Issues of Language Minority Students
Journal of Educational and Behavioral Statistics
Journal of Educational Computing Research
Journal of Educational Measurement
Journal of Educational Research
Journal of Educational Statistics
Journal of Educational Thought
Journal of Experiential Education
Journal of Experimental Education
Journal of General Education
Journal of Humanistic Education and Development
Journal of Industrial Teacher Education
Journal of Instructional Development
Journal of Literacy Research
Journal of Moral Education
Journal of Negro Education
Journal of Outdoor Education

Journal of Philosophy of Education
Journal of Reading Behavior
Journal of Reading Research
Journal of Research and Development in Education
Journal of Research in Mathematics Education
Journal of Research in Reading
Journal of Research in Rural Education
Journal of Research on Computing in Education
Journal of Rural and Small Schools
Journal of Teaching in Physical Education
Journal of Thought
Language Arts
Language Learning Journal
Learning: Creative Ideas and Insights for Teachers
Learning and Individual Differences
Learning and Instruction
Liberal Education
Mathematics Teacher
National Association of Laboratory Schools Journal
Negro Educational Review
New Directions for Teaching and Learning
New Frontiers in Education
New Schools, New Communities
New Zealand Journal of Educational Studies
Orbit: Ideas about Teaching and Learning
Oxford Review of Education
Peabody Journal of Education
Pennsylvania School Boards Association Bulletin
Performance and Education
Philosophy of Education
Preventing School Failure
Progress of Education
Radical Teacher
Reading and Writing Quarterly
Reading Horizons
Reading Improvement
Reading Research and Instruction
Reading Research Quarterly
Reading Teacher
Reading World
Research and Teaching in Developmental Education
Research in Middle Level Education

Research in Teaching
Research Papers in Education
Review of Education
Review of Educational Research
Review of Research in Education
Rural Educator
Russian Education and Society
Scandinavian Journal of Educational Research
Scholastic Scope
School and Community
School Review
Science and Children
Science Scope
Science Teacher, The
Social Studies and the Young Learner
Sociology of Education
Spectrum: Journal of School Research and Information
Studies in Educational Evaluation
Studies in Music
Studies in Philosophy and Education
Support for Learning
Teacher
Teacher Educator
Teacher Magazine
Teaching Pre-K thru 8
Techniques
Technology and Learning
Theory into Practice
Theory into Practice
Urban Education
Western European Education
Writing Center Journal

Resources

American Educational Research Association
1430 K Street, NW, Suite 1200
Washington, DC 20005
202/238-3200
www.aera.net

SUBJECT INDEX

A

Accommodations, 5, 73, 88, 97, 98, 118, 130
Age appropriateness, 12–13, 57, 73, 111–112
Antecedent control procedures, 190–193
Assessment, 27, 33, 35, 40, 87–92, 106, 117, 126, 148–150, 153, 159

C

Choice making, 20, 57, 107, 115, 117, 118, 127, 128, 135, 149, 166, 167, 168, 169–170, 173, 175
Competence, 6, 14, 15, 19, 20, 47, 106, 107, 108, 190
Context relevance, 7
Corrections, 51–53
Cost, 109
Criterion of ultimate functioning, 9, 11, 12, 19, 69, 70, 73, 111, 112
Cues, 48–51

D

Data collection, 33–42

E

Ecological inventory, 27–29
Errors, 42

F

Financial skills, 119–121
Functional skills, 6, 7, 8, 10, 69–70

G

Generalization, 17, 18, 40, 43–43, 47, 51, 60–63, 69, 71, 72, 78, 79, 90, 106, 107, 136, 137, 153, 155, 157, 158, 188, 191

I

Inclusion (*see* Integration)
Instruction domains, 6
Integration, 5, 10, 11, 20, 47, 84, 85, 86, 117, 146, 147
Interviewing skills, 96–97

J

Job analysis, 95–96
Job exploration, 93–94

M

Massed trials, 53–55, 136
Math skills, 69, 72, 77–78, 112, 120, 170
Modifications, 5, 42, 73, 79, 88, 97–98, 129, 134

N

Normalization, 18–19, 84

O

Objectives, 8, 33, 47

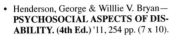